SAFELY REST

---★---

Books by David P. Colley

SOUNDWAVES

ROAD TO VICTORY

BLOOD FOR DIGNITY

FACES OF VICTORY
(WITH OTHER CONTRIBUTORS)

SAFELY REST

DAVID P. COLLEY

BERKLEY
CALIBER

A Caliber Book
Published by the Penguin Group
Penguin Group (USA) Inc.
375 Hudson Street, New York, New York 10014, USA
Penguin Group (Canada), 10 Alcorn Avenue, Toronto, Ontario M4V 3B2, Canada
(a division of Pearson Penguin Canada Inc.)
Penguin Books Ltd., 80 Strand, London WC2R 0RL, England
Penguin Group Ireland, 25 St. Stephen's Green, Dublin 2, Ireland (a division of Penguin Books Ltd.)
Penguin Group (Australia), 250 Camberwell Road, Camberwell, Victoria 3124, Australia
(a division of Pearson Australia Group Pty. Ltd.)
Penguin Books India Pvt. Ltd., 11 Community Centre, Panchsheel Park, New Delhi—110 017, India
Penguin Group (NZ), Cnr. Airborne and Rosedale Roads, Albany, Auckland 1310, New Zealand
(a division of Pearson New Zealand Ltd.)
Penguin Books (South Africa) (Pty.) Ltd., 24 Sturdee Avenue, Rosebank, Johannesburg 2196, South Africa

Penguin Books Ltd., Registered Offices: 80 Strand, London WC2R 0RL, England

This book is an original publication of The Berkley Publishing Group.

Copyright © 2004 by David P. Colley
Text design by Tiffany Estreicher

First edition: November 2004

Library of Congress Cataloging-in-Publication Data

Colley, David.
    Safely rest / by David P. Colley.
        p. cm.
Includes bibliographical references.
ISBN 0-425-19835-9
    1. World War, 1939-1945—Repatriation of war dead—United States. I. Title.

D810.D4C63 2004
940.54'6—dc22   2004045691

PRINTED IN THE UNITED STATES OF AMERICA

10 9 8 7 6 5 4 3 2 1

To Mary Liz
And to Pad, Chris, Erin, and Jack
For all their wonderful support and love

Acknowledgments

My thanks for this book must first go to my agent, Richard Curtis, and my wife, Mary Liz, for their inspiration and support for *Safely Rest*. Richard recognized the merit in the story of the return and final disposition of America's dead from WWII. It had never been related before, and Richard saw its force if told through the eyes of those who experienced loss in the war. And it was through Mary Liz's many readings of drafts and her insightful suggestions that the book improved immeasurably. She edited and managed to plod through at least six works in progress.

Red Franks provided the power and poignancy to this story. I have never forgotten his photograph that appeared in 1966 in the second volume of the *American Heritage History of World War II*. Red epitomized the strength of the American citizen soldier of World War II with his steady, determined gaze. There were millions like him, and they won the war.

Instinctively I turned to Red when I began the book, but I never imagined the depth of his story and that of his father, Dr. Jesse Dee Franks. It unfolded in its many dimensions.

Red Franks hailed from Columbus, Mississippi, and so many of the citizens of that wonderful town were of invaluable help in my research for *Safely Rest*. Foremost was Mrs. Fran Fuqua, member and historian at the First Baptist Church. Fran was indefatigable in uncovering material from Dr. Franks's years at the church from 1921 through 1947 and in introducing me to many Columbians who knew both Dr. Franks and Red. She and her husband Bob extended their hospitality and that of the church on our visit to Mississippi.

I also owe so much to Nancy Lee Franks Goodall of Gallatin, Tennessee, Red Franks's sister, who related the life of the Franks family in Columbus in the years they lived there, particularly during the war. Nancy indulged me for many hours on the phone and in person and introduced me to her friends in Columbus.

Dawn Furr Garakaris, daughter of Dottie Turner, Red's fiancée, also shared many thoughts and memories of her mother.

Bernie Imes, editor of the *Columbus Commercial Dispatch*, ran a story in the newspaper reporting that I was working on the book and asking any Columbians who remembered Red and his father to come forward. Through these contacts I developed a network of old friends of Red and Dr. Franks. Among them was Mrs. Chebie Bateman, director of the library in Columbus, who sent me material from the archives. Wanda Sumner, local history librarian, and Russell James, archivist, provided me with historical information.

There were many friends of Red Franks whom I interviewed, among them Jake Propst, Howard and Riley Noland, Shield Sims, Dick Burts, Herbert Gabhart, J. W. Fagan, and Nannie Kate Smith.

Those who helped are not limited to Columbus. A number of people from Pontotoc, Mississippi, who remember Red and Dottie Turner, passed on memories to me: the Anderson sisters, Julia Holmes, Eleanor Rayburn, Genevieve Yancey, and Sarah Gillespie. Sarah and David Naugher invited us into their home and related their personal experiences with loss in WWII. Old classmates and friends of Dottie's, including the writer Elizabeth Spencer, shared their memories with me.

ACKNOWLEDGMENTS

Thanks also to the Easton Area Public Library and Mrs. Dottie Patoki who retrieved numerous books through interlibrary loan, and the Skillman Library of Lafayette College.

Finally, thanks to my editor, Tom Colgan, for his insight and support, and to Leslie Curtis, Richard Curtis's wife, for her enthusiasm for the manuscript and for suggesting the title, *Safely Rest*.

Col. Walter Stuart, retired in Benjamin, Utah gave me valuable information about the Ploești raid and recounted the battle as he flew on *Euroclydon's* wing. So too did retired Gen. Jacob Smart, who planned the Ploești raid.

The staff at the Central Identification Laboratory, Hawaii (CILHI) in Honolulu assembled in an interview at Hickham AFB to fill me in on the workings of the organization that searches for America's missing war dead. Among the staff that spoke to me were Col. Paul A. Bethke, commander, CILHI, Johnnie Webb, senior advisor at JPAC (Joint POW/MIA Accounting Command), Ginger Couden, public affairs specialist with JPAC, and Sgt. Sebastian Harris. Brian Moon also provided information about the search for the missing from WWII.

Ellie Pope Dodwell related the trauma of her brother's death in Normandy. Alita Howard spoke of her communications with her late husband Cory, shot down and killed over Germany, and Brenda Scalf Birchfield told of her search for her father. I owe much to Jack Davis of Easton, Pennsylvania, a highly decorated combat medic who served with the 5th Division in Europe, and to Dr. John A. Kerner who took time for a lengthy interview about his days as a combat medic during the war. He tells his story in the book *Combat Medic World War II*. Col. Wallace Hale offered his personal memoir, *Battle Rattle*, about his experience as a division chaplain in WWII. Dick Austin also gave permission to quote extensively from the book *Letters From the Pacific, A Combat Chaplain in World War II*.

Darrell C. Richardson of Memphis, Tennessee, a friend, summer camp mate, and Baptist seminary classmate of Red Franks provided information and photographs of Red as a boy and as a young man. Lt. Col. Deborah Skillman, assistant chief, Mortuary Affairs, and Casualty Support Division, Department of the Army, went to great lengths to obtain Red Franks's military file. Karen Warner Pearce gave permission to use Jack Warner's photograph of the crew assembled in front of the B-24 *Euroclydon the Storm* taken a few days before the battle of Ploești, along with excerpts of several of her father's letters. John F. Kane and his wife Donna gave permission to use quotations from Col. John R. Kane's papers. Williams College gave permission to quote from the war memoirs of Irving Fish, Jr.

Contents

CONTENTS

"ONE NEVER KNOWS WHAT TOMORROW MAY BRING."

—LT. JESSE D. "RED" FRANKS, JR.

Prologue

It was a parade of sorts that began shortly after the *Joseph V. Connolly* sailed past Ambrose Light, through the Narrows, and glided slowly into New York harbor in the early morning haze of October 26, 1947. Two sleek navy destroyers, the USS *Bristol* and the USS *Beatty,* and the gleaming white Coast Guard cutter, *Spencer,* wheeled into position to escort the Liberty Ship as their crews snapped to rigid attention along the guardrails. On the *Connolly's* boat deck an honor guard surrounded a solitary flag-draped coffin that stood out in the defused autumn light, a swatch of red, white, and blue against the ship's gray flanks. The *Connolly* approached the towering mass of New York City as the huge 16-inch guns of the battleship, USS *Missouri,* boomed a salute that echoed off the New Jersey Palisades and back through Manhattan's man-made canyons. The thunder of the guns rolled away, and a flight of fighter planes roared overhead before gracefully turning to leave the city's streets in an unnatural quiet. To fill the sudden void, a lone marine on the

Bristol's fantail raised his bugle and sounded "Church Call." As the notes drifted away, a somber voice broke the silence to deliver a prayer.

The *Connolly* slipped into Pier 61 at West Twenty-first Street in Manhattan with a reassuring nudge, marking the end of a journey to fulfill a long-held promise of a grateful nation in bringing her cargo safely home. The accompanying tugboats reversed screws and withdrew in a rush of churning water and pounding engines as the crew cast the *Connolly's* lines ashore and she was firmly secured. In her reinforced holds she carried 6,248 coffins containing the remains of American soldiers killed in the European theater of World War II. The casket on deck, bearing an unnamed medal of honor winner killed in the Battle of the Bulge, was a symbol of all the young men who were coming home on the *Connolly* and of the scores of thousands more American dead who also would be returned in the months and years ahead.

At 12:45 P.M. the heavy steel sarcophagus was carried ashore by pallbearers representing all the nation's armed services and placed on a caisson that was hitched to a turreted armored car. A bugle sounded, onlookers wiped away tears, and the procession began, solemnly, quietly, 6,000 men strong, as it moved up Fifth Avenue, past the first ranks of 400,000 New Yorkers who lined the sidewalks on this warm autumn day to pay final tribute to the nation's war dead.

This was very different from the victory parade and celebration two years earlier in 1945 when frenzied, elated, and war weary New Yorkers welcomed the return of their proud and triumphant fighting men, who marched along the same route in battle dress. The war had been won and all thoughts were to the future and to the living, not to the past and to the dead. General of the Army Dwight D. Eisenhower was among the soldiers, seamen, and airmen passing in review in 1945, and a smartly dressed, khaki clad "Ike," seated in the back of an open limousine, greeted the throngs in his typical public salute of outstretched arms and broad smile. The din from the cheering crowds had filled the avenue, and a festive blizzard of ticker tape and confetti swirled down to blanket the street along the way. The parade route was festooned with signs: "Welcome Home" and "Well Done." The people of New York were delirious.

In October 1947, the old welcome signs from '45 were still visible, but faded, and an eerie silence greeted the marching ranks as they filed up Fifth Avenue, stopping briefly in Madison Square at Twenty-second Street. They moved on, through the shadow of the Empire State Building on Thirty-fourth Street, past the public library on Forty-second Street, and on toward Central Park. There was no confetti or ticker tape and no roaring crowds, only the sound of muffled footsteps and the hollow clop of horses' hooves. Many in the crowd sobbed openly and prayed as the military formations passed, led by mounted New York City policemen, followed by contingents of West Point cadets and Naval Academy midshipmen, soldiers from the Eighty-second Airborne Division, marines and sailors, and members of civic groups from the city of New York. Behind them came the caisson bearing the flag-draped coffin.

A band in the procession struck up a funereal, "Onward Christian Soldiers," and muted bells tolled as it passed St. Patrick's Cathedral with its flag at half-mast. At Sixty-third and Fifth Avenue a diminutive city street sweeper raised his broom rigidly with his left hand in a present arms and snapped a salute with his right hand as the coffin went by. The marchers turned into Central Park at Seventy-second Street and advanced into the Sheep Meadow where forty thousand mourners had assembled to see the casket lifted from its caisson by pallbearers, who solemnly carried it forward and placed it on a purple and black catafalque. As the day wore on and a heat haze settled over the Sheep Meadow, the crowd swelled to 150,000.

Chaplains of three faiths offered prayers for the souls of the war dead and for solace and peace for their loved ones. Speakers eulogized the fallen warriors of World War II; Secretary of the Army Kenneth C. Royall represented the nation, Governor Thomas E. Dewey came on behalf of the state of New York, and Mayor William O'Dwyer appeared for the city. Maj. Gen. Harry H. Vaughan, President Harry S. Truman's military aide, placed a wreath on the coffin. At 4 P.M. a seven-man honor guard fired a three-volley salute, a drummer began a slow roll, and a mournful taps sounded across the Sheep Meadow as the setting sun backlit the skyline to cast ever lengthening shadows across the park. Another, distant bugler beyond a stand of trees echoed with the same faint quivering notes. The pallbearers returned the casket to the caisson as the West Point band played "Nearer My God To Thee." The public ceremonies ended, and the assembled on-lookers filed home to continue their lives. The casket was carried away and returned to the *Connolly* from whence the body would make its way home to Ohio or maybe Alabama, where a mother, a father, a brother, and a wife would accompany the remains to a final resting place. For these American families, life would never be the same.

In San Francisco, a similar ceremony took place under an overcast October sky as the army transport ship *Honda Knot* slipped through the frigid waters beneath the Golden Gate Bridge into San Francisco Bay. An aerial escort of forty-eight fighter planes flew over the vessel before dipping their wings in salute and banking away. Surface ships from the Coast Guard and the Navy approached the *Honda Knot* and led her through a misting rain to anchorage off Marina Point, where a gathering of five thousand mourners waited to pay tribute to the war dead that the ship was delivering home to American soil from the Pacific theater. A navy launch approached the *Honda Knot* and offered another massive wreath from President Truman. Dignitaries in the audience included Army General Mark Clark, who had led American troops in Italy during the war, and the Secretary of the Navy John L. Sullivan, who honored these fallen heroes, many of whom had passed under the Golden Gate Bridge on ships bound for the Pacific war.

Six of the 3,012 flag-draped coffins aboard the *Honda Knot* were removed the next day to lie in state in the rotunda of San Francisco's city hall, where the ordinary citizens of a sorrowful nation paid their last respects. The six dead represented servicemen from the Army, the Navy, the Marine Corps, the Air Force, and the Coast Guard, along with a civilian, all killed in the war. From early morning until late that night, thousands of mourners filed by the coffins or knelt in prayer by their sides.

The arrival of the *Honda Knot* and the *Joseph V. Connolly* officially initiated what one observer called the "most melancholy immigration movement in the history of man," the return to the United States of 233,181 American dead after the end of World War II.[1] America's army of fallen warriors was coming home from the four corners of the earth, from Guadalcanal and Australia, from New Guinea, Japan, China, and Burma in the Pacific theater. From the Mediterranean theater men were returned from Libya, Sicily, Italy, Yugoslavia, and Romania. The bodies of men who had died in France, Belgium, Luxembourg, and Germany also came home. Most had been killed in action or had died of wounds from direct combat against the enemy.

In New York, the day after the symbolic funeral for all the nation's dead, the *Connolly* moved to the Brooklyn army base, where longshoremen began unloading her cargo of steel caskets and preparing them for shipment. Workers also began unloading the *Honda Knot* the day after the viewing in San Francisco's city hall. Her cargo of dead had gone to war expecting one day to return to friends and family. They would be home within ten to thirty days.

At the war's end families who lost sons, brothers, and husbands in the conflict were asked where they wished the remains of their sons to be interred, in the United States or overseas in an American military cemetery. Congress had passed legislation authorizing repatriation of the bodies, and the majority of the families wanted their boys returned to private burial plots or to a national cemetery nearby.

Not all the dead were returned to U.S. soil. An additional 93,242 men were buried in overseas American cemeteries because the families believed it more appropriate for them to rest with comrades near the battlefields where they had died.

The families of 78,976 dead soldiers had no choice; their sons were listed as missing in action, and their remains were never recovered. Today the number of missing has been reduced by only a trifle; about seventy-eight thousand Americans who went off to World War II are still listed as lost. Among those still missing are about eight thousand men whose bodies had been recovered but whose identities are unknown. Their remains are buried in American cemeteries overseas.

The entire repatriation and overseas reburial program took six years to

[1] Figures from American Battle Monuments Commission.

complete, from 1945 to 1951, at a cost of $200,000,000 in 1945 dollars—several billion today. It wasn't the first American repatriation program following a foreign war, but it was the most extensive. More than twelve hundred U.S. dead were returned for burial after the Spanish-American War, and about 46,292 were repatriated from France after World War I. Another 30,921 U.S. soldiers who died in World War I were buried in eight American military cemeteries in France following that conflict.

The vast reburial program after World War II is all but forgotten today. There is no glory in the saga of the dead, and this operation was not connected to any massive invasion armada or to a victorious battle or campaign where heroes were made. It was conducted for the most part in obscurity, and the men of this huge army of the dead were mute.

Today we think of these men, many merely boys, but once a year and not so much as real individuals but as part of the fabric of myth on which the nation is built. We think of them as abstractions and we do not know the details of their return.

The retrieval and burial of American dead from World War II still goes on and will go on for centuries. Every year the bodies of missing American soldiers from that conflict are recovered, some in the remote jungles of places like New Guinea where hikers or tribesmen discover them. Others are found in isolated village cemeteries as was one American flyer who had been interred anonymously in Sicily for years. They are found in the waters of the Zuider Zee in the Netherlands, where the bodies of American flyers are regularly recovered from wrecked aircraft found years after the war. All remains are carefully analyzed, relatives sought and found, and then these once lost soldiers are returned to their hometowns or buried in national cemeteries abroad.

The nation glorifies World War II; it was called the Great Crusade, and we now idolize the men of the Greatest Generation and immortalize the dwindling legions of these heroes constantly in film and in literature. In so doing we have lost touch with the immense pain and suffering caused by the war and the ripples of sorrow that still flow across America from that devastating conflict. We know little of the men who gave their lives and nothing about the struggles of their families. This is their story.

1

Target Ploeşti

They rose from a wasteland, enormous and lumbering four-engine machines with slender, delicate wings ascending into the chilled desert air just after dawn. Some were sand pink, some mud brown, and all reflected the golden rays of the early morning sun as they built up speed in takeoff and left the earth in great clouds of swirling orange-red dust. The bombers groaned upward, their engines throbbing in the crystalline, frozen brightness where they began to circle like raptors above the vast plain of Cyrenaica, climbing higher and higher to assemble in loose formations before wheeling in a great migration that rumbled northward above the trackless Sahara. They flew over a ribbon of Mediterranean shoreline embroidered with gauzy white strands of breaking surf, onward over the dappled sea toward their distant target.

For centuries armies and invaders had crossed the Mediterranean. Phoenicians, Greeks, Romans, and Carthaginians had come before, and most recently, Germans and Italians had traversed this sea of antiquity from the north to be vanquished just months before in the vast deserts of North Africa. On this day, August 1, 1943, 178 American B-24 Liberator bombers lifted off from bases that dotted the barren landscape around Benghazi, Libya, on a mission to soar twenty-four hundred miles over sea and land to strike deep into Nazi-occupied Europe and destroy the oil refineries at Ploeşti, Romania. Never before had an armada so numerous and powerful crossed these waters to attack from on high. The four-engine Liberators, with boxlike bodies and cumbersome-looking twin tail stabilizers, were se-lected because they could fly faster and farther and carry a greater bomb load than any other plane in the American arsenal, including the vaunted B-17 Flying Fortress. The B-24s lugged a destructive force of 311 tons of high explosives and enough incendiary bombs to create a fiery tempest amidst Ploeşti's refineries.

The fifteen-hour round-trip mission, code named Operation Tidal Wave, would tax the aircrews to their physical and psychological limits. But the men were young, eager for the impending clash, and able to withstand the wear and punishment of the long flight. The German air defenses that ex-tended over the Mediterranean and deep into Eastern Europe were the greatest concern to the aircrews. The oil refineries were the most heavily de-fended targets in the Nazi empire, and on the flight to Ploeşti the Amer-icans could meet enemy fighter planes winking death from 20 mm nose cannons. Around and over the target they would encounter an array of an-tiaircraft guns, including nests of dreaded 88 mm flak guns and scores of rapidly firing, smaller caliber guns that spewed out fiery streams of explo-sive projectiles. Once the planes completed their bomb runs and turned for home, enemy fighters would resume their relentless attacks all across Roma-nia, Bulgaria, and Greece to the sea.

The allied high command regarded Ploeşti as the single most important target in Nazi-occupied Europe and sought its destruction despite the ex-pected cost. An attack on the oil fields had utmost priority and was dis-cussed by Roosevelt and Churchill at the Casablanca Conference in January 1943. The two leaders recognized the critical importance of cutting off Hitler's oil supplies to impede his war-making capabilities.

Churchill urged that the oil fields be taken by land armies invading through the Balkans, the region the British prime minister dubbed Europe's "soft underbelly." The Americans demurred and counseled that Ploeşti could be destroyed from the air, and Churchill threw them the challenge.

The man selected to plan the destruction of the Ploeşti refineries from the air was thirty-three-year-old Air Corps Col. Jacob E. Smart, a West Point graduate and bomber pilot who was assigned to the staff of Air Corps Chief of Staff General Henry H. Arnold. "You do it," Arnold ordered, and Colonel Smart enlisted the best minds he could find to plan the operation: Air Corps specialists, civilian engineers who knew the workings of refineries, and a British petroleum engineer who had worked in Ploeşti before the war.

Several plans were considered, but Colonel Smart believed a low-level raid at fifty feet would inflict the greatest damage. A high-altitude mission at twenty-five thousand feet would require many more aircraft to achieve the same results, and in 1943, the Air Corps didn't have enough bomb groups to attack Ploeşti repeatedly from on high.

To the men who would fly against Ploeşti, Colonel Smart's plan smacked of insanity. The B-24 was a high-altitude bomber, not a single-engine ground-attack plane, and the experienced airmen selected for the mission knew there would be terrible losses. Col. John Riley Kane, commander of the Ninety-eighth Bomb Group that would join the Ploeşti mission, complained, "It was some wild-eyed dreamer sitting at a desk in Washington who devised this mess of a low-level raid." But Smart stuck to his plan. "Nobody with any sense wanted to fly a B-24 in low, but we had no choice," he said. "It was the only way we could do it. I was about as popular as the illegitimate one at a family reunion."

By May 25, the Ploeşti raid was given its first code name, Statesman, and shortly thereafter Smart took his plan to be approved by high-ranking allied commanders including Gen. Dwight Eisenhower, the overall commander of allied operations in North Africa and the supreme Allied commander in Europe later in the war. Statesman subsequently became Soapsuds and later Operation Tidal Wave.

Air commanders estimated that casualties among the American aircrews could be 50 percent or greater, and some believed they could approach 100 percent. But if the refineries were left in ruins, the mission would be deemed a success regardless of the losses.

Lt. Gen. Lewis Brereton, commander of the North African based U.S. Ninth Air Force that would carry out the raid, visited the crews the day before the mission to inspire his men. That afternoon they had completed their last practice run over the desert and were roused and ready to take the war deep into Eastern Europe. A young pilot from Utah, Lt. Walter Stuart, who would be in the lead of the attack the next day, remembered Brereton's address. A young bombardier from Mississippi, 2nd Lt. Jesse D. Franks, Jr., also heard the general's remarks: "You are going in at low level to hit the oil refineries . . . and leave your powerful impression," General Brereton said. "The roar of your engines in the heart of the enemy's conquest will sound in the ears of Romanians—and, yes, the whole world, long after the blasts of your bombs and fires have died away."

Despite the stirring commands to duty and honor, the men knew that their chances of returning from the mission were slim, and as the sun set over the western desert in a red-gold glow the night before the attack, 1,729 American flyers felt the specter of death by their sides as never before. On this mission all were expendable, from Maj. Gen. Uzal Ent, who would command the attack from the B-24 *Teggie Ann,* to the lowliest waist gunner.

Ploeşti had been the first place in the world to refine crude oil in 1857, and its production of gasoline and lubricating oils fueled the German war machine from the Wehrmacht's panzer divisions at the gates of Moscow to its diesel-powered submarines prowling the coastal waters off the United States. The oil fields yielded an estimated 60 percent of the total German production, or about ten million tons of petroleum products annually, including large quantities of ninety-octane aviation gasoline. The Allies believed that if this supply of oil was cut off, the armies of the Third Reich would wither and collapse.

Tidal Wave was not the first U.S. raid against the Romanian oil fields. That mission, code named Halpro, was launched a year earlier on June 11, 1942, when thirteen U.S. Liberators took off from a Royal Air Force base in Fayid, Egypt, and flew across the Mediterranean, over Greece and Bulgaria, to bomb Ploeşti. The raid took the Germans by complete surprise; they had not expected the Americans to strike so soon after Pearl Harbor, on December 7, 1941. The enemy perceived the Americans as militarily too weak in mid-1942 to mount a raid as complex in its undertaking and as distant as the oil fields. But the Americans dropped their four thousand-pound bomb loads through cloud cover from ten thousand feet against little resistance. Not one B-24 was lost; seven of the bombers reached their intended return base in Iraq, two landed in Syria, and four landed in Turkey, where the crews were interned for nearly a year because of Turkey's status as a neutral nation. The men were eventually returned to U.S. custody.

The Halpro mission was a lift to the badly battered U.S. fortunes early in World War II. The Japanese had driven the Americans from their Pacific bases on Guam, Wake Island, and the Philippines, and the United States had little hope of launching a ground attack against Hitler in Europe until 1943, at the earliest. Halpro was a similar but unpublicized counterpoint to the famous April 18, 1942, Doolittle raid on Tokyo when American B-25, twin-engine bombers, took off from the aircraft carrier USS *Hornet,* some four hundred miles off the coast of Japan, and bombed the home islands to the astonishment of the complacent Japanese. The Halpro and the Doolittle raiders did little damage, but both buoyed America's hope for ultimate victory.

Halpro also proved the worth and capability of the long-range bomber. If the B-24s had hit Ploeşti once without loss, they could do it repeatedly until the target was destroyed. But Halpro served to alert the Germans to the vulnerability of their primary fuel source, and they hastily fortified Ploeşti's defenses with hundreds of antiaircraft guns and increased the number of fighter interceptors guarding the refineries.

The Americans had planned the Tidal Wave mission for months and gathered the armada of B-24s at bases all around Benghazi. To flesh out the ranks of the North African based Ninth Air Force, four bomb groups from the Britain based U.S. Eighth Air Force were dispatched to Libya. They included planes from the 93rd Bomb Group (BG), nicknamed the Ted's

Traveling Circus, the 44th BG, the Eight Balls, and the 389th BG, the Sky Scorpions. All flew Liberators and they would reinforce Colonel Kane's 98th BG, the Pyramiders, and the 376th BG, the Liberandos, already assigned to the Ninth.

The Army Air Corps had been developing the concept of high altitude bombing since the 1920s and in the late 1930s began designing and building the big B-24s and B-17s that could bomb from heights of twenty-five thousand feet. Every plane carried a trained bombardier, and in World War II each aircraft was equipped with the new supersecret Norden bombsight. Together, bombardier and bombsight were supposed to be able to place a bomb in a pickle barrel thousands of feet below. But that kind of precision was achieved only under ideal conditions. In combat, massive barrages of antiaircraft fire and hundreds of enemy fighter planes attacking from all angles distracted bombardiers and pilots, and the bombers frequently missed the target by hundreds of yards, sometimes by miles.

To improve accuracy the Liberators would go in low over Ploeşti. A bomber, skimming the treetops, could not miss the refineries, but the downside of this tactic was that the B-24s would make huge targets and would be vulnerable to heavy machine gun and small-caliber antiaircraft fire, which could not have reached them at twenty-five thousand feet.

The attacking Liberators would bomb Ploeşti at fifty feet, but many would drop to twenty feet off the ground, with the intent of surprising the German and Romanian antiaircraft crews and avoiding their fire. The enemy gunners usually preset their large-caliber antiaircraft shells to detonate around twenty-five thousand feet in "box barrages," confined areas at the same altitude as the bombers. The Americans had to fly through these concentrated zones of fire and were unable to take evasive action because they were committed to their bomb runs in tight formations.

Low-flying Liberators would force the enemy gunners to reset the fuses and deflect their heavy guns downward as bombers bore in on them. The Americans also hoped to slip beneath the enemy's radar defenses, reach the target undetected, and release their bombs and incendiaries before the Germans had time to react. Additionally, the most deadly of German antiaircraft guns, the 88 mm, was believed to be too cumbersome to swivel rapidly enough to track a fast-moving B-24 at low level and would be limited to firing at planes head-on. The bombers would still be subject to intense small-caliber antiaircraft fire, but Col. Smart and his planners expected to get in and get out before the enemy could organize coordinated defensive fire.

The B-24s going into Ploeşti also would be less vulnerable to enemy fighters. At twenty-five thousand feet German interceptors darted around U.S. formations to shoot at the unescorted American planes. The U.S. still didn't have fighters with the range to escort the bombers all the way to distant targets and back. That was still months away. In 1943 fighters often accompanied them partway to the target and then tipped their wings and made for home, and the bombers fended for themselves against German Me 109s and the Focke Wulf fighters as they flew deep into enemy territory.

At fifty feet or lower over Ploeşti, the enemy fighter planes would be deprived of maneuver room. They could not come up from below, and if they attacked from above, they risked slamming into the ground. Despite the advantages, it would be difficult for the B-24s, nicknamed "furniture vans" by the Germans, to dodge enemy fire. They were not agile aircraft, they presented a huge target, and they would have to fly directly into the sights of the enemy guns.

The Americans also hoped that the bulk of the soldiers manning the antiaircraft guns around Ploeşti were Romanian, and this prospect raised expectations for a successful attack. Romanian troops were said to lack the motivation, the dedication to duty, and the training of the German gunners. The U.S. aircrews had watched an instructional film, narrated by the well-known American publicist Tex McCrary that belittled Romanian resolve and abilities in the defense of Ploeşti. "All the antiaircraft guns are manned by Romanians," McCrary said in his stern, authoritative voice. "So there is a pretty good chance there might be incidents like there were in Italy at the beginning of the war, when civilians could not get into shelters because they were filled with antiaircraft gunners. The defenses of Ploeşti may look formidable on paper, but remember, they are manned by Romanians." But

McCrary was expounding on supposition, not fact. The Americans had sparse intelligence information on Ploeşti, not even up-to-date aerial photographs. The Air Corps was using old picture postcards and artists' sketches of the refineries to acquaint the crews with the layout of the target. Reconnaissance flights over the oil fields would tip the Germans to the coming attack.

The Tidal Wave aircrews had practiced low-level missions for weeks. In England, the Eighth Air Force bomb groups that were soon to be transferred to Libya began training for the raid by flying over the fens of East Anglia so close to the ground that they snapped tree branches, startled farmers, and scattered dairy cattle on the flat, verdant landscape. At least one B-24 was damaged beyond repair when a wingman's number three and four props tore into her and nearly ripped her in two. The plane barely made it back to base.

Later, in North Africa, the full armada of planes resumed the low-level practice flights over the desert, starting at five hundred feet to allow the pilots time to adapt to nearly zero altitude in formations of six or more aircraft. The pilots brought the B-24s down to two hundred feet, and then dropped to twenty feet as they shot across the desert floor and dropped practice bombs on a full-scale, though crude, mock-up target of the refinery complex erected in the desert from discarded oil barrels. Their aim was excellent and the "damage" was deemed to be extensive.

The B-24 was a hard plane to control for many pilots at high altitude, and flying on the deck was even more difficult, particularly in the hot, humid, and turbulent air just above the desert floor. Colonel Smart flew a number of the practice missions over the Libyan desert with the 93rd BG and recalled losing weight flying the plane. "Flying a B-24 was so intense," he said. "You worked hard to control it, and at low altitude you certainly had to be keenly alert."

While flying against the mock target, one of the bombers hit a downdraft and slammed into the desert floor. The pilot dragged the belly in the sand for a few yards before yanking the plane back into the air. She made it back to base, but the impact of the crash bent critical bulkheads and the plane was no longer airworthy.

Flying on the deck soon became great sport for B-24 pilots who zoomed along the Libyan beaches around Benghazi at ten feet off the ground to scatter their naked comrades partaking in a peaceful swims in the Mediterranean. Sometimes the planes flew so low over their airfields that the pilots had to pull up to clear parked aircraft, and Arab tents became fair game to be grazed and knocked down by careening bombers. Anywhere else these cowboy tactics would have meant instant grounding and court-martial.

Small, precisely fabricated models of the refineries were constructed and displayed in restricted tents where every pilot and every bombardier memorized the silhouette of his assigned target area. These mock-ups had been meticulously constructed to a three dimensional, 1:5000 scale and were detailed down to individual trees and hedges around the target. But these models were flawed. They too were copied from the picture postcards and did not depict up-to-date enemy defenses such as blast walls built around critical parts of the refining operations.

Past experience and training would be of little benefit to the bombardiers. They had trained with the Norden bombsight and had learned to manipulate the horizontal and vertical crosshairs and course knobs as they took control of the bomber from the pilot at high altitude as it approached the target. Once the objective was in the sights, the bombardier released the bombs and followed them down until they became dark specks erupting in seemingly innocuous puffs thousands of feet below.

For the Ploeşti raid the bombardiers would use a simple reticule-type sight they peered through as though aiming down a rifle barrel. Once the target was framed, the bombardier released the bombs. At fifty feet over Ploeşti, the run would be, in the words of pilot Lt. Walter Stuart, "like lobbing basketballs onto the court from the bleachers."

Several B-24s made practice runs at twenty feet over the Allied-controlled Benghazi harbor to test the ability of the planes to outrun the imaginary flak from British antiaircraft crews. The lesson the Americans learned was sobering. The British gunners poured their "fire" into the broad bellies of the Liberators as the gunners swiveled their guns in time to lead the planes. The "Tommies" joked at the ease with which they shot down the American bombers even before they completed their runs. Despite this evidence that disaster might be lurking over Ploeşti, the raid would go on.

The intense training continued, and the large formations of thirty or more aircraft skimming the desert floor were broken into groups of six aircraft and then into flights of three planes flying abreast. Each flight of three was expected to come in over the target from a different angle. The first trio of B-24s came in straight, the second from the left, the third straight in, the fourth from the right, the fifth straight, and so on until an entire bomb group had passed over the target. The objective was to spread the bombs and to do it as quickly as possible.

Would the plan work? Colonel Smart and his planners knew it was risky, but they believed it had a chance to succeed. Much depended on timing and execution. "The charm of the plan was that the planes would go over in waves only a few seconds apart. The entire force would pass over the target in a matter of two, three, or four minutes and would be in the heavily defended zone only about fifteen minutes," Smart said.

The aircrews were assembled on the evening of July 31 and were briefed about the details of the attack. Tidal Wave would begin the following morning at dawn with the bomber force heading north over the Mediterranean to a point south of the island of Corfu, where it would turn northeast onto the mainland along the coast of Albania. The planes would climb over the mountainous Albanian coast and proceed over northern Greece and southern Yugoslavia before dropping down as they flew over Bulgaria and across the Wallachian plain in Romania. As the force closed on Ploeşti, the Liberators would fly at three hundred feet, and when they reached the target area, they would drop to fifty feet or below, barely clearing the tops of the refinery smokestacks when they released their bombs. The surviving planes would pull up and away and head toward the welcoming Libyan Desert.

Each man was given a survival kit that contained a handkerchief map of the Balkans, a British gold sovereign or a twenty-dollar U.S. gold piece, ten one-dollar bills, and six dollars worth of drachmae and lire. Also included were pressed dates, water purification tablets, biscuits, sugar cubes, and chocolate. The crews had been taught escape and evasion tactics in case they were shot down and were issued revolvers and carbines and tiny compasses to guide them out of enemy territory. But many crew members left the firearms behind, knowing that any attempt to shoot their way to freedom would probably be futile and fatal.

The airmen were subdued and quiet after the last practice-mission briefing, knowing that the following day might be their last. The officers in charge informed the assembled flyers at the various airfields around Benghazi that casualties could be heavy. These were alarming thoughts for young men whose average age was not much older than twenty-two. In the game of war, men in their mid to late twenties frequently acquired the nickname "Pops." Men who had survived numerous missions were "old-timers."

The men reflected, and many prayed. Lieutenant Stuart, a former Mormon missionary, gathered about thirty men around him. "We talked about death, resurrection, and the life to come," Stuart said. "I told the boys that no Nazi gunner could end that which has always been—the soul and intelligence of man. I was convinced beyond question that this life was just part of a great, everlasting, progressive existence that ruled before we came here. . . . This testimony was much appreciated by the warriors of the Ninety-third. It does not remove fear, which is fixed by nature, but it gives great purpose to this life."

Most of the men wrote home. The young bombardier, Lt. Jesse D. Franks, Jr., twenty-four, from Columbus, Mississippi, assigned to the B-24, *Euroclydon the Storm* wrote his sweetheart and fiancée Dottie Turner from Philadelphia, Mississippi, a farewell letter that he hoped she would never receive. They had begun their courtship when he was a student at Mississippi College in Clinton, Mississippi, and she was enrolled at Belhaven College in nearby Jackson. Lieutenant Franks decided upon graduation in 1941 to enter the ministry like his father and began his pastoral studies that fall at the Southern Baptist Seminary in Louisville, Kentucky.

Lieutenant Franks and Dottie planned to be married after she graduated from Belhaven in 1942. Everything was in readiness for the wedding; they had even picked out their silverware pattern and begun buying a few pieces. But Pearl Harbor changed their lives, as it changed the lives of every American. In January 1942, Lieutenant Franks decided that duty to country came first, and he left the seminary to join the Air Corps. He and Dottie postponed their marriage until after the war.

As Lieutenant Franks wrote Dottie that night, he gazed at the two small snapshots of the two of them taken in January 1943 at a training base near Tucson, Arizona. He was dressed in his Class A uniform, khaki pants known as "pinks," brown tunic, and an officer's garrison hat. They were smiling and happy, side by side and holding hands as they looked into the camera. Lieutenant Franks took both photos and carefully returned them to his thin leather wallet where he had kept them since coming overseas. They would be pressed against his body over Ploeşti.

Lieutenant Franks also wrote a farewell letter to his father, the Rev. Jesse Dee Franks, Sr., the presiding minister at the First Baptist Church in Columbus, who was immensely proud of his son. Back home Dr. Franks was known as "Jesse," and his son was nicknamed "Red," because of his flaming hair. Red was the center of Dr. Franks's universe, and his letters home were reassuring, brave, and mature for a young man of twenty-four. On the night before Ploeşti, however, there was a foreboding tone in his letter. Red asked his father and Dottie to carry on if he did not come back. He told them that the upcoming mission was critical to the outcome of the war.

Like all parents of soldiers in times of war, Dr. Franks worried desperately about his son. On Red's last visit home in May 1943, just before shipping out to an Eighth Air Force base in Norfolk, England, Dr. Franks had gathered the family, his second wife Augusta, Red, and his daughter, Nancy Lee, in the living room of their Victorian-style parsonage next to Columbus' First Baptist Church at 705 Second Avenue North, and invoked the Ninety-first Psalm. Devotionals were common in the Franks family, but that night they prayed as earnestly as they ever had for Red's safe return. His crisp officer's uniform belied the freckle-faced little redhead they all remembered. Dr. Franks fell to his knees and began his prayer, emphasizing the lines that most touched his soul:

You shall not be afraid of the terror of the night, nor of the arrow that flies by day.

Nor of the pestilence that walks in darkness, nor of the destruction that lays waste at noonday.

A thousand may fall at your side, and ten thousand at your right hand; but it shall not come near you.

No evil shall befall you, nor shall any plague come near your dwelling.

For he shall give His angels charge over you, to keep you in all your ways.

With long life I will satisfy him and show him My salvation.

The next afternoon Red Franks left for war, and Dr. Franks framed in memory his son's smiling face through the window of the departing bus. Red waved; it was the start of his son's long and perilous journey, and Dr. Franks held back his emotion and tears. The tristate bus headed down Main Street in Columbus and crossed the trestle bridge below the bluffs above the Tombigbee River. He knew Red and he would travel a long journey before the war was over, and he prayed to God he would see him again in this life.

Dr. Franks continued to bestow on Red all the blessings and protection he could invoke from afar. On July 17, 1943, he wrote Red a chatty letter about life at Camp Ridgecrest, North Carolina, the Baptist boys' camp where Red had been a counselor and later its youth director. Dr. Franks mentioned some of Red's boyhood friends who were serving in the military in strange and exotic places around the world. He included an envelope-size card listing passages in the Bible that offered Red solace and comfort in the days ahead.

Red wired his father a week later: "I am fine. Hope all well. Tell Al Hi. Love. Jesse D. Franks, Jr." It was lighthearted, as though there were no war.

Dr. Franks mailed Red a booklet, "On to Victory," a compendium of biblical sayings and passages along with the words to well-known hymns, euphemistically called "victory songs." He did not include an accompanying letter, but jotted down an inscription on the inside page: "Thought you would enjoy this little pamphlet. Love, Dad."

On the night before the Ploeşti raid, Red also wrote a letter to a boyhood pal, Jake Propst of Columbus, from the tent city where the men of his Ninety-third Bomb Group were housed in the Libyan Desert. Each group had its own base in this desolate landscape surrounding Benghazi, where the men baked in the blazing sunlight by day and froze under a nighttime dome that was speckled by silvery white stars. They slept on hard cots and struggled against the talclike sand, flies, and scorpions. Bomb fin casings served as tables and oil drums, seats. The Air Corps had set up a bar for the crews and permitted gambling, but Red did not drink nor did he approve of gambling. The Mediterranean Sea beckoned every day, but an afternoon swim hardly compensated for the harsh conditions of the desert, nor did it release them from the growing anxiety.

And on this night pilots, navigators, bombardiers, and gunners tried to sleep, but many could not doze off. They were tense with excitement and anticipation and accosted by terror and all wondered if they would live to see the sun setting over the Libyan Desert the next day as they brought their B-24s home from Romania. But they also experienced elation and pride at the importance of their mission. If Tidal Wave were successful, it could break the back of the Nazi war machine and shorten the war. Red laid down his pen, sealed the envelopes, and turned in to sleep. The crews would be awakened at 2 A.M. for take off at 7 A.M., just after sunup.

Some men thought of home and some spoke among themselves of loved ones in murmurs or rose to stroll and contemplate the coming day, their voices sometimes carrying across the flat landscape. Colonel Kane, nicknamed Killer Kane by the Germans for his aerial exploits as commander of the Pyramiders, the Ninety-eighth BG, wandered through the group's encampment in the powerful blackness and penetrating chill of the desert night. Beneath his veneer of rugged individualism and bravado, Colonel

Kane was a deeply religious man and a sensitive observer. He recorded his thoughts that night as he prepared for combat:

> There was a quietness, quite unlike the usual buzz. Some crews were quietly giving away their belongings. I sat on my favorite perch on an old engine and stared for a long time at the stars. In my short lifetime, the stars have stayed in their places as they have for countless lifetimes before mine. They have remained unaffected whether I and the men with me lived or died. Whether we died in the near future or years later from senility mattered not in the great scheme of things. Yet the manner of our dying could have far-reaching effects. I have a young son I may never see again, yet I shall be content if I feel that his freedom is assured and he is never forced to be humbled in spirit and body before another man who proclaims himself master.

2

As Ready as I'll Ever Be

The desert air carried the vibrating roar of aircraft engines as mechanics readied bombers that stood out as silhouettes in the predawn blackness of August I, 1943. At 2 A.M. ground personnel drove jeeps through the tent city blowing horns and barking wake-up calls through tent flaps to rouse the men for the day's mission. The crews rose, shaved away beard stubble that would irritate their skin under oxygen masks, dressed, and then strode briskly into the mess tent for breakfast. The hall hummed with subdued conversation and clattered from kitchenware and metal mess trays as Red Franks sat down and ate pancakes with comrades and crewmates. He ate quickly and returned to his quarters where he had neatly piled his personal belongings at the end of his cot. The letters to Dottie and his father were on top to facilitate their mailing if he did not return. His crewmates had done the same.

Red pushed his heavy flying gear aside and donned his suntan khaki trousers and khaki shirt on which the Eighth Air Force insignia stood out colorfully on the left upper sleeve as did the gold bar of a second lieutenant on the collar. He pulled an OD (olive drab) sweater over the shirt and slipped into his gabardine flying coveralls. He would carry his A-2 leather jacket, lighter but similar looking to the fleece-lined one he had worn for the portrait taken in bombardier school at Victorville, California, near San Bernardino. Red had peered straight into the camera to look rugged and casual, but the camera caught a touch of melancholy in his eyes. His overseas cap was slightly tilted and his earphones were clamped to the sides of his head. It was a jaunty photo that would make his dad and Dottie proud.

When he left the seminary, he had hoped to become a pilot, but he had "washed out" of flight school. This turn of events was a disappointment, but Red took it in stride and jokingly told his boyhood friend, Frank Noland, that on two occasions he had run out of runway and cracked up the old Stearman biplane trainer when his eyesight failed him. The Air Corps wanted only steady hands in the cockpits of bombers. Red had retrained and qualified to fly as a bombardier in the huge four-engine B-24s the Americans were producing by the thousands.

Red slipped into his parachute harness knowing it would be useless during much of the mission. The planes were going into Ploeşti too low for a parachute jump. But there was always the chance that over the target the pilot could bring a damaged plane up at the last minute to give the crew the opportunity to bail out. And over the Mediterranean and over most of Eastern Europe the planes would be at three thousand feet or higher.

Red boarded a truck with his fellow crewmen, which carried them out to *Euroclydon* as she sat low and massive looking in the darkness. Her mud brown color identified her as one of the planes on loan to the Ninth Air Force from the Eighth Air Force in Britain, where the planes were camouflaged against attacks from German marauders that occasionally slipped through British air defenses and bombed Allied airfields. The Ninth Air Force planes, permanently stationed in Libya, were painted a putty color or "desert pink" to blend with the landscape.

Every man on the mission reminded himself of the day's target. For Red it was the Concordia Vega refinery code named White 2 on the northern edge of Ploeşti that produced more high-octane gasoline and lubricating oil than any of the other refineries. His specific aiming point was the front door of the distilling plant, a structure as familiar to him now as his own home in Columbus. As a bombardier Red had memorized the features of all the key structures in the twenty-two-acre refining complex and the three tall chimneys near the center of Concordia Vega. The Air Corps had also provided films of the refinery areas and simulated a bomb run in motion pictures. Red had watched them until he felt as though he had already made scores of missions over the target. When he stepped from the truck, he carried more photographs of White 2 to study on the way to Ploeşti.

As Red approached the aircraft, *Euroclydon*'s pilot, 1st Lt. Enoch M. Porter, Jr., from Great Falls, Montana, greeted him, "Are you ready?" Lieutenant Porter asked.

"As ready as I'll ever be," Red replied in his deep southern drawl as he stepped into the plane through the rear hatch. *Euroclydon* was laden with bombs and extra fuel and sat lower to the ground than usual. "The Traveling Circus is gonna wow 'em in Ploeşti today," Red added.

He made his way to the nose, past the waist positions where the gunners were installing their machine guns on mounts and inserting belts of .50-caliber bullets that hung from the breach to the steel deck. Red squeezed into the bomb bay, where there was hardly room on the narrow catwalk for a normal-size man.

Euroclydon carried four thousand pounders in the rear bay, two on each side of the plane while the front bay on this mission held two four hundred-gallon auxiliary gas tanks for the extended flight. Red checked to see that the bombs were properly attached to their shackles and that the fuse safety pin in the nose of each bomb was in place. Otherwise, these inert projectiles could turn deadly and detonate during takeoff or in flight. Each Tidal Wave B-24 also carried several hundred pounds of incendiary sticks to ignite a conflagration.

Red moved on, stepping out of the bomb bay and looking up to the pilots' platform before kneeling down to crawl through the space below the cockpit. He squeezed past oxygen tanks, generators, hydraulic lines, and control cables that ran along the inside skin and wiggled his way to the front of the plane, past the navigator's station and into the glassed-in nose.

Lieutenant Porter also greeted 1st Lt. Howard Dickson, a gunnery officer and a desk jockey with the 93rd BG who trained waist and ball turret gunners for aerial combat in the security of an air force base. Dickson often hitched rides on bombing missions to experience combat, and to pass the hours of boredom that characterized most missions prior to reaching the target, he carried reading material; today it was Shakespeare.

"What's the book?" Lieutenant Porter asked Lieutenant Dickson.

"*As You Like It*," Lieutenant Dickson replied.

"Well, don't get into it too deeply," Lieutenant Porter added. "You're going to see some sights. We're going over in the first wave with Colonel Baker." Lt. Col. Addison Baker commanded the 93rd Bomb Group.

Dickson would be more than an observer in *Euroclydon* on Tidal Wave. He had been assigned as the top turret gunner to fill in for the regular gunner who had been sentenced to thirty days of KP (kitchen police) duty for stealing another crew member's whiskey ration the night before. It was an odd punishment. Many of the men would grab at the opportunity to avoid this mission; they were looking for a way out, and KP duty might have been a blessing and lifesaver. But Lieutenant Dickson was game to fight and climbed into the top turret behind the pilot.

Except for Lieutenant Dickson and a spare pilot, 2nd Lt. John Minogue, *Euroclydon*'s crew had been together since the States when they all reported to the 539th Bomb Squadron at Davis-Monthan Field near Tucson, Arizona. Lieutenant Porter, from Great Falls, Montana, was the pilot; the copilot was 2nd Lt. Joe S. Boswell, from Del eon, Texas; 2nd Lt. Jack Warner, from Lexington, Kentucky, was navigator; Red was the bombardier; S.Sgt. Frank Farrell, from Lueders, Texas, was the flight engineer; Sgt. Bernard R. Lucas, from Hanna, Wyoming, was the radio operator; and the gunners were sergeants Earl A. Frost, from Geneva, New York; Charles A. Reed, from Ridgewood, Long Island, New York; and James R. Vest, from Belle Plaines, Iowa.

The new team was greeted at the Tucson railroad station in late January 1943 by the sight of several coffins containing the bodies of B-24 crewmen killed on training missions. The men of *Euroclydon* had come to Davis-Monthan to hone their piloting, navigating, and bombing skills, and the ghosts of these dead airmen were warning that the preparation for war could be as deadly as combat itself.

The crew flew practice bombing missions over prairies, dams, and cities, plotted long-distance flights over the vastness of the American west, and, at the end of March 1943, traveled to Topeka, Kansas, to pick up their new plane, a B-24D that had been assembled in Fort Worth, Texas. She might be homely on the ground, drab brown with machine guns protruding from her nose like whiskers on an old hag, but in the air she flew with grace and speed.

Euroclydon would be home to her crew for many months. The men would get to know their plane's quirks and become comfortable in her confined spaces. They would learn to move quickly in an emergency around and over tanks, cables, guns, and bombs and to scamper across the bomb bay catwalk.

The crew had turned to Red, their preacher-bombardier, for advice in naming the plane. He asked his dad for an appropriate name, and Dr. Franks suggested that they call it *Euroclydon the Storm*, after the biblical tempest that had engulfed the eastern Mediterranean as the Apostle Paul was being conveyed by galley to Rome as a prisoner of the emperor. The name came from the New Testament, the Book of Acts, Chapter 27, and the crew seemed pleased with the image of a huge hurricanelike force enveloping the enemy from on high. It also was appropriately masculine and warlike, yet virtuous. So many of the bombers had names that alluded to loose women and sex, such as *Vulgar Virgin*, *Pink Lady*, *Strawberry Bitch*, and *Hadley's Harem*. *Euroclydon* was said to be the most erudite name for a plane in the entire Air Corps.

Dr. Franks also knew that Paul had survived the tempest and had comforted those on his vessel by assuring them that they all would be safe. "I now bid you to take heart; for there will be no loss of life among you, but only of the ship," Paul had said. He also assured his fellow travelers that the Almighty was watching over them: "For there stood by me this night an angel of God." In Dr. Franks's deepest prayers was the hope that the same angel sat on Red's shoulder and would guide him through the storm of war. But the elder Franks could never have imagined that *Euroclydon*, the B-24, would soon cross the path of Paul's meager vessel that sailed from Alexandria in Egypt to Italy as it weathered the fierce storm nearly two thousand years before.

Red and his crewmates flew *Euroclydon* across the Atlantic, over Ireland and Scotland, and down the length of England in May 1943, to an air base at Hardwick in Norfolk. Just before they landed, they were introduced to the dangers in a war zone. As the plane approached their new base, Lieutenant Porter picked up the "squeaker" radio signals emanating from barrage balloons that bobbed over the nearby town of Norwich. The base was frequently socked in by fog and drizzle, and the balloons were a deadly hazard for low-flying planes, friend or foe.

Euroclydon was assigned to the 328th Bomb Squadron of the Ninety-third Bomb Group that was headquartered at Hardwick. The base was a series of mile-long runways, constructed in a triangle around which were barracks, hangars, bomb storage areas, mess halls and the control tower. Up to three thousand men lived on the base that also was home to forty or fifty bombers.

The Ninety-third was the oldest serving B-24 group in the Eighth Air Force and had flown its first mission over German occupied France in October 1942, under command of Col. Edward Timberlake. The Eighth Air Force was comprised mostly of the better-known B-17s, nicknamed Flying Fortresses. The Ninety-third and its Liberators soon became known as Ted's Traveling Circus because the bomb group had already been transferred once before to North Africa and had returned to England. The name was similar to the German fighter group of World War I, The Flying Circus, made famous by Manfred von Richthofen, the Red Baron.

As *Euroclydon* touched down on the plains of Norfolk, Red was immediately awed by the beauty of the English countryside, the quaint villages, the rich green fields, the wildlife and birds, and the bleakness of nearby North Sea. Except for the sea, the landscape was not unlike Red's home country around Columbus, Mississippi, green and flat. All around Hardwick, B-24 and B-17 airfields were being carved out of former pastures and croplands, and there were days when the skies vibrated from the engine noise of hundreds of aircraft flying out on bombing missions to France or Germany, the Americans by day and the Royal Air Force (RAF) at night.

In the States the crew had counted, in wary anticipation, the days until they went into combat. Now the reality of the war was upon them, and they concentrated on surviving the twenty-five missions required of each crew member before he could rotate back home. But few men completed the mandatory number of missions. A majority were killed, wounded, or shot down to become prisoners of war before their tours of duty were up. The aircrews tried not to think of their probable fate, but the dangers also made them proud of their status as combat flyers. They were an elite vanguard of America's armed forces that was carrying the fight to the enemy. The average life expectancy of an Eighth Air Force crew and bomber was only fifteen missions, which prompted one navigator to exclaim to his pilot, "Skipper, mathematically there just isn't any way we're going to live through this thing."

Red and his navigator, Lt. Raymond "Jack" Warner, noticed immediately that bombardiers and navigators were in great demand in England, and they soon understood why. The Germans had discovered that the B-24s and the B-17s were lightly defended in the nose, and the Me 109s and Focke Wulf fighters attacked American bomber formations from the front. The nose sections, where the bombardier and navigator were positioned, were the most vulnerable part of the aircraft, and casualty rates for the two were higher than for other bomber crewmen. It was terrifying during fighter attacks to be stationed in the front of the B-24D with its 180-degree Plexiglas surround, dubbed the greenhouse, where the bombardier sat on his flimsy stool or on his haunches as though suspended from a girder atop the Empire State Building. In later B-24 models, a turret replaced the greenhouse and housed twin .50-caliber machine guns.

In the greenhouse, whichever way he looked, down, up, or sideways, Red saw nothing but a vast expanse of air, and he could see the enemy fighters climbing into the sun to get into position to streak down through the bomber formations with cannons blazing. And he watched helplessly as the plane flew into barrages of exploding antiaircraft shells. No one else in the plane had such a bird's-eye view of impending death. The pilots were sighted forward, but their windshields were narrow slits compared to the glass surround of the bombardier's position. By the time they flew on the Tidal Wave mission, Red and Jack had survived ten missions, all but one against targets in Italy. But none promised to be like Ploeşti.

As dawn broke around Benghazi and takeoff time for Tidal Wave approached, *Euroclydon*'s engines coughed to life, shooting flame from exhaust stacks and spewing clouds of white smoke that hovered above the wings momentarily before being whisked away by prop wash. The pilots of the heavily laden bombers taxied into position for takeoff, engines revving and idling as fuel trucks darted around the bombers to top off their gas tanks. As sunlight streaked the desert sky, the thirty B-24s of the 376th BG, the Liberandos, in their putty-colored desert camouflage, were the first to roll down the runway, leaving trails of swirling sand and dust. The thirty-six planes of the Traveling Circus also took off, as did the Pyramiders, the Eight Balls, and the Sky Scorpions from the various airfields that ringed Benghazi.

Among the Pyramiders taking off was the B-24 *Hadley's Harem*, piloted by 2nd Lt. Gilbert Hadley, twenty-two, of Arkansas City, Kansas, who had also just picked up his plane in Topeka fresh from a production facility in San Diego. The crew had flown the *Harem* to Cairo after a long trek of island-hopping through the Caribbean, across the Atlantic to Africa and then over the lifeless Sahara to Egypt. On July 2, 1943, the *Harem* was assigned to the Ninth Air Force outside Benghazi, and two days later she flew her first mission to bomb Vibo Valentia, Italy. It was a milk run with sparse flak and little fighter opposition, but the crew had tasted aerial combat. Two Macchi 202s came buzzing in but stayed clear of the B-24s and their eleven .50-caliber machine guns.

THE *Harem* flew her next raid against the chain of Axis air bases around Foggia, Italy, where the two waist gunners were given four-pound firebombs to throw out their gun windows when they were over the target. The *Harem*'s first mass raid was against Rome in mid-July, and by the end of the month, the crew members had flown nine missions. Despite her limited combat experience the *Harem* was assigned to fly on Killer Kane's left wing as he led the Pyramiders over Ploeşti. The colonel and the young Lt. "Gib" Hadley had quickly developed a fast friendship when the *Harem* joined the Ninety-eighth's 344th Bomb Squadron in early July. Kane and Hadley were flamboyant types who jockeyed their B-24s around the sky as though they were fighter planes. Hadley used to buzz grazing animals on training flights over the vast plains of the Midwest and once flew the *Harem* under a bridge as his incredulous crew watched in amazement and held their breaths in terror as the big bomber cleared the gorge.

The lead Liberandos rose skyward from Benghazi and began to assemble in staggered formations as they flew out over the Mediterranean Sea toward Ploeşti. The sheltering desert rushed away beneath them, and the planes, seemingly nimble despite their heavy bomb loads, rose higher and higher to swarm above Homer's "wine dark" sea. Just behind the Liberandos came the first groups of the Traveling Circus led by Lt. Col. Baker in the B-24 *Hell's Wench*. To his right was Lt. Walter Stuart, the former Mormon missionary, piloting *Utah Man*. To the left was *Euroclydon*. The three planes would lead the Traveling Circus into Eastern Europe and over Ploeşti.

In *Euroclydon's* chilly snout, spiked by .50-caliber machine guns, Red Franks busied himself to ward off boredom and fear and to prepare for the attack. Later, it would be his mission responsibility to see that the four thousand-pound bombs were armed just prior to reaching the target and then to drop them on Concordia Vega. Each bomb carried a delayed action fuse to prevent its instant detonation when it hit the ground. The force of bombs exploding on contact could bring down oncoming B-24s in the rear formations still approaching the target at only fifty feet. Some of the bomb fuses were set to detonate hours after being dropped to impede and kill enemy repair crews.

As the bombers reached their cruising altitude at three thousand feet in staggered formations, Lieutenant Porter ordered his gunners to test fire their weapons. Normally there were three machine guns in the nose of a B-24D, one pointing forward through the Plexiglas, usually manned by the bombardier, and two "cheek" guns on either side of the nose. Red and navigator Lt. Jack Warner gripped the gun handles and squeezed off staccato bursts that sent orange-red tracer rounds curving into the firmament and arching downward into the vastness of the Mediterranean. *Euroclydon*, like the other lead planes on the mission, had been equipped with another set of stationary twin .50s installed in the nose, controlled by the pilot and designed to send streams of bullets at targets of opportunity as the plane flew over the target.

All around the formation tracers danced and twisted away, silent and mysterious, like streaks of summer lightning, as each plane tested its guns. Every fourth round in a belt of machine gun bullets was an illuminated tracer to enable the gunner to follow the bullet's trajectory and more accurately aim at the target. Over Ploeşti the tracers would facilitate hitting ground targets as the gunners aimed to kill enemy soldiers and to puncture the huge oil tanks and distilling plants with armor-piercing, incendiary bullets. Enemy fighter pilots too were wary of the flashing tracers that darted out at them from large formations of B-24s. Only veteran Axis pilots had learned to ignore the streams of lethal projectiles, and they approached with respect.

Euroclydon shook and reverberated to the blast of its eleven machine guns all firing at once, and the acrid smell of spent powder drifted through the frigid plane. The shooting ceased, and Red settled back to watch and wait. For much of the flight he would sit perched on a small canvas-covered seat attached to three wheeled legs that enabled him to swivel quickly about the nose and gave him leverage on high-altitude missions to peer down into the Norden bombsight.

Red looked out at the sea stretching away in all directions. The preacher's son had learned the history of this ancient region three thousand feet below from years of historical and biblical instruction from his father. Off the right wing, to the east, as the Circus flew northward over the Mediterranean, was a shadowy and low silhouette that rose from the sea, most likely the distant island of Crete, the land of King Minos and the Minotaur. *Euroclydon* and the Circus flew on into the mythical world of ancient Greece profiled on their right in the rugged, jutting peaks of Sparta. Below too was the ancient port of Pylos on the west coast of the Peloponnesian peninsula, the home of Odysseus's legendary friend, King Nestor. The flight traversed the Ionian Sea where Odysseus made his home on the island of Ithaca from which he set out for the Trojan War. Beneath them, the waters of the Middle Sea were indifferent to this new army of men and machines that soared above on yet another journey to war.

As the Tidal Wave force closed on the coast of Albania, the crews felt relief that no enemy fighters had been sighted and there had been no anti-aircraft fire. The only disturbance was the drone of the turbo-supercharged, twelve hundred-horsepower engines that forced the men to communicate through the intercom. Talk between the bombers was forbidden to prevent the Germans from picking up radio chatter and learning of the impending attack. But the secrecy was in vain. The Germans had broken the Allied code and knew as the first planes took off that a large force of B-24s was headed toward southern Europe. Spotters on Corfu and at other points along the flight path called in as the bombers flew over, and German radar operators locked onto the Tidal Wave blip. The enemy waited, watched, and plotted. "Many wings," reported one radar operator. "Many big bombers," reported a ground spotter. The only question for the Germans to answer was where the attack would fall, the Me 109 fighter plane plant at Weiner Neustadt in Austria, targets in Sophia, Bulgaria, or the oil refineries at Ploeşti?

When the B-24s reached the Balkans, Bulgarian fighter planes shadowed the force, but only a few B-24 crews saw the enemy, and radio silence precluded warning the rest of the formation. By the time the Tidal Wave planes made Romania, the Germans were preparing for an attack on Ploeşti.

Three hours out from Benghazi the lead planes of the Traveling Circus discerned the shadow of Corfu, snug against the rugged coastline of Albania and Greece. With the Liberandos up ahead, Tidal Wave would soon be executing a right turn over the mainland into Eastern Europe, territory that for these men was as uncharted as the surface of the moon.

Near Corfu, the official Tidal Wave leader, Col. Keith Compton leading the 376th Liberandos in his ship, *Teggie Ann,* gave the signal for the force to climb to ten thousand feet above unexpected cloud cover that hovered over the Pindus Mountains, the coastal range in southern Albania and northwest

Greece. *Wongo Wongo*, the mission's lead ship and the Tidal Wave navigator, began her turn and climb. But the plane suddenly nosed upward and stalled, then banked sharply to the left as sister ships scattered to avoid collision, and fell into the sea. Her death struggle had lasted less than a minute.

Lt. Walter Stuart, piloting *Utah Man*, felt a tug on the shoulder of his flying jacket. "Look at that," his copilot exclaimed as Lieutenant Stuart saw a bomber flash by the windscreen. Lieutenant Stuart watched *Wongo Wongo* career downward, as did Red Franks in *Euroclydon*'s nose. Men tensed and fidgeted with their guns and looked for German fighters lurking off the Albanian coast that may have sniffed out the force and begun an attack.

The pilot in the plane carrying the backup lead navigator inexplicably defied standing orders that forbade any plane to leave the formation and descended to a few feet above the water to search for survivors. None were seen and the plane turned for home. She could not regain altitude and rejoin the bomber team. As the backup navigator aborted the mission, men in the oncoming bombers pondered the fate of Tidal Wave. 2nd Lt. William Wright in the B-24 *Brewery Wagon* now became the lead navigator for one of the most critical operations of the war.

Red instinctively checked the forward guns and scanned the skies. The heavens were empty except for the bomber stream that stretched back five miles until the distant B-24s were mere silvery specks almost lost in the frosted blue of the heavens. As *Euroclydon* plodded onward, the smudge in the sea left by *Wongo Wongo* became a column of black smoke rising to greet the oncoming Tidal Wave bombers.

The eyes of every man in the attacking waves focused on this pillar of doom, knowing that *Wongo Wongo*'s crew had perished. They had died in a flash, but not so quickly that they did not have time to contemplate their fate. Sergeant Russell Page, the engineer in *Hadley's Harem*, saw the fire in the sea and winced as the Pyramiders flew by. It was one of their own, the second ship to go down since the start of the operation. The aircrews fought back a fear that left a distinct metallic taste in their dry mouths as it sucked the blood from their faces. The B-24's fate only reinforced an earlier ill omen. At takeoff *Kickapoo* had crashed trying to land after an engine failed.

Laden with bombs and thousands of gallons of aviation gasoline, *Kickapoo* hit a light pole on its return to base and exploded in flames. The bomb group's planes were still taking off and flew over the funeral pyre on the runway. Only two of the ten-man crew survived.

As Tidal Wave pressed on, occasional B-24s feathered propellers when engine cylinders failed, and the planes peeled out of formation to return to Benghazi. Before the Tidal Wave force reached the target, more than a dozen bombers would abort the mission and wing their way back to base with crews barely suppressing their relief. They would live another day. Wind-blown desert sands had ruined many engines, and there was no place for a limping bomber on the flight to Ploeşti.

The bomber force swept past *Wongo Wongo's* fiery tomb, and each man pondered in apprehensive silence the fate of his ship and its crew and the fate of all the men of Tidal Wave in the hours ahead. Red Franks and his comrades prayed and soothed themselves with thoughts of home and loved ones.

3

Just One More Day

"Give me just one more day back home," Lt. Walter Stuart mused the night before the Tidal Wave bombers rose in attack. For Lieutenant Stuart, home was Benjamin, Utah, a small town nearly a mile above sea level in the rugged uplands south of Salt Lake City, with the peaks of the nearby Rockies jutting to the sky. And as Lieutenant Stuart in *Utah Man*, Lieutenant Porter in *Euroclydon*, and Lieutenant Colonel Baker in *Hell's Wench* piloted their B-24s in the lead of the Ninety-third Bomb Group over the rugged Balkan terrain towards Ploeşti, many men in the bomber force dreamed of home. Red Franks could look at his watch and imagine the beginnings of the day back home where it was just before dawn on Sunday. His father would be rising at almost this exact moment to put the finishing touches on his sermon for the day; he would deliver it to his congregation at 11 A.M. from his usual jumble of handwritten notes jotted down on scrap paper and on the backs of old envelopes. As Dr. Franks began Sunday school classes at 9 A.M. in the church education building, Red and his comrades would be fighting for their lives over Ploeşti.

Home for Red was in the fertile and gently undulating prairie country around Columbus in northeastern Mississippi, a place, some said, where there was room to breathe. The setting was quintessentially mid-twentieth century rural American: the city was small, about ten thousand residents, and isolated amidst vast tracks of farm and open land that stretched for miles to the next sizable metropolis. Memphis, Tennessee, was 171 miles to the northwest, and Birmingham, Alabama, lay 120 miles due east.

The landscape in midsummer was a patchwork quilt of never-ending fields, green with prairie grass and alfalfa, yellow from waving corn tassels, and fluffy white from the miles of ripened cotton balls quivering in the shifting breezes. Cattle basked in pastures grazed smooth as alpine meadows, and dust rose from the dirt and gravel roads that stitched the countryside together.

Columbus was a city of wide, tree-shaded streets. Seen from above, it resembled the cozy, welcoming town of a model-train set. There was little industry although the city was home to the Columbus marble plant that occupied a plot between Seventh and Eighth Avenue South and cut Georgia and Alabama marble into building blocks, slabs, and headstones. There were a few other small industrial establishments, but the city's main purpose was to be a hub for this rural region of Mississippi.

The downtown was compact in five or six blocks and the buildings were low lying, mostly two- and three-story brick structures with detailed cornices that housed two movie theaters, drug and clothing stores, a bakery, restaurants, and a firehouse. The massive four-story Gilmer Hotel that overlooked the Tombigbee River below the bluff where the city's forefathers had built their city anchored the commercial district at its western end. The Lowndes County Courthouse, with the traditional monument to the Confederate dead of the Civil War erected near the front entrance, was at the north end. Across the street from the courts was a neat line of Federal style, two-story townhouses converted to law offices and appropriately named Lawyer's Row.

The commercial district flowed into Columbus's residential areas to the south and to the north where one found numerous porticoed mansions some topped with widow's walks. These had once dominated the blocks where they stood, but over the years the large lots had been parceled off, and smaller homes now occupied ground that had once been wide lawns and sumptuous gardens. Most of these stately houses dated from the thirty years before the Civil War, Columbus's most prosperous period, when cotton production was at an all-time high. Many were built in a style that became known as Columbus Eclectic and featured a combination of the Greek Revival, Italianate, and Gothic styles. Their furnishings were imported from Europe and had been transported to Columbus by barge up the Tombigbee from Mobile, Alabama.

The great homes had once served as town houses for the outlying plantation owners who spent part of the year in the city to escape the boredom of the countryside. It was these southern patricians who later became stalwarts of the Confederacy. Among them was Gen. Stephen D. Lee, who reportedly fired the first shots of the Civil War when he ordered rebel guns to open up on Fort Sumter in 1861. Stephen Lee was such a favored son that the citizens of Columbus named the high school in his honor, and his old mansion on Seventh Street North, across from the First Baptist Church, was used as a classroom building for Lee High.

Columbus was proud of its antebellum heritage, and until the outbreak of World War II many of the old mansions were open during Pilgrimage Week in April to tourists who flocked to the city to view a slice of the Old South. The tour promoted Columbus as the Sleeping Beauty of the Deep South, with its architectural splendor augmented by stands of japonicas, jonquils, and jessamine. Wisteria and azaleas were also abundant. The city's leading citizens volunteered to staff the houses when they were open to visitors, and Red's sister, Nancy Lee, used to dress in a Civil War–era hoopskirt and frilly blouse and play the piano at estates with names like Hickory Sticks, on Seventh Street North, and Magnolia Hill, on Twelfth Street North, as tourists filed through.

The city had been spared during the Civil War when Yankee raiders burned and pillaged other Mississippi towns. Federal troops did not venture into Columbus, and the grand homes survived, and many served as hospitals for Confederate wounded from the Battle of Shiloh in Tennessee in 1862. The only other town that had as many antebellum homes the equal of those in Columbus, so it was said, was Nachez, Mississippi, but Columbus residents were sure their hometown's stock was superior.

The citizens of Columbus were a cultured lot who valued education. Columbus was the site of Franklin Academy, the first free school in Mississippi, founded in 1821, and before the Civil War, the school reflected the forward thinkers of the South and was open to all races and creeds. In 1847 the city became home to the Columbus Female Institute, later renamed Mississippi State College for Women (MSCW), the first state-supported college for women in the United States. Any Yankee who thought the South was backward had only to look at the emphasis Mississippians and Columbians placed on educating their young people, including women. Most of Red's friends, even a number of the young ladies in his high school class, as well as Nancy Lee, had gone to college, and most had attended institutions within the state of Mississippi: Mississippi College, MSCW, Milsaps, Belhaven, and Mississippi State University.

Visitors to Columbus who wandered down College Avenue came upon MSCW's massive brick and ivy-covered Calloway and Columbus Halls. In appearance the college seemed more like a Victorian place of incarceration than an institution of higher learning, but this image suited many Mississippians who sent their daughters there. They welcomed MSCW's strictness along with its high educational and moral standards. The campus was off limits to young men, unless they walked in one side and kept on moving right out the other side, and MSCW women were forbidden to date until they were seniors. The girls all wore the same uniform, a simple blue dress and black cotton hose, and the educational director at the First Baptist Church remembers their carefully chaperoned weekly walks to Sunday morning services: "They were a tide of blue," she noted. One of the young women who attended MSCW in the late 1920s when Dr. Franks was involved in the college's Baptist Youth Organization was a budding writer named Eudora Welty. She later transferred to the more liberal environment of the University of Wisconsin.

It was said by outsiders that the people of Columbus looked down their noses at their neighbors in the surrounding countryside and didn't speak to newcomers until they had lived in the community for at least a year. But Red knew the people of his hometown as the friendliest and most caring anywhere; in fact, Columbus was often called the Friendly City, where total strangers greeted each other on the street and asked how they were getting on. Red mentioned their kindness and thoughtfulness in the letter to his father that was sitting at the end of his cot in Benghazi.

In fact, Columbus was small enough that most everyone knew everyone else. Red could walk the three blocks to Main Street when he was in high school and in college and drop by to chat with merchants or converse with passersby who were friends of his father or members of the First Baptist Church. There weren't many young men left in town now that Red had known growing up. Most were in military service.

August in Mississippi was a time of such heavy heat that the land became shrouded in a sweltering humid haze, slowing life to a languorous pace. Massive thunderheads collected in the domed sky, the locust screeched, and the mourning doves cooed soothingly. As a boy Red escaped the soaring temperatures of summer in the YMCA pool a block from his home on Second Avenue North, where for a dime he and his friends swam all day. Better still, they often wandered down by the trestle bridge on the edge of town and walked up the Tombigbee River to one of their favorite swimming holes where they swung from vines and cannonballed into the muddy waters. Many of Columbus's leading citizens had cabins—they called them "camps" in Mississippi—on the Tombigbee or on the nearby Luxapalila where the wives and children of professional men spent their summers lolling by the rivers.

The slowness of a Mississippi summer seemed to be reflected in the lilting drawl and kindly manners of the townsfolk. Nannie Kate Smith, one of the Frankses' closest neighbors, personified these courteous southerners.

The Smith home was on Third Avenue North, behind the Frankes' parsonage, and next to the First Baptist Church where Dr. Franks had been pastor for twenty-two years. Nannie Kate called everyone "honey" in her deep Mississippi drawl. "What, honey," "Hello, honey," and "Bye, honey." When Nannie Kate said, "Bye," it came out "Baaa," soft and sweet, like the bleating of a lamb, far different from the jargon of those Yankees whom Red met in the Air Corps.

If Red were home right now, he might see Nannie Kate's daughter, Eleanor, and Nancy Lee conversing with the intensity of gossiping spinsters over the wooden back fence that split the residential block behind Nannie Kate's house and the Baptist parsonage. The fence had been more rallying point than property divider, and the neighborhood kids met by it, chatted and argued there, and easily climbed over it on a makeshift ladder built from discarded pieces of lumber.

The block where Red lived was bounded by Second Avenue North and Third Avenue North and Seventh and Eighth Streets, and it teemed with children. The church and its educational building filled half of the block, and the other half was taken up by homes, including the parsonage, and all had backyards that converged on the wooden fence. Besides Red, there was a gang of boys about his own age, Rufus Ward and his two brothers, Edward Hudson, Albert Pippin, and Howard, Frank, and Riley Noland who lived next door to the Franks. Across Second Avenue North from the Nolands and the Frankses were the McGahey brothers. When they were children, the din of their voices was constant from dawn till dusk, and whenever they moved it seemed to be en masse, over and through backyards and flower beds. Albert Pippin's grandmother was constantly gathering up her switch to chase boys from her backyard, where they disturbed her laying chickens. And the neighbor woman across Second Avenue North was always on the lookout for prowling bands of boys who trampled her flower beds.

The Frankses did their share of shooing children from their own yard, which was given over in summer to a large vegetable and flower garden that Dr. Franks tended with the same fervor as he administered the word of God to his parishioners. The family table was never without his big ripe tomatoes, radishes, cabbage, and squash, while the parlor always sprouted tulips and roses. They might even be eating a squirrel or a rabbit that Dr. Franks bagged on a seven-acre plot in the country outside Columbus where he had built a small cabin to find solitude away from the needs of his congregation on his days off.

To escape the summer heat the Franks were served meals by their black cook, Nora, on the screened porch just behind the kitchen. From their dinner table they could watch their cow in the backyard as she grazed contentedly near the small barn that backed against the Nolands' property. Dr. Franks kept her to supplement his meager preacher's salary, and Red's job in high school was to care for her and pick up her plops that oozed in the lawn, drawing flies and sprouting new blades of bright green grass. Cow droppings made excellent fertilizer for Dr. Franks's garden.

Behind his dapper façade, Dr. Franks was a country boy who had once been used to getting down and dirty with animals. Having been raised on a farm, he knew how to care for livestock, and he fed his backyard cow bran and cottonseed whenever possible. His father had been a farmer and carpenter, and young Jesse learned to work with his hands and might have followed in his father's footsteps had he not received a college scholarship. He had paid part of his way through Mississippi College at the turn of the century by working in the college dairy.

Red was awake every morning before dawn to collect and sanitize the cow's milk in an electric pasteurizer and then bottle it for delivery to families around the neighborhood. Red marketed his dairy products under the name of his small enterprise, "Columbus Ice Cream and Creamery Company," written out in big bold letters on a sign tacked on the side of the barn in the backyard. But he had never gotten around to starting the ice cream operation.

The cow had another function besides giving milk; she taught the neighborhood boys their first lessons about sex. They gleefully gathered to follow Red whenever he marched her out of town into the prairie to a nearby farm for an appointment with a local bull, and later they returned to accompany her back home. The Frankses' cow was eventually banished to the countryside when a neighbor complained about farm animals being housed in the city just a block from the courthouse.

Having a cow in the backyard was part of the innocence that Red and his friends experienced growing up in the late 1920s and during the height of the depression in the early 1930s. It was an era that now seemed to be light-years away from the war and the icy, well-ventilated B-24 that droned on towards Ploeşti. In the often raucous, hard-drinking, poker-playing environment of the Air Corps where death and mayhem lurked with every dawn, Red could look back to quiet evenings at home as a boy playing Old Maid or Rook with Nancy Lee and his father and listening to *Amos and Andy* and *Little Orphan Annie* on the Atwater Kent radio. In summer he would sometimes sit on the front porch with his father and sister as the cool breezes of evening washed across them and the children's chatter slowly died away as night descended on the neighborhood.

The mores of Columbus and the Baptist South were strict and straight laced. Still the neighborhood kids were often up to mischief. But it was an innocent kind. One favorite pursuit of Red's block gang when they were young children was to stuff an old black sock with newspaper, tie it to a string, and, just at dusk, drop it on the other side of the sidewalk that ran past the parsonage. The children rushed to hide on the front part of the wraparound porch of the parsonage and waited for some unsuspecting pedestrian to pass. Red or Howard Noland or Albert Pippin pulled the string and the sock slithered across the sidewalk to frighten the passerby. Red and his friends would guffaw loudly, and Nancy Lee and Eleanor Ward would giggle at the startled yelps of passing neighbors.

As he grew older, Red was known for his red hair, freckles, disarming smile, and deep, friendly brown eyes that were just like his father's, and Columbians regarded him as a good boy. He and his friends could still be a handful. Dr. Franks one day peered out from the back of the parsonage to see smoke pouring from the clubhouse that Red and his friends had built in the Frankses' backyard. The dutiful father dashed out to quench the fire, but arrived at the clubhouse door to see Red and his friends sucking on pipes.

They had puffed up so much smoke that their clubhouse appeared to be on fire. He grabbed Red and sent him to his room and ordered the other boys home. When he gathered up the smoking paraphernalia, he was surprised to see that, instead of tobacco, his son and his friends had filled their pipes with coffee grounds pilfered from the kitchen pantry.

Dr. Franks tried to promote sugarcane sticks for Red as a tobacco substitute and bought a few stalks each week from an elderly black farmer who hawked vegetables and produce door-to-door. Dr. Franks split the cane into pencil thin slivers with his penknife and handed them out to Red and Nancy Lee to suck on while keeping a few for himself. But that didn't stop Red and his friends from continuing their experiments with smoking. They puffed on corn silk and lopped off sections of vine stems, dried them, and lit them up as well. Even Nancy Lee and her friends experimented with corn silk.

The antics of the children continued. Dr. Franks again sent Red's friends packing when he caught them snaring pigeons that roosted in the crawl space in the church attic. But they returned to the potentially dangerous occupation when Dr. Franks wasn't looking. Red, Frank Noland, and others in the neighborhood gang carried flashlights to blind their quarry to gather more birds. Their plan was to turn the pigeons into house pets, and they soon had so many captive birds that they had to let most of them go. Pigeons as house pets! Augusta, Red's stepmother, was mortified. She wasn't fond of animals and had banished the terrier she inherited when she and Dr. Franks were married.

Red and his friend Jake Propst, who lived on the city's more sumptuous south side, were almost nabbed by the city police one Halloween night. They joined a group of rowdy teenage pranksters and went trick-or-treating through the neighborhood, throwing corn kernels at houses, rattling windows, and taking chairs off front porches and hauling them up telephone poles. Red and Jake scurried home just before the police arrived to nab the rest of the gang. The next day Jake's father, the right honorable mayor of Columbus, was informed about the roundup and warned his son that if he ever got caught doing the things those other boys were doing the night before he'd be in for a good whipping.

Red didn't fit the mold of the strict Southern Baptists of the day; he was too independently minded, not demonstrably religious, certainly not pious, and not above flouting some of the strict rules of the Baptist Church. No one pegged him as a preacher's son. Rumor even had it that Red had once gone for a dip to cool off in the church's massive baptismal pool behind the pulpit. "There's no way you could say he was pious," Betty Holland remembered. "He was just a barrel of fun, and he had a gay little smile and mischievous eyes."

If there was one place where Red and the neighborhood children were well behaved, it was in and around the synagogue, and they gave it wide berth. The synagogue was next to the parsonage and had once been a Christian house of worship, the First Presbyterian Church, built in the mid-1800s. The congregation moved two blocks away to a new building, and the old church soon was taken over by Columbus's expanding Jewish community.

Unexposed to different religions and cultures, all the children glanced furtively at the old rabbi with his strange ways and his even stranger yarmulke and manner of dress. But it was the red light that burned continuously inside the temple day and night that intrigued and frightened them most. After dark, Red and Nancy Lee could peer from her bedroom window through the synagogue windows to see the eerie glow. It was avowed by many of the children that if the red light ever went out, it would portend the end of the world, and every kid was preternaturally attentive to the light as they passed by. If it still burned, the safety of the world was assured. Even as teenagers, Red and his friends would cast wary glances at the red light, still somewhat taken in by its supposed powers.

But Nancy Lee and her friend Betty were unfazed by the synagogue, and they sometimes eluded the rabbi and snuck inside to play the organ. Nancy Lee was too small and her feet did not reach the foot pedals, so Betty crouched beneath her to push them with her hands. The old rabbi was startled to hear Christian hymns suddenly radiating from a Jewish house of worship, and he rushed out to scold them and shoo them back to Baptist territory. Nancy Lee was certain her father never found out about her escapades in the synagogue with Betty, but Dr. Franks may have known anyway, but said nothing.

He knew Nancy Lee to be a well-behaved little girl, growing up in the image of her dead mother, Sallie, and in the traditions of southern ladies.

Nancy Lee and Betty's playground was also the Baptist Church where they would sail their toy boats in the enormous baptismal pool that was sometimes left filled with water following a service. And they sometimes snitched grape juice left in cups after communion. Nancy Lee once dripped juice on her dress and tried to cleanse the stain with bleach only to leave an even larger blemish that made her transgression easily visible to her father.

Red called Nancy Lee "Sis," and she too was remarkably fearless and free spirited for the daughter of a Baptist minister. As a child of hardly more than four, she would stride, barefoot in summer, the mile or so down Military Road to the more tumbled down black section of town to visit her black nurse, and nannie, whose name was Laura. Nearby was the Queen City Hotel where blacks congregated to imbibe bootleg liquor and listen to jazz. Dr. Franks said nothing, although parishioners almost surely would have reported her adventures back to him.

Nancy Lee loved to run to the church when she heard the chimes and climb into the steeple to help William, the black janitor, ring the bells. He would lift her up to the rope, and she would swing freely across the belfry, moving up and down and from side to side with the motions of the bells.

In an era before the sustained civil rights movement of the 1960s, some in the city and the state might have cringed and others might have been angered by Dr. Franks's acceptance of Nancy's associations. But Dr. Franks was a tolerant man and preacher with a vision that surpassed that of most of his contemporaries. He could preach the strictures of the Bible and the conservative Southern Baptist philosophy, but he was a believer in the equality of man even though he could not be overly demonstrative about his feelings in a Mississippi that practiced rigid segregation and where many citizens thrived on racial divide. He provided space for blacks in the Baptist Church, and although they were confined to the balcony, many white southern churches of any denomination denied access to blacks. When Sallie died, Nancy Lee attended the funeral service with Laura, and the two sat in the balcony.

In the 1920s and 1930s, Dr. Franks was years ahead of his Baptist colleagues and light-years ahead of most Mississippians in his belief that the two races would begin to mix sooner than most could visualize. "He foresaw that white people would be marrying black people," Nancy Lee said.

"If it is God's plan that the development of the human race should come from the cultivation of many racial types and cultures as Babel teaches, then God must be working toward the creation of a glorious worldwide racial mosaic, one in which all racial peculiarities and endowments are to be remembered, recognized, selected, and made to contribute towards working out of his masterpiece, a harmonious brotherhood of man in the family of nations," Dr. Franks wrote in 1939. He added: "Certainly God's way as taught in Genesis 11 leaves no room for racial or national boasting." He referred to the Tower of Babel and stated, "They were seeking to establish racial superiority and power by entrenching themselves in favor of the good land and erecting many barriers to keep out the rest of the world. But God said, 'No, that is not my way,' and he scattered them abroad." Dr. Franks's liberal philosophy on race was not lost on Red, or on Nancy Lee.

Nancy Lee's talents had always impressed Red. She was an A student and became the class valedictorian from Lee High in 1941. She also played the piano beautifully and was now majoring in music at Shorter College in Georgia. Her musical talents were a far cry from Red's. He played the trumpet in high school and was a member of the Lee High band, where he gained a reputation for his brand of play; he was louder than he was polished. Nancy Lee's friend Betty laughed behind his back whenever he hit a high note. "His face gets as red as his hair when he blows real hard," she once whispered to Nancy Lee. Every house on the block knew when Red practiced the trumpet. His playing didn't have his sister's delicate tone and touch when she practiced the piano. Red would often turn on the radio and blast big band music to the outdoors and play along with the likes of Louis Armstrong or other well-known trumpet players. His favorite jazz piece was "Sugar Blues."

High school for Red was half a block away on the corner of Third Avenue North and Seventh Street North. The school had been built around the turn of the century, and as the enrollment grew, the city purchased the Stephen D. Lee house next door for additional classrooms and a cafeteria. In the mornings many of Red's friends on the block poured out of their homes and into Lee High as the last bell rang. They had learned to time their rising just right, to have a few minutes more of sleep. They were out of bed at the sound of the first bell and clothed and on their way to class at the sound of the final one.

Red was an average student, not particularly interested in academics. Where he excelled was in athletics. "Red was no intellectual. He was a football player," remembered Dick Burts, a boyhood pal from summer camp. Every afternoon after school Red went home to drop his books and then ran off to the locker room at the Magnolia Bowl, the Lee High stadium. He played football in the fall, participated in basketball in winter, ran track in the spring, and played baseball in the summer. In high school Red was well respected for his football prowess and was a sizable enough kid in high school at five foot eight inches and 155 pounds to have an impact as a guard for the Lee High School Generals. "He was really eager and aggressive. Determined, that's what Red was on the field," was the way Jake Propst described his friend.

The year 1936 was a mythical one for the Lee High squad, and Red was one of the players. The Generals won all their games against local opponents and drew large crowds to the Magnolia Bowl, a concrete stadium on the northern edge of Columbus where the city gave way to rolling prairie. The team went on to beat tough squads in the regional playoff, and by season's end they found themselves facing Chicago's powerful Austin High School for a championship game that would decide the best high school team in the country.

Red and the Generals were up against Bill DeCorrevont, who was considered the best high school football player of the 1930s and who would later play on championship Northwestern teams and for the Chicago Bears. He could do everything: run, block, and pass, and he always found a way to score. The Generals met Austin High for the championship game at Crump Stadium in Memphis before a crowd of forty thousand. Red had never seen such tumult. It was wet and the temperature was near freezing as the two teams slugged it out in the Tennessee muck. The Generals scored a touchdown early and kicked the extra point. Austin did everything it could to best these southern boys from Mississippi, but the Lee High squad contained DeCorrevont and held his Austin teammates to only six points. The Generals emerged as national champions.

The next year Red had filled out and was a strapping first-string guard for the Generals. "He sure could 'whup 'em,'" Jake Propst remembered. Red was proud that he could tangle with the biggest and the roughest of the "old southern boys" on the line, and he pushed as much as he was shoved.

In the Baptist South, religion was as important as education, and Dr. Franks saw that Red and his pals were in the congregation every Sunday. He had baptized most of them and instructed them in Sunday school classes held in the education building.

Red and his friends were regulars at the Baptist youth gatherings held on Sunday nights in the education center next to the church. They were always well chaperoned because Dr. Franks would not stand for inappropriate behavior. His strictures seemed harsh, but he lived by them. Sunday was the Sabbath, and he frowned upon going to the movies, participating in athletic events of any sort, and dancing on God's day of rest, and he would not budge from his convictions. The family didn't even keep playing cards in the home. Certainly his children should not indulge in these pastimes on the Sabbath, nor was it appropriate for them to be seen "carrying on" at any time in Columbus. The children of a Southern Baptist minister were expected to set examples for all the children in the parish.

But Red flaunted a number of the Baptist rules. "He went the other way from his father," Burts remembered. Red loved the movies, particularly since the preacher's son got into the show for the cost of the entertainment tax— one cent. Red often went with Frank Noland on Sundays, and sometimes Frank's loyal bird dog followed them all the way downtown to the Princess Theater. On one occasion the boys paid their fare, and Frank pointed towards home and told the hound to vamoose. Red and Frank went in, sat down, and the movie began. A few minutes later Red looked up to see the bird dog staring intently at them from the aisle.

Sunday in the summer was the day of pickup baseball games at a nearby park, and Red played catcher. Whether it was misguided bravado or distaste for cumbersome equipment, he refused to wear a mask and paid the price when a foul tip broke his nose. He sported two huge shiners for several weeks. But Dr. Franks didn't need to see Red's black eyes to know that his son was violating the Sabbath. Tattletale parishioners always managed to report these infractions to his father. But Dr. Franks never punished Red.

Red also loved to go dancing with Dottie when he was in college, and when he came home for a weekend, he would turn on the radio to dance music, roll up the rug, and teach Nancy the basic steps of the fox-trot or the waltz. As a preacher's daughter, Nancy Lee was unschooled in the art of dancing. "Stand on my toes," Red instructed his sister as he led her around the room, "and just follow my lead." Nancy Lee wouldn't dare take up dancing at any time, anywhere in Columbus. But Dr. Franks never uttered a word about Red's lessons. Red wasn't teaching Nancy Lee to dance in defiance of his father; he was doing it because he always took an interest in his kid sister's needs and looked after her following their mother's death.

As Red grew up, he came to admire his father even with his unyielding principles, and Red developed strong opinions and principles of his own. His friend Dick Burts remembers him as a young man of strong character who expected strength of character from friends. Red knew Dr. Franks to have that strength. But his father was also a gentle, forgiving, and sympathetic man, and Red remembered times when Dr. Franks asked his children, and sometimes their friends, to attend church funeral services of poor parishioners to flesh out the ranks of mourners. In the nearly empty church, the children sat in the rear, their heads hung low in well-rehearsed mourning and prayer. There was no mockery intended. It was a kindly gesture reflecting Dr. Franks's compassion. He just wanted to make it appear as though the deceased had had friends of all ages and from all walks and to comfort the bereaved family.

Dr. Franks did not intimidate his children with threats of eternal damnation or criticize them for their behavior. Maybe it was because he knew that both Nancy Lee and Red had suffered from their mother's early death. But Red knew that Sallie's death was a cruel blow to his father as well. Everyone missed Sallie.

4

Remembering Sallie

Life in Columbus seemed a lifetime away as Red steadied himself in the nose compartment of *Euroclydon* and the big plane bounced and skidded along in the updrafts rising from the chiseled ridges and deep valleys below in Albania and Yugoslavia. Soon the formations would be approaching Bulgaria, and Romania was not far beyond. The people below were enemies, and like many of the Tidal Wave crewmen, Red wondered what they were like. Were they truly hostile? Whatever they were, he knew they were compelled to fight.

Red searched the horizon for enemy fighters as Lieutenant Dickson spun in his Plexiglas gun turret behind the pilots, looking for Me 109s. If enemy planes appeared, the intercom would suddenly crackle with shouts of "bandits," with a fix of their position in the sky—twelve o'clock high or three o'clock high. But in all directions the heavens above them were vivid blue, empty except for B-24s flying along ahead, to the sides, and to the rear, sparkling in the sharp rays of the bright morning sun. The big bombers seemed to have assumed the characteristics of angry birds, as the narrow windows of their cockpits resembled the fierce, glinting eyes of eagles.

As the son of a Baptist preacher, Red often pondered the notion of everlasting life; he certainly believed that the souls of the dead rose to heaven, and in the frigid clarity of the stratosphere, Red was reminded of his mother. He never really knew Sallie; she had died when he was a boy of eight, and she was the sweet-faced and tender young woman who had always comforted him. Everybody in Columbus remembered Sallie Graham Franks as a "lovely, charming girl." "She was a darling woman, a lovely lady whom everybody adored," Nannie Kate said.

Sallie and Dr. Franks met when he became the pastor at the First Baptist Church in Ripley, Mississippi. He was a young preacher with hair as flaming red as his son's would one day be, and he fell in love with Sallie the minute he laid eyes on her. But Jesse, as friends called him even late in life, was shy and had to contrive a way to meet this pretty and gentle young woman who taught music at a Synodical College near Ripley. His investigations revealed that Sallie played the piano beautifully and was a member of the Ripley music club that met weekly. Jesse began attending their concerts, and when Sallie was featured to play a piano sonata by the Russian Anton Rubinstein, he brushed up on the composer's work and was prepared to converse knowledgably about her selection after the recital. He knew little about music, but the plan worked. He approached her, introduced himself, and even had the courage to ask Sallie on a date. Their relationship flourished and Jesse soon nicknamed his bride-to-be "Graham." They were married in 1915.

The couple had a baby girl in 1916, Graham Elizabeth, whom they adored, but she died during the flu epidemic of 1918. Red was born in 1919 and Nancy Lee came along in 1923. By all accounts it was a happy family, and the Frankses moved to Columbus when Dr. Franks became pastor of the First Baptist Church.

Sallie was diagnosed with ovarian cancer shortly after she gave birth to Nancy Lee and became an invalid rarely able to attend church functions. She died in 1927 at the age of 35. Her death was such a severe blow to Dr.

Franks that he sent his children to live for the summer with Sallie's sister, Aunt Annie Laurie in Abingdon, Virginia, while he took time to heal. Red never forgot Sallie and tried to impart what little he remembered of her to Nancy Lee, who had no recollection of her mother except for the one memory of being raised in the arms of her nannie to give Sallie a farewell kiss as she lay near death.

Sallie's youthful portrait, taken when she was in her late 20s, revealed much about her charm to Red. She looked back at her son, her head turned slightly and her gaze steady. Her face was oval; her eyes reflected her gentle personality, and her hair was swept back over the right side of her forehead. Pince-nez glasses were perched on her nose and were attached to a delicate chain that disappeared behind her ears. She wore a soft, cottony dress open at the throat, and a heart-shaped pendant hung from her neck. Yes, she was lovely and Red had mourned terribly at her death, and everybody in Columbus grieved for little Red Franks. Sallie was buried in Ripley next to Graham Elizabeth, and the family's visits to her grave were infrequent.

Dr. Franks mourned for his children as much he did for his wife. They survived the years immediately following Sallie's death in large part because of Aunt Millie, Dr. Franks's sister, who came to Columbus to care for Nancy Lee and Red. Aunt Millie was a kindly woman who helped Red through his mourning, but she and Dr. Franks knew that Red had suffered a wound that would never completely heal. Only time would soften the blow and ease the anguish.

In 1930 Dr. Franks married Augusta Fort, a home economics professor at MSCW. Augusta had ideal credentials to be a good stepmother; she held a master's degree in home economics and credits towards a PhD at Columbia University and the University of Chicago. She had received her bachelor's degree from MSCW and had gone on to teach at Baylor College in Belton, Texas, where she was appointed chairman of the home economics department. In 1927 Augusta accepted a teaching position at MSCW. "I did not realize for one moment, at that time, that my whole life would soon change, and that I would spend the next nineteen years in Columbus, seventeen of these years as the wife of the pastor of the First Baptist Church of Columbus," Augusta wrote in a diary. She met Dr. Franks through their mutual interest in the MSCW Baptist student organization.

Everyone in Columbus believed that Augusta would know how to run Dr. Franks's household, but she ruled with an iron hand. Old Gussy, as Red called his stepmother behind her back, or Miss Fort, in public, knew nothing about nurturing; she was more drill sergeant than mother. If Red arrived late for dinner, Augusta was waiting for him by the door with a stick in hand, and she would swat at him as he came in. Augusta's mother came to live with the Franks for several months and the two made Red even more miserable.

Nancy Lee knew that Red had strong disagreements with his stepmother, and Nancy and Red would discuss what they should do. That was when Nancy Lee asked Red about her real mother, and Red told her that Sallie Franks would never have been so mean spirited. As a child Nancy Lee would approach her father on the wide porch of the parsonage and climb into his lap and ask about Sallie. If Augusta were not nearby, he would tell Nancy stories about his earlier life with Sallie at parishes in Mississippi and in Louisiana where Red was born.

Dr. Franks had hoped that he and Augusta could recapture the sense of family that had been lost when Sallie died. In those first months of marriage he believed she just needed to settle down and learn to live with Red and Nancy Lee. She meant well, but somehow things went awry. Augusta just didn't know anything about children. All the degrees and courses had left her ignorant and totally unprepared to care for Dr. Franks's children.

Friends and neighbors dismissed Red and Augusta's antagonism as typical conflict between a stepmother and a growing, rebellious teenage boy. Dr. Franks tried to dismiss it as well by looking the other way, but he knew his children were suffering. Every summer he sent Red out of Augusta's reach, away to Camp Ridgecrest in North Carolina. And he tried to comfort his daughter when she came to him complaining about her stepmother's behavior. Nancy Lee soon followed Red to Camp Montreat, a few miles down the road from Ridgecrest, where she waited tables to pay her way. But Dr. Franks knew there was nothing he could do about his marriage to Augusta.

Divorce for him was out of the question. A Baptist minister could not break the solemn vows of marriage, he told his daughter.

Augusta did have strong points. Although some in the congregation referred to her as a spinster, Augusta was strikingly handsome, dark haired with strong facial features. She enhanced Dr. Franks's career in the Baptist organization with her resolve and her faith. During a Baptist revival in one rural Mississippi community, Augusta was invited to dine and spend the night with a poor farm family. They had little to offer her for dinner, and when bedtime came, she was shown her quarters in the hayloft. She accepted everything with grace.

Dr. Franks gave Augusta credit for helping in the management of the church and for his appointment to the Baptist World Congress in Prague, Czechoslovakia, and as "unofficial observer" at the World Conference of Life and Work and Faith and Order in Oxford, England, and in Edinburgh, Scotland. He was proud of those and other prestigious appointments.

When he wanted to build a new educational center for the church, Augusta supported him even as the church's board of elders declined to continue construction of the project when the depression struck. Parishioners who had pledged substantial sums of money withdrew their contributions, but Dr. Franks was determined to see the project through to completion. The board balked and threatened to terminate his salary if he pursued his dream.

But he pressed on and went without pay for more than a year while the new three-story educational center was constructed. He approached a friend, a Methodist banker in Columbus, who loaned him a hundred dollars a month for thirteen months until his salary was restored. He would see that his family was fed; he had the cow in the backyard that Red milked every morning, and the vegetable garden was expanded.

The antagonism between Red and Augusta dissipated as Red grew older and he enrolled at Mississippi College in Clinton in 1937. MC, as it was nicknamed by alumni, was Dr. Franks's alma mater and was located just outside of the state capital in Jackson. It was the oldest college in Mississippi and the nation's first coeducational college, having granted two women degrees in 1831. It also was a magnet for Southern Baptists from the state where young men were educated in the liberal arts as well as "the Christian tradition." Several high school mates accompanied Red to college in 1937, Shields Sims, for one, who was now a B-24 pilot in the Pacific theater.

Jackson was 175 miles south of Columbus, and while a sleepy little southern city by most standards, it was a thriving metropolis compared to Columbus. There were all kinds of diversions including girls. Red had seldom dated in high school, but he soon joined his MC classmates in thumbing rides to Belhaven College. The young ladies were chaperoned for every activity, but a boy could at least talk to a young lady. Red often made the trip to Jackson to see Dottie Turner.

Red's classmates immediately accepted him as a leader and an athlete. He played freshman football and in his sophomore year moved up to the varsity and lived with his teammates on the second floor of the athletic dorm. Red was a solid 165 pounds, more than adequate in size for a football guard of his day, and he was eager to play. In the opening game of the 1938 season against Louisiana Tech, the Choctaws' coach, Stanley Robinson, affectionately nicknamed "Robby," looked down the row of eager sophomores waiting their turn at play. His eyes rested on his redheaded guard. "Warm up, Red," Robby ordered, and before the words were out of his mouth, Red was halfway across the field and hunkering down on the line of scrimmage.

The Mississippi College Chocktaws were well coached and usually triumphed over most of their opponents from Mississippi and Louisiana. The Chocktaws' main rival was Milsaps College in Jackson, and the nights before the annual games the MC campus reverberated to the constant pounding of a tom-tom that often went on till dawn.

Coach Robinson regularly took his team on a biannual cross-country trip to play solid clubs in the South or Northeast, and during Red's junior year the Choctaws traveled to Hamilton, New York, to play Robby's alma mater, Colgate University. Robby always treated his boys to a good time and exposed them to a new region of the country. The Choctaws were given a rousing send-off by the student body that accompanied the team through Clinton to the railroad station to board Pullman cars for the two-day trip to Syracuse. From there they took the bus to Hamilton.

The game was a mismatch as the Raiders drubbed the Choctaws 31 to 0. But the real highlight of the trip was a train ride to New York City through the blazing foliage of upstate New York in late autumn. Red had never seen anything like Manhattan with all its commotion and irreverence. Coach Robby took his boys out to dinner and then on a subway ride to the Polo Grounds to see the New York Giants take on the Chicago Bears. One reason for the Choctaws' interest in the game was a Mississippian playing end for the Giants.

The homespun boys from the small towns of Mississippi were out of place in the hustle and bustle of New York. Red and some of his mates became separated from the team in the stadium, and Red approached a hardboiled New York City cop for help: "Have you seen any guys around here that look like they come from Mississippi?" Red asked in his best southern drawl. The cop's tough demeanor softened and he laughed as he jabbed his thumb over his shoulder. "They went that way, son."

Red strived to do his best in class, but he was never an A student. At the end of his junior year, however, he aced a few final exams and was stunned by his newfound academic prowess. He wrote his father about the good news. "I hope that you have fully recovered from the shock," he reported. "I think I shall save the report and show it to my grandchildren. It made me feel good; I could have done anything after I heard from my finals."

His letter also revealed how busy he was at college. "We have a full week this week. B.S.U. (Baptist Student Union) installation service tonight, dramatics club play Thursday, Blue Mountain opera, with final practice game of spring football Thursday. *Gone with the Wind* is in Jackson, and they say it is really good.

"I was elected president of next year's senior S.S. Class, 100 members. I think this is going to be too much if I get the student body president. I was hoping that I would not be in the B.S.U. for next year, but I will do my best.

"We have a bunch of parties coming up before Spring Holidays. Son."

Red was unanimously elected president of the student body his senior year, and he was also voted best leader and most popular student and was included in *Who's Who among Students in American Universities and Colleges*, but he never appeared imperious. He was quiet, serious, and thoughtful in public but was assertive and well spoken when called up to voice an opinion. And he found time every day for devotionals, often outside under a tree, where he and friends would pray and give thanks.

Red and Dottie Turner decided to marry when Red was a senior. Dottie was a Mississippi girl, from Philadelphia, some seventy-five miles northeast of Jackson, and she came to Belhaven in the fall of 1938. Red had met her the summer before his freshman year when he was a counselor at Camp Ridgecrest and she was a counselor at the nearby Camp Montreat, the girl's camp that Nancy Lee attended. Red had gone to Ridgecrest for years and had progressed from camp bugler to camp director in 1941. His jobs paid his way, and he was delighted to leave the bugler's job behind. Every morning he was up before anyone else for reveille and every evening he sounded taps. Nancy Lee remembered the day he was promoted to counselor; he flung his bugle into a nearby lake.

Red surprised everyone when he graduated by deciding to attend the Southern Baptist Theological Seminary in Louisville. At MC he had majored in economics and seemed more interested in a career in business, or even athletics, than in the role of a Baptist minister.

Certainly most people in Columbus were surprised by Red's decision; they were amused that he was even Dr. Franks's boy. He was relaxed and approachable with his fuzzy, brushlike crew cut whereas Dr. Franks had a somewhat stern demeanor that was accentuated by his white-tinged black hair that was parted right down the middle. As a young man Dr. Frank's red hair had turned black. In his early 20s, Red's hair was beginning to show strands of black as well.

Columbians also got a good laugh trying to imagine the good and pious Dr. Franks slugging it out as a football guard and enjoying it as Red did. Red had been a three-sport letterman every year at Mississippi College while Dr. Franks, in his years at MC, had been a member of the college choir and had won his awards on the debating team. The one area where Dr. Franks and Red seemed alike was in their ability to persuade. Dr. Franks had gone on to become an inspiring evangelist throughout Mississippi and the surrounding states, and while Red was not yet as articulate a mediator, he could bring people together with his quiet logic.

Red approached the ministry with the same gusto and verve as he approached football. Elizabeth Spencer, Dottie's freshman year roommate at Belhaven College, remembered that when Dottie expressed reservations about being the wife of a poor, Baptist minister, he straightened up and announced: "I'm going to be a minister like you've never seen!" And everyone, including Dottie, believed that he would be true to his word not only because of his conviction, but because he was so warm and understanding and related well to people.

Dr. Franks was surprised as well but he was proud and pleased when Red decided to follow in his footsteps. Southern Baptist Theological Seminary was also Dr. Franks's alma mater, where he had completed his ministerial studies twenty-five years before.

Twenty-five years. That period of time exactly paralleled Red's life. Suddenly Red's reverie into the past seemed far away as Lt. Jack Warner's voice broke the tense silence that had gripped the crew. Lieutenant Warner's words crackled over the intercom to inform the crew that the plane was somewhere over the northwest corner of Bulgaria. *Euroclydon* passed over the landscape of Eastern Europe with her crew still looking for the first sign of the enemy.

Tidal Wave flew on. The force would rendezvous over the battlefield in little more than an hour.

5

Sweetest Girl in the World

The B-24 formations rose to twelve thousand feet above the threatening landscape of Albania and Yugoslavia after leaving behind the basalt smooth Ionian Sea that sparkled like a bed of diamonds in the yellowish Mediterranean light. The bomber force was down to 163 planes as they began to descend over Bulgaria and crossed the legendary Danube. Barge traffic jammed parts of the river that many crew members expected to be a ribbon of blue on the verdant plain, but to their chagrin it was neither blue nor beautiful, but a mud-colored, meandering strip glinting in the sunlight of early afternoon. Sgt. William Leonard, the radio operator in *Hadley's Harem*, muttered to his comrades over the intercom that the Danube was like Kentucky bluegrass: "It just ain't blue."

The bombers swept lower as they shot over the fertile and sleepy landscape of the Wallachian plain, gold from the summer harvest and covered with a light haze. This was Romania, home to a Latin people in a sea of Slavs, descendants of the Roman soldiers who once protected the eastern frontier of the Empire from the barbarian hordes. The American airmen took particular note of the countryside racing by beneath them. It seemed to stand out in greater relief, its contours seemed more ominous, and it conveyed a sense of doom.

Lieutenant Porter eased *Euroclydon's* nose closer to the ground to fly beneath threatening rain clouds and to drop below German radar signals that would detect the presence of approaching aircraft. If the blips of Tidal Wave planes appeared on enemy radar screens, the Americans could expect an eruption of accurate and deadly antiaircraft fire the moment they reached the target. Red peered out of the greenhouse nose, studying the folds of the terrain, intent on catching the reflection of sunlight from enemy gun barrels or from the wings and fuselages of approaching enemy planes. He was aware, as never before, of his exposure in the glassed-in front of the plane, of being suspended in midair, as he anxiously awaited the first flashes from the guns of enemy fighters that would be aiming right at him. He gripped the handles of the gun, ready to return German fire. His mouth was dry and he could feel his heart thumping faster than normal in his chest. Instinctively he patted his right hip pocket and felt the bulge from his tan leather wallet. It was stuffed with dollar bills and strange, colorful foreign currency engraved with distinguished looking heads of state. If *Euroclydon* went down and the crew bailed out, the money might buy him passage to Allied territory. The desk jockeys back in Benghazi had told the crews that the ten dollars in American bills they carried represented three months wages for a Romanian peasant eager to help a downed American flyer. But would they help and could the Americans trust a Romanian peasant? Red's wallet also contained the two snapshots of Dottie; just the thought of her lessened his anxiety. In both photos she was smiling her beautiful smile.

When Red had told Dottie that he was joining the Air Corps, she was stunned and silent, but she supported his decision. Before Pearl Harbor their future was clear; she and Red would marry, he would find a parish somewhere or he would teach theology, and they would raise a family. They were already planning their wedding, and Dottie had made the first entries into her sterling diary in November 1941. Her pattern was Prelude by Towle Silversmiths.

In February 1942, Red left the seminary in Louisville to join the Air Corps and was shipped first to a training base in Tampa, Florida, and later to Maxwell Field in Alabama. He and Dottie wrote to each other regularly and were together as often as possible when Red had leave. She savored every moment of their meetings, knowing that Red would be ordered overseas once he finished bombardier school at Victorville, California. The war had altered everything in life. Young men like Red were serving in the far reaches of the world, in places they had never dreamed of, in places that they never knew existed.

Dottie began living the reality of all women in wartime that Red could be shot down or killed. She struggled to keep such thoughts from her mind and relied on her faith in God that Red would come back. She too knew the Ninety-first Psalm by heart and prayed over and over that it would protect Red wherever he served. Her mother, "Miss" Lila Turner, and her aunts Genevieve Anderson and Julia Maxidon, and her Anderson cousins all rallied around her and offered reassurance and comfort when she came to visit Pontotoc near Tupelo in northeast Mississippi. Dottie carried on with the usual quiet dignity that Miss Lila had instilled in her, and she kept her fears and sadness to herself. But never before had her faith in God and life been so tested. She felt alone without Red, more alone than ever in her life.

Dottie reminded herself that she was a Turner, and the Turners were a self-reliant family that had always survived despite adversity. Miss Lila had demonstrated that pluck after her husband, Jim Turner, died suddenly in 1934 when Dottie was fourteen. Jim was one of several brothers who had moved to Philadelphia, Mississippi, at the turn of the century and had established various businesses.

At that time, not long before Dottie was born in 1920, Philadelphia "was a rough, raw town. A few wooden houses were perched up on a red clay hill, and down by the new railroad tracks was a Negro section called Froggy Bottom. There were no sidewalks, nor water nor sewage system, and pigs roamed the streets," wrote Turner Catledge, a member of the clan and Dottie's cousin who would later become managing editor of the *New York Times.*

Dottie's uncles, Homer and Joe Turner, ran a grocery store, and Homer later opened a lumberyard with his father-in-law after returning from World War I. Sam had a Ford automobile agency, and Dottie's father, Jim, opened a drugstore.

"Few of the Turners ever worked for anyone else; it was a sort of tribal system with the family determined to take care of its own," Catledge wrote. "The Turners had not been born rich. They were born poor. The Turners were not interested in politics, only in the church and material success. They achieved it."

Jim Turner's death was devastating for Dottie and her mother. Death seemed to stalk Miss Lila. She had lost a child, a boy, before Dottie was born, which made Dottie's life even more precious to her. Miss Lila responded to her husband's death by attending the University of Alabama to obtain a degree in education and become a teacher. She also worked summers as an adult counselor at Camp Montreat where Dottie was a junior counselor. Dottie and Lila began spending their holidays with Aunt Genevieve Anderson, Miss Lila's sister in Pontotoc. The six Anderson daughters adored the diminutive Dottie whenever she came to visit. She was always immaculately dressed and so well behaved that the Anderson girls referred to her as "our little princess."

Pontotoc became Dottie's second home. She and Miss Lila spent every Thanksgiving and Christmas with the Andersons and many steamy and fragrant days during summer vacations after they returned from Camp Montreat. Pontotoc was a whisper of a community of some two thousand residents with a center about four blocks long and three streets wide. The town was nestled in the gently rolling countryside of Pontotoc County with its population of about twenty thousand people, mostly farming families.

The two-story county courthouse dominated the downtown with its eclectic architectural style that made it resemble both a hacienda with a red tile roof and a Greek temple with Doric columns holding up the front portico. The structure took up the entire south side of the town square while the north side housed a drugstore, a five-and-dime, and the general store. In the center of the square was a grassy plot with the obligatory monument to the Confederacy that honored the Pontotoc boys who had given their lives in the Civil War. The names of veterans from the world wars were added later.

Nothing much happened in Pontotoc or in the county. The last time there was real excitement was over one hundred years before when there were fights with the Chickasaw Indians. Later there were skirmishes with Yankee soldiers who came in raiding parties during the Civil War. Pontotoc residents had to drive for miles to shop in the "big cities" of Oxford, the site of Old Miss, the University of Mississippi, sixteen miles west, and of Tupelo, about sixteen miles east.

In between Oxford and Tupelo, and all around, was farmland, cotton fields, and pastureland. In summer the landscape was rich green and wooded, and the native plants and trees had been invaded by kudzu, a fast-growing vine that covered many of the trees with a thick web of broad leaves to create monsterlike shapes or friendly blimplike make-believe figures lurking by the roadsides.

While visiting her cousins Grace, Julia, Eleanor, Genevieve, Sarah, and Roberta, Dottie was the picture of good manners, attired in spotless, freshly laundered dresses and shiny patent leather Mary Janes, accented by clean white socks. In Miss Julia Anderson's house that gleamed with well-polished silver and antiques, she sat with her legs crossed at the ankles and her hands folded daintily in her lap. Around adults she was expected to be polite, to make interesting conversation, and to speak only when spoken to. Her speech was flawless; Dottie had been drilled by Miss Lila to utter only impeccably correct English, albeit with a rich and thick Mississippi accent, and she knew her syntax and grammar backward and forward.

But once out of reach and earshot of the adults, Dottie would romp about the yard and garden with the abandon of her cousins, especially at dusk when the impending night brought breezes to cool the sweltering day. The Andersons lived in a large three-story, gabled brick house on the southern end of Pontotoc with a wide front porch and lawns that stretched to Main Street and back to woods in the rear.

The girls played croquet on the front lawn, shot marbles, or organized games of kick the can. The biggest thrill was the cable slide that stretched from a tree in the backyard over a gully to the base of a tree at the edge of the woods. They climbed the tree to grab a section of pipe covering the wire and zoomed down into the woods. For all her daintiness Dottie was athletic, particularly good as a tennis player, but the courts were across town and the rules set by Uncle Dabney Anderson were strict; his daughters and his niece could not break southern sartorial conventions by bicycling through Pontotoc wearing tennis shorts. They had to wear dresses. Dottie also learned to ride horses. Uncle Dabney ran a pharmacy in Pontotoc but also operated a farm about fifteen miles from town where he kept his steeds.

When the girls were bored, they squeezed into the large swing in the front yard that faced Main Street and lazed away the hours chatting among themselves and watching the comings and goings of the townsfolk. Or they wrote plays and dressed up as the characters of their imaginations. Some days they wandered uptown to the drugstore in the courthouse square to sip Cokes and gossip with friends, and afterward they returned home to gather around the piano in the living room to sing and perform. They listened to Dottie play the piano masterfully and mesmerize her cousins with the sweetness of her voice and the maturity of her skills.

By the time Dottie was in her teens, every young man was in love with her. She was a classic southern belle at just over five feet, with a soft voice, smiling eyes, and shining dark brown hair that framed her face and touched the nape of her neck. Sarah Carter, a friend of the Anderson cousins whose father was the superintendent of schools in Pontotoc, remembered Dottie: "She's just the prettiest little thing, so small and so dainty."

"Young men just really paid attention to her," Eleanor Anderson remembered. "I never saw anyone who wasn't ready to drop everything and do something for her."

One of Dottie's suitors was Dick Furr, whose father had been the mayor of Pontotoc. Dick's mother, Estelle, operated her own floral business, and Dick was planning to take a degree in landscape architecture when he attended Mississippi State. Dick fell madly in love with the fourteen-year-old Dottie shortly after she began coming to Pontotoc.

But Dottie had also caught Red Franks's eye in the summer of 1937 when he was a counselor at Camp Ridgecrest and Dottie and Miss Lila were counselors at nearby Camp Montreat. Dottie and Red were drawn together because Dottie was in charge of Nancy Lee's cabin and the two camps occasionally had joint gatherings. Red was smitten by Dottie the moment he laid eyes on her.

A strong, romantic attachment was an entirely new experience for Red. He'd never had a steady girlfriend before, and Jake Propst used to kid him about not pursuing more girls. But Red was too involved in sports and milking cows and was reluctant to bring a young lady home to be scrutinized by Augusta. His friend Dick Burts remembers that one summer at Camp Ridgecrest he was "sweet" on a young lady in Asheville, but the relationship didn't last long.

It was under Miss Lila's watchful eyes at the occasional parties between Camps Ridgecrest and Montreat that Red noticed Dottie. They began a courtship that continued when Dottie attended Belhaven and during the summers while both were at camp. Whenever Dottie returned from a date with Red, she would tiptoe over to Nancy Lee's upper bunk to tell her of the marvelous times she and Red had had that night. They'd even gone to Asheville to hear the Ink Spots, Dottie whispered one night to Nancy Lee in the dark of the cabin.

This quiet and serious young man intrigued Dottie; he was strong looking and held strong opinions and was a leader. In 1938 she enrolled in Belhaven, which had the look of a southern plantation in the heart of the city. Belhaven was where well-brought-up Mississippi girls were sent to get a proper education. The campus opened out from a white-pillared mansion "and faced a twin edifice across a pond, where large goldfish lazed and water lilies bloomed. . . . Pine trees towered up on the rolling land; meadows and playing fields provided the aspect of an estate," wrote Elizabeth Spencer, a roommate of Dottie's. The rules were austere. One student was grounded for eighteen weeks for smoking a cigarette while several others suffered similar punishment for the high crime of dancing. The young women of Belhaven were required to wear hats, white gloves, and silk stockings whenever they ventured into downtown Jackson, a short distance from the college campus. And if any were being courted by a young man, the rules dictated that the couple be accompanied by a college-approved chaperon, except to

Primo's, the campus hangout a block from campus where the dress code and rule requiring a chaperone did not apply. It was not unusual for a young man and a young Belhaven woman to have a date by simply remaining in the dorm lounge and chatting the evening away. Dancing was considered by those in charge at Belhaven as the Devil's entertainment, and sex was unspeakable.

Dottie majored in English at Belhaven and continued to pursue her interest in music. Elizabeth Spencer, an aspiring writer, introduced her to the young novelist, Eudora Welty, who lived across the street from Belhaven's main gates. Spencer would later become an award-winning short story writer and novelist.

Dottie's friends and cousins at Belhaven knew Red, and they followed the couple's romance approvingly. "Everybody kept up with Red and Dottie," remembered Dottie's cousin, Sarah Anderson, who attended Belhaven at the same time as Dottie. "And everyone knew when he came on campus. He's just as cute as he can be," Genevieve Anderson drawled, "just a great big wonderful teddy bear, and he treats her like a little flower."

Red adored Dottie. He sent her a book of poetry, *Light of the Years*, by Grace Noll Crowell and inscribed it "To Dottie from Red." She kept a photograph of Red on the dresser in her dorm room on which Red wrote: "Sweetest girl in the world. I really do love her and always will.—The way she holds her head and that smile. Then when her left leg is all tucked under."

Red was always buying presents for Dottie. On the football trip north to play Colgate University in New York state, Red bought her a chic raincoat with matching umbrella.

"Red, where on earth did you find such a wonderful outfit?" Dottie asked.

Red blushed and admitted he'd seen it advertised in a woman's magazine on the train north.

"What magazine was that?" she asked.

He was unfamiliar with the Yankee women's magazine, *Harper's Bazaar*.

"Harper's Brassiere," Red replied.

Dottie frequently visited Red at Mississippi College for weekends, and as often as he could, Red hitchhiked the eight miles into Jackson to visit

Dottie. Afterward he wandered back out to the Illinois Central viaduct on the outskirts of town and stuck his thumb out for the ride back to Clinton.

Miss Lila gave her blessing to Red and Dottie's engagement in 1942 despite reservations about her daughter marrying a Southern Baptist preacher. She always believed Presbyterians had more class and Southern Baptists took their religion so seriously. But Red was special. She knew that he was unique among ministerial candidates. He was devout, but quiet and thoughtful. But beneath his calm exterior was a streak of masculine aggressiveness. Miss Lila had heard about Red's exploits on the football field when he played guard for Mississippi College.

Dr. Franks also approved of Red and Dottie's engagement and consecrated it by offering his son the ring he had given to Sallie when he asked her to marry him in 1915. When Red presented it to Dottie, he had it engraved on the inside: "D.T., J.F."

Dottie graduated from Belhaven in June 1942, and with marriage postponed, she left Mississippi to join C&S Airlines, the forerunner of Delta Airlines that serviced the central United States from the upper Midwest to the Deep South. She would join Red as one of the pioneers of flight. Commercial flying was hardly more than a decade old, and not overly safe. But Dottie loved it. She was even issued business cards with her name: "Dorothy Turner, Stewardess, Chicago and Southern Airlines." She looked stunning in her new uniform and cap and happily took up residence in a large house in New Orleans with other C&S stewardesses.

Red was finishing his bombardier training in California and would soon be assigned to a new B-24 crew. In May 1943, the men received orders to proceed to England to join the Eighth Air Force.

Dottie found her work as a stewardess uplifting; it gave her a sense of independence after the restrictions of college. "She was growing up, spreading her wings and growing into herself," said her daughter, Dawn. And she was unafraid in the air. The flights in twin-engine, noisy DC-3s and even smaller Lockheed Electras could be terrifying as the planes bounced and swayed along at five thousand feet with passengers expecting momentary death or experiencing violent airsickness that had them throwing up into vomit bags. But Dottie didn't bat an eye. She had faith that she would survive just as she had faith that Red would come through the war. She loved flying over the patchwork of farms and prairies of the South and Midwest on flights between Chicago and New Orleans, with stops in places like Memphis and Nashville. No matter what the weather or flying conditions, her warm smile and reassuring voice comforted all passengers.

Dottie maintained her ties to Pontotoc; Miss Lila had finally moved there from Philadelphia while Dottie was in college and bought a house two doors down from her sister Julia. It was a modest-size home constructed to look massive with four Ionic columns with capitals that supported a balcony and second story. Inside, the living-room ceiling was graced with hand-carved and delicate plasterwork, fine moldings, and crystal chandeliers. Miss Lila had retired to antebellum elegance.

But Pontotoc was too quiet a place for Dottie, too far from the bustle of the outside world and without the crowds. She wanted to experience the more vibrant life in New Orleans and Chicago. The war had changed everything as well. Americans were uprooted and on the move. It was one thing to be from Pontotoc and another to spend a lifetime there. Dottie would stay in the house on Charles Street in New Orleans and wait for Red's return.

6

Hell's Dominion

The planes were now in Romania, rumbling along, seemingly in a never-ending procession, over open plain, deep valleys, and clustered villages. They roused the curiosity of the startled inhabitants below, some hardly advanced in thought and ways from their ancestors in the Middle Ages. These were superstitious peasant farmers who toiled endlessly in their fields and prayed for deliverance in steepled churches erected before the United States was proclaimed a nation. The Yanks looked down and saw people like themselves, as human as they were, living in a Shangri-La of lush fields with flowing rivers and tree-lined roads.

Some Romanians waved and smiled up at the passing tumult of wings and roaring engines, while others fled. The airmen saw farm women in brightly decorated skirts riding in horse carts with big painted wheels. One plane passed over a swimming hole where young women sunbathed in the nude, eliciting cheers of delight from airmen seeking relief from their anxieties, and a B-24 soared over a buggy in which a man looked up and shook his fist at the Americans, and the girl beside him pulled her skirt over her face. The radio operator in Lieutenant Stuart's *Utah Man* saw a woman stop her wagon and dive underneath it as the bombers passed. When the plane shot by, the horses bolted leaving the woman lying exposed and face down on the road.

The bombers skimmed over the Wallachian plain toward the distant and rugged Transylvania Alps. The ground below was once the domain of Count Dracula, notorious for slaughter and pillage, and a land of myths that were as threatening as the lurking Germans. These young American flyers were mostly from rural and small-town America, many from the South and from the West for whom even Manhattan was alien ground.

Just behind the Liberandos the crews of the Traveling Circus began preparing for their bomb runs. The men continued to watch the skies for enemy aircraft and the ground for antiaircraft guns but saw neither, and the ranking officers in the bomber force remained confident that the mission would achieve surprise. But they had not been informed about the Axis fighters that had shadowed several Tidal Wave planes over Bulgaria. The enemy had avoided a fight; their purpose was reconnaissance only. Like most of the crews at this point in the mission, the men in *Euroclydon* were buoyant and optimistic as they closed on the target after more than seven hours of flight without any sign of the enemy. They had anticipated heavy enemy attacks all the way in, but so far it was a milk run.

Euroclydon's good fortune ended abruptly when Flight Officer Frank Farrell's voice sounded over the intercom. A fuel pump needed to transfer gasoline from the bomb bay tanks to the wing tanks had malfunctioned, and *Euroclydon* would not have enough gas for the return flight to Benghazi. The news was stark and frightening, but the crew absorbed it in silent fear as they steadied themselves. They had trained to deal with equipment failure and combat damage and were prepared to put in to emergency landing fields in Turkey and Cyprus or even in the Soviet Union. Turkey would now be *Euroclydon*'s destination, if they made it through the maelstrom of Ploeşti. The men knew they faced internment once they landed, possibly for the duration of the war.

The leading Liberandos had reached the critical juncture, the first IP, or initial point, over the town of Pitesti, one hundred miles west of Ploeşti, where the Tidal Wave formations were to begin their descent to treetop level and increase their speed. They were now headed toward the second IP over Floresti, where the air armada was to make a right turn over a set of railroad tracks, heading southeast, to approach Ploeşti from the northwest. The refineries were fifteen minutes away.

Before reaching Floresti, however, the planes had to overfly the town of Targoviste that was also bisected by a set of railroad tracks. Air Corps intelligence had neglected to warn the mission chief that the railroad tracks at Floresti would appear identical to those at Targoviste. Without *Wongo Wongo's* lead navigator, and without his designated backup, the Tidal Wave force was flying partially blind.

When the mission commander, Brig. Gen. Uzal Ent, passed over Targoviste in Lt. Col. Keith Compton's *Teggie Ann,* he peered at the tracks below and concluded that he had reached the second IP over Floresti. On General Ent's command, Lieutenant Colonel Compton dipped his wings, and the Liberandos turned south and headed down a valley bordered by steep ridges. The Traveling Circus was forced to follow, and the two leading Tidal Wave bomb groups pointed their planes at a distant haze that spread out along the horizon. General Ent was leading his men to what he thought was Ploeşti.

The turn past the second IP was the cue for Lieutenant Stuart to pull *Utah Man* above *Hell's Wench* and *Euroclydon* to his left and signal to the crews in the oncoming echelons to arm their bombs and for the men to don their helmets, standard issue just like an infantryman's, but few wore these bulky "tin pots." In *Euroclydon,* Red Franks called to the flight engineer to pull the pins from the fuses to arm the bombs in the cavernous bomb bay. They were now ready to be dropped.

As the stream of aircraft turned, the planes of the Traveling Circus dropped to about five hundred feet above the ground, where they skimmed along at speeds of 200 mph. *Euroclydon* was on the extreme left in the first wave of Circus bombers.

But crew members in both bomb groups realized immediately that General Ent had steered *Teggie Ann,* and the entire mission, on the wrong course. *Teggie Ann's* navigator, Capt. Harold Wicklund, a veteran of the Halpro raid, yelled into the intercom that they had turned too soon. General Ent ignored his navigator, but the cries and curses from the pilots who wheeled their planes southeast behind the leader became a torrent. Two bold crew members broke radio silence. "Not here! Not here!" one navigator screamed over the airwaves. "Mistake! Mistake!" bellowed pilot Ramsey Potts in the B-24 *Duchess.* Others joined in but the flight was committed. Lieutenant Stuart heard the protests of his navigator in *Utah Man.* "We're going wrong; we're going wrong," he yelled through the intercom just after the planes had made their turn. But *Hell's Wench* and *Euroclydon* were following with the rest of the Ninety-third.

"Look at the tracks," the navigator yelled to Lieutenant Stuart in *Utah Man.* "We're heading for Bucharesti," he said, emphasizing the Romanian *e* sound at the word's end. Lieutenant Stuart knew Tidal Wave was supposed to turn on a set of railroad tacks heading southeast, and he looked down to see that the ones they followed were in a state of disrepair and had been abandoned to rust. The smoke in the distance spewed from stacks around the Romanian capital city. Tidal Wave had turned too soon and was headed away from the target.

Lieutenant Stuart's rear gunner yelled out: "Look at nine o'clock, Lieutenant, smokestacks to the rear. That's Ploești!" Lieutenant Stuart waved frantically through *Utah Man's* narrow cockpit window and dipped the plane's wings up and down to get the attention of Lieutenant Colonel Baker, the Ninety-third's commander in *Hell's Wench.* He had to somehow inform the bomb group leader of the error without breaking radio silence. Lieutenant Colonel Baker had already realized the mistake and pondered whether to abandon General Ent and lead the Ninety-third alone back to Ploești. He acted quickly and countermanded the general's order and began to wheel the planes of the Traveling Circus back on a northeast course, towards the refineries. If he were mistaken and was turning the Ninety-third toward the wrong target, he would face court-martial, disgrace and possibly time in Fort Leavenworth Prison.

The Liberandos drove on toward Bucharest alone, streaking in over the suburbs of the capital until they realized their error when they were met by intense antiaircraft fire blackening the sky around them. There was nothing below the 376th that resembled the models of Ploeşti that the crews had studied back in Benghazi, and a frustrated General Ent turned his formation north toward the target. But the mission plan was now badly disrupted with the lead B-24 groups approaching late, from the wrong direction, and forced to drop their bombs on targets designated for the follow-up groups. General Ent's navigational error had compromised the outcome of Tidal Wave.

On Lieutenant Colonel Baker's command the planes of the Traveling Circus pulled away from the 376th BG and made a perfectly executed turn back toward the northeast. *Euroclydon* became the pivot of the turn as the B-24s, with wings spanning 110 feet, flying less than five hundred feet from the ground at breathtaking speed, maneuvered toward Ploeşti and maintained exact formation as they homed in on the target. More than a half century later Lt. Jack Warner would marvel that this incredible feat of airmanship was one of the most amazing aspects of the entire mission.

In *Euroclydon's* nose Red Franks was kneeling behind the riflelike bombsight, taking aim at the distant stacks that grew larger as the Circus approached Ploeşti. He could feel his body tense as the plane bounced and yawed toward the target that now seemed more unreal than the models of the refineries back in Terria, the Ninety-third base outside Benghazi. Red had wisecracked to Lieutenant Stuart about how he would sight on Concordia Vega. He would take off his boot and sock and place his foot on the bombsight rest and aim between his big and second toe. They had laughed, but Red could find nothing now to alleviate his rising tensions. The Ninety-third's leading echelon of *Euroclydon, Hell's Wench,* and *Utah Man* would be the first to bomb the refineries, and all hope of hitting their preassigned targets was gone. Coming in from the southwest, not from the northwest, the

Ninety-third would attack the Astra Romana and Columbia Aquila refineries originally assigned to the Ninety-eighth and Forty-fourth bomb groups still miles behind in the approaching bomber stream. Other B-24 squadrons would have to take out the Concordia Vega refinery, so carefully committed to the memories of the Ninety-third bombardiers. Red and his comrades would now drop their bombs by instinct as they crossed over the refineries and unloaded their ordnance on targets of opportunity.

The target was indistinct in a haze that blanketed the city and refineries as the Circus streaked over farmland, colored golden in the late summer with harvested wheat lying in bundles. The phalanxes of planes were within minutes of the target, and ten miles from Ploeşti, the B-24s dropped to fifty feet and increased their airspeed to 245 mph, 65 mph faster than the usual cruising speed. The engines screamed in protest as beneath *Euroclydon* the ground raced by in a kaleidoscope of color—ten miles, nine, eight, seven miles. The haze suddenly gave way to reveal clusters of buildings, stacks, and tank farms that looked serene in the instant before the battle began.

Around Ploeşti the enemy flak batteries had been waiting for the raid since dawn, and when the flights of B-24s passed over Albania, the Germans were almost certain the target was the refineries. The wrong turn toward Bucharest momentarily threw them off; German commanders thought it was a crafty ploy, but they weren't fooled. As the planes approached, German antiaircraft gunners searched the skies for telltale vapor trails left by U.S. bombers grazing the stratosphere, and the enemy welcomed the chance to take out the American planes with their 88s.

Suddenly several groups of German and Romanian gunners were startled by shouts and cries of alarm and arms pointing to cornfields adjoining the refineries. The gunners at first were perturbed, then terrified. Huge and strange looking silhouettes seemed to hover just above the tops of the stalks with overhead wings and bellies slung so low some were slashing through the cornrows. Momentarily the enemy heard the roar of the engines from scores of B-24s that were suddenly upon them.

The enemy gunners frantically ran to their batteries and cranked their guns down almost parallel to the ground, slammed in shells and began to fire.

The blasts from their guns were answered by the brittle crackle of .50-caliber machine guns from airmen in the onrushing B-24s taking aim at the enemy troops, and tracer bullets zipped and ricocheted back and forth over the refineries.

The fight began suddenly. Within a few miles of the refineries the aircrews discerned barrage balloons suspended on steel cables a few hundred feet above the ground to snare oncoming bombers, clip their wings, and stagger the planes to send them crashing into the ground. Some of the cables were laden with explosives to detonate when struck by a plane. Hidden enemy antiaircraft guns began spitting flashing small-caliber rounds, and heavier shells exploded in black bursts around the lead planes to shock the aircrews by the incongruity of the moment as the once pastoral setting disintegrated into conflagration. Lieutenant Stuart saw the tops of haystacks pop off and quadruple ack-ack guns appear with their barrels flaming as they rotated with the speed of the planes. The sides of a chicken coop fell away, exposing an 88 mm antiaircraft gun.

Euroclydon, Utah Man, and *Hell's Wench* were the leading edge of the attack; they would be the first targets for the German and Romanian gunners who opened fire from hidden gun emplacements. The men in the lead planes were quick to return fire. "Fire at anything you see!" Lieutenant Stuart shouted to his crew over the intercom. *Utah Man* shook and vibrated from the coordinated fire from the ship's machine guns, blasting out armor piercing and incendiary rounds to ignite the oil and gasoline storage tanks and to kill enemy antiaircraft crews and destroy their emplacements. *Utah Man's* gunner, John *Connolly,* riddled an enemy soldier raising a barrage balloon and saw them disappear in a puff of smoke. He swung his gun towards a locomotive and opened fire as the B-24 winged over it. He looked down to see a flak gunner cradling a shell and staring up with gaping mouth and another soldier grinning and waving his cap on the end of a bayonet.

Lieutenant Stuart looked left to see *Euroclydon's* guns spewing tracers. She was so close to the ground that the tunnel gun position in the belly was useless, and gunner Sgt. Charles Reed stood between waist gunners Sergeants Bernard Lucas and James Vest, pointing out enemy gun emplacements and flak towers for his comrades to shoot at. In the tail position, Sgt. Earl Frost swung his guns back and forth as *Euroclydon* shot over the refineries.

Lieutenant Stewart looked right to see a B-24 hit the ground and careen through a cornfield, twisting back and forth as it skidded to a stop. He was thankful that the plane did not explode. Dead ahead he saw an 88 mm gun fire point-blank at *Utah Man* from forty yards away. The din of the engines drowned out the gun's blast, but he saw a tongue of flame leap from the barrel, and his body instinctively tensed as he awaited the projectile's impact in the plane's nose. It crashed instead through one of the rear stabilizers and ripped a hole the size of a large wash bucket. *Utah Man*'s tail gunner screamed to his skipper when he saw the gaping gash, "Don't do that, Lieutenant." Lieutenant Stuart pushed his B–24 as low as she would go to where the cumbersome bomber skimmed along at "cornstalk altitude." With their overhead wings the planes still had lift even as their bodies nearly scraped the ground.

Ploeşti was a rough ride at almost zero altitude as pilots and copilots wrestled their planes to keep them under control. Yet they went lower for safety, down to twenty feet, some to five feet, and the buffeting intensified from prop wash from the planes ahead, from the blast of exploding 88 mm and 105 mm shells and from the whirlwind of blazing oil tanks After the battle at least one B-24 returned to base with a corn stalk stuck in its belly.

Just behind Red Franks in *Euroclydon*'s nose, Jack Warner was awestruck by the mêlée and froze behind a .50-caliber machine gun as he looked out into the surreal battlefield and into the barrels of so many German guns, all of which seemed to be firing directly at him. No ground battle in history had ever looked like this, nor had any aerial battle either. General Ent had estimated the Germans would have fewer than one hundred antiaircraft guns positioned around Ploeşti. In fact, there were more than one thousand of all calibers including forty six-gun batteries of 88s along with batteries of 37 mm and 20 mm guns. The antiaircraft defenses around Ploeşti were denser than at any other target in the world and were more concentrated than at Berlin, and Tex McCrary was wrong. They were manned by as many Germans as Romanians.

Lieutenant Warner was suddenly brought to his senses by Lieutenant Porter's impatient voice over the intercom demanding to know when the navigator was going to open fire. Immediately the machine gun vibrated like a jackhammer in LieutenantWarner's hands as he swung the gun back and forth, firing at anything that moved.

The battle was joined. Flak gun crews had reset their fuses to detonate almost instantly after they left the barrel, and they waited for more of the big bombers to appear in their sights.

The Americans continued to fire back. In the Ninety-third's B-24, *Tupelo Lass*, the copilot called out the position of flak gun batteries for his gunners. "Eight o'clock.! Twelve o'clock! Three o'clock." He finally ordered: "Shoot all over!" In the tempest of steel, flame, and smoke he saw "pink stuff, white stuff, red stuff, black stuff." The planes were flying through a hailstorm of exploding shells, flying shards of metal and Plexiglas glittering in the light as they tumbled to earth, and the detritus of disintegrating B-24s. The debris slammed into the flanks of the oncoming bombers like the crash of pebbles against sheet metal.

Men were dying in the planes even before they reached Ploești, and several bombers were trailing smoke as they bore in on the refineries. In *Euroclydon* the din of the battle was the background accompaniment to the foreground rattle of the .50-caliber machine guns ejecting searing shell casings that clattered on the metal deck by the waste gunners and from the top turret. In the nose Lieutenant Warner continued to fire his guns as Red Franks took aim at the oncoming buildings.

Red and Lieutenant Warner were too focused on the enemy to notice when *Hell's Wench* on *Euroclydon's* right wing took a severe hit and began to falter. Lieutenant Stuart saw it: "Look at that, Lieutenant," his co-pilot exclaimed as Lieutenant Stuart glanced up to the left to see flame spewing from *Hell's Wench's* number three engine. The plane struck a barrage balloon cable and took hits in the wing and wing root, and the cockpit became enveloped in flame. Lieutenant Colonel Baker had an open wheat field beneath him in which to crash-land but he flew on, jettisoning his bombs, determined to lead the Circus over the target.

An airman tumbled out of *Hell's Wench*'s nose wheel hatch and was seen shooting over the bomber formation so close that his burned legs were visible to crewman in the oncoming aircraft. His chute snapped opened and he disappeared from view. Lieutenant Colonel Baker struggled to keep *Hell's Wench* level and in the lead as the Circus approached the target. When the stricken bomber reached the refinery area, he pulled back on the wheel and the bomber climbed for altitude. She made it up to three hundred feet and several more crewmen bailed out. Then the bomber drifted to the left and back through the oncoming formation, her cockpit engulfed in flame. Her wing struck the ground, and *Hell's Wench* disappeared in a cartwheeling ball of flaming debris.

"Bombs away," Red Franks yelled over the intercom as the lead planes flew over the refinery. The other bombers also were dropping their thousand pounders, which sailed toward the earth, skipped along the ground, and punched through buildings, leaving gaping holes in the brickwork.

Utah Man dropped her bombs and tail gunner Paul Johnston yelled back to Lieutenant Stewart, "Saw two bombs go into the target. Didn't see any more fall out. The incendiaries hit on top."

In *Euroclydon* the noise and excitement of battle obscured all but what took place within the limited scope of each man's vision and hearing. The ship had taken hits and her radio operator, Sargeant Lucas, who was manning a waist gun on the raid, was killed. A large-caliber shell had exploded in the bomb bay, and *Euroclydon* was trailing smoke and fire, and tracers chased her as she streaked over the target. A 37 mm shell exploded in the nose near Lieutenant Warner and jammed his gun but left him unhurt. Red and Lieutenant Warner peered back toward the bomb bay to see it consumed by fire and flames shooting towards them in the tunnel-like fuselage. They looked at each other and instinctively reacted. They had to bail out.

Flight Officer Russell Longnecker in the oncoming B-24, *Thundermug*, looked ahead to see *Euroclydon* become engulfed in flame. "Two red streams poured out the sides around the tail turret and joined in a river of fire flowing behind for two hundred feet," Longnecker remembered. In *Euroclydon* Lieutenant Porter sensed the end as the ship lost trim. He hit the bail out alarm and pulled hard on the wheel. *Euroclydon* still had enough life and speed to respond and the aircraft rose slowly.

Lieutenant Stuart in *Utah Man* looked up and to his right and saw *Euroclydon* start to climb, her engines straining for altitude to give her crew time and altitude to escape. *Euroclydon* was still climbing when the two waist gunners, Sergeants Charles Reed and James Vest, bailed out. "Two men out, two men out!" Lieutenant Stuart's left waist gunner yelled over *Utah Man's* intercom.

Flight Officer Longnecker described the crippled *Euroclydon* as "hanging like a cloud of fire" as the bomber rose to about one hundred feet, then faltered, and began to fall. To the oncoming bomber crews she appeared like a blazing star vanishing over the horizon. Flight Officer Longnecker saw Lieutenant Warner jump from the plane, and seconds later he saw Red Franks tumble through the hatch. Then *Euroclydon* disappeared from Flight Officer Longnecker's view as he flew over the exploding world of Ploeşti.

Lieutenant Stuart drove his bomber onward over the refineries and gave the stricken *Euroclydon* one last glance as he left it behind. "Ship broke in two, broke in two," the waist gunner yelled over the intercom as he watched *Euroclydon* plunge to earth. *Utah Man* was now alone in the lead as the ship shot over the refineries dodging antiaircraft fire and barrage balloons, on over the rooftops of Ploeşti, leaking gasoline from flak holes with two big bombs still stuck in her belly. The complex slipped by below, but dead ahead was a radio tower. Lieutenant Stuart dipped the left wing almost to the ground, and the right wing rose perpendicularly as the bomber barely skirted the stack. He leveled out and struggled to control the bomber as he pointed *Utah Man* toward home and began climbing to clear the deadly fire and to make for the sea. In the distance streams of bombers were still homing in on Ploeşti while those who had completed their runs were congregating in defensive formations to fend off enemy fighters on the trip back to Benghazi. As they headed for North Africa, the aircrews in the surviving planes looked back to see the entire quadrant of the sky above Ploeşti black from raging oil fires.

Lieutenant Stuart looked for comrades among the returning bombers and sidled up to a loose formation of B-24s heading back to Libya. Lieutenant

Stuart was completing his twenty-fifth mission and realized that the airmen in the planes were strangely silent. Normally there would be chatter between the planes, but the Ploeşti raid was different. Lieutenant Stuart realized that many of the bombers contained dead and wounded flyers, and those who had survived were traumatized or were frantically tending to bleeding and dying comrades. Lieutenant Stuart knew that there was little the survivors could do for the wounded.

The Ninety-third had been mauled. Thirty-nine planes from the bomb group took off from Libya that morning, and thirty-four made it to the target. In the aftermath, Lt. Col. George S. Brown, a future Air Force chief of staff, took command of the Ninety-third when Lieutenant Colonel Baker went down with *Hell's Wench*. Lieutenant Colonel Brown had barely made it through the maelstrom as his plane, *The Blasted Event*, took hit after hit and was shot through with holes and a wingtip was crumpled from striking a church steeple. As the Ninety-third's survivors formed up around Lieutenant Colonel Brown for the trip back to Benghazi, he was shocked to see just fifteen planes, only five relatively undamaged.

Utah Man had been hit in her number three engine and could make no more than 145 mph, and the crew watched in dismay as the protective formation of bombers moved ahead of them at 185 mph. She was on her own, exposed to enemy fighters, her fuselage laced with deadly fumes from leaking aviation gasoline, her torn flanks and bomb bay doors rattling in the slipstream. She still carried two monstrous bombs fused and waiting to explode. The engineer and bombardier struggled in the bomb bay, desperately working to release the bombs, their curses drowned out by torn and screeching metal that slapped against the plane's belly. The rest of the crew listened to the men's frantic hammering until it finally it stopped. The bombs were released and exploded in an open field. Lieutenant Stuart and his crippled bomber flew on towards home praying they would not be spotted by enemy fighters.

Hadley's Harem was also one of scores of damaged planes struggling to make it back to base as she made her way south over plains and mountains to the safety of the sea. The *Harem* had come in with Killer Kane after *Euroclydon* had reached the target, and her crew spotted the crash sites of the preceding B-24s, now heaps of rubble burning furiously in and around of the refineries. The *Harem* had just begun her bomb run on Killer Kane's left wing when the plane was rocked by a flak burst that smashed the greenhouse and killed bombardier Lt. Leon Storms and badly wounded navigator Lt. Harold Tabacoff. The plane shuddered from more hits as it drove through raging oil fires that enveloped the crew in searing heat and sent up impenetrable smoke that cast the fuselage in absolute darkness. As the *Harem* plunged back into daylight, her crew watched as a B-24 slithered along the ground while another, burning wingtip to wingtip, climbed in desperation and disappeared in a blinding flash.

The *Harem* staggered along at twenty-five feet off the ground, her hydraulic system shot out and gasoline pouring from the number one engine and from the bomb bay tanks. The engineer worked furiously to transfer the fuel to undamaged tanks. The number two engine was also damaged and began to burn while Lieutenant Hadley wrestled to keep his plane in the air as it bucked like a raging bronco. Her crew was stunned as the B-24 pulled away from the firestorm that soared up from the burning refinery and licked the plane's underside.

Hundreds of miles to the southwest the sun was setting over Benghazi as *Utah Man* touched down on the runway at Terria, the last Tidal Wave Liberator to make it back. As she rolled along the runway, the tire on the right main landing gear went flat from a flak hit and Lieutenant Stuart pulled the ship off to the side. For the first time in sixteen hours, the men were greeted by the silence of the Libyan Desert. Their ears rang and their bodies vibrated to the hammering rhythms of the bomber, but they could finally relax into the state of euphoria that often settled on aircrews after they had hit their target and made it safely back to base. Lieutenant Stuart knew the sense of loss would come the next day as the casualty figures of men and planes were tallied. The crew heard the voices of Red Cross girls approaching the forlorn and battered *Utah Man* with cigarettes, coffee, and candy. A nonsmoking non-coffee-drinking Morman, Lieutenant Stuart traded his cigarettes for everyone else's candy, and the crew took a coffee break on the side of the main runway at Terria. They were home and they were safe.

Capt. William D. Banks, who piloted the B-24 *Sad Sack* over Ploeşti and made it back to Cyprus, later wrote of the moment when he brought his plane to a stop and cut the engines after the Ploeşti raid. "We didn't speak a word—just leaned back in our seats and absorbed the sedative quiet of the pilot's compartment. For fifteen hours we had been in an earsplitting roar, weaving, climbing, diving, praying our way over mountaintops . . . every nerve strained and on the alert. Now there was calm, almost sacred peacefulness. It is one of the most beautiful things I remember." The crew of *Sad Sack* could barely climb out of the aircraft; they were stiff from hours of sitting and had to hold on to the plane to keep from collapsing.

Back in Benghazi as a new day dawned on August 2, 1943, the survivors of Ploeşti took stock. One crewman in Killer Kane's *Hail Columbia* summed up his experience on the raid: " I guess we'll go to heaven when we die. We've had our purgatory." Fifty-three of the 178-plane Tidal Wave force had been shot down, and 446 airmen were listed as killed or missing in action. Only thirty-three planes of the total force were fit to fly after the mission. The survivors went about their business in glum silence. In the tents where the airmen had lived, bunks were empty, uniforms and shoes would never be worn again, decks of cards would never be played, and last letters lay waiting to be sent home. Many hearts would be broken—forever.

7

Regret to Inform You

The midday sun beat down unmercifully on the landscape around Columbus on August I, 1943. Dairy cattle sought the shade of solitary trees
on the pasturelands, cornfields stood withered, and the prairies were turned
brown in the relentless heat. By midafternoon life in northern Mississippi
was at a standstill while eight thousand miles to the east the last of the Tidal
Wave bombers touched down in the rising chill of a desert night descending
around Benghazi.

Drought occupied the attention of Columbians and Lowndes County
residents in August 1943 as much as the advances and retreats on the battlefronts. Mississippi was in the grip of the worst dry spell of the century, and
the countryside baked in temperatures above one hundred degrees Fahrenheit.
The Columbus Army Airfield (CAAF) refused to reveal the temperature because commanders feared it would offer valuable military information to the
enemy. The rainfall level of 19.6 inches was nearly half that of normal, and
farmers usually anticipated at least 35 inches of precipitation this late in the

summer. The people of Columbus and the surrounding communities prayed as much for deliverance from nature as from their Axis enemies; they hadn't had a crop failure in fifty years.

As the war grew in intensity on battlefields like Ploeşti, it became routine news, and everyday life once again vied for space on the front page of the *Columbus Commercial Dispatch*. City and country residents flocked to the downtown Princess Theater to forget their cares with Gene Autry in *South of the Border* and Henry Fonda and Maureen O'Hara appearing in *Immortal Sergeant*. The Mississippi Music Company in Columbus advertised recordings of "Coming in on a wing and a prayer," and "You'll Never Know," two songs that had ironic meaning for the Franks family and for young women like Dottie Turner.

On August 3, a short piece in the *Commercial Dispatch* mentioned that several American Liberator bombers had made emergency landings in Turkey after a raid on Ploeşti, Romania, a place few people on the home front had ever heard of. All the planes that landed had been severely damaged by anti-aircraft fire and one of the pilots had been killed. Three days later, the newspaper displayed a dramatic front-page photograph of Killer Kane's B-24, *Hail Columbia*, and two other Liberators, one possibly being *Hadley's Harem*, flying low over the Ploeşti refineries against a backdrop of towering flames and billowing smoke from the fires set by the bombs and incendiaries of the preceding planes. *Euroclydon* had made its bomb run near the same spot, but no one in the Franks family knew that Red had been on the fateful raid or that they were looking at the battlefield where he had been shot down. Nor could anyone in Columbus have imagined the carnage at Ploeşti, the bodies strewn about, the burns and injuries of the wounded, the disorientation of the prisoners of war, and the wrecks of thirty of the total number of fifty-three lost B-24s littering the landscape around the refineries.

For nearly three weeks after the raid, no word came from Red and that was unlike him. Dr. Franks tried to ignore the absence of letters and telegrams from his son and he threw himself into his work. Nancy Lee was home for the summer and would soon be returning to Shorter College. Life had some of the trappings of normalcy.

August 16 was a typically hot afternoon when the doorbell rang at the parsonage. Nancy Lee went to answer and saw the figure of a young man framed in the doorway. It was the Western Union deliveryman; he was informally dressed with a busman's hat perched above an expressionless face. When Nancy opened the door, he raised his arm and held out a yellow envelope and spoke one word: "Telegram."

Nancy's heart raced as she signed for the message and began to read its contents. The Franks had received several similar communications in recent weeks from Red, and their hearts had momentarily stopped as they fumbled to open them with trembling hands. Most likely this was another of Red's telegrams saying that all was well and apologizing for failing to write; all of the previous messages had brought good news. The first from Red came May 8, just after he had arrived at Hardwick, and it was short and reassuring: "My thoughts are with you all. Well and safe. Jesse Franks Jr." There was another on July 23 from somewhere in the Mediterranean theater that indicated Red was in good spirits.

Nancy Lee saw that the words were typed in capital letters on the yellow sheet of paper, and she read them so quickly that at first she did not absorb their full meaning. They were laid out on the page without punctuation, which added to the difficulty of comprehending the text. She read the telegram over again, and this time the words hit her with staggering force:

I REGRET TO INFORM YOU REPORT RECEIVED STATES YOUR SON SECOND LIEUTENANT JESSE D FRANKS JR MISSING IN ACTION IN MIDDLE EASTERN AREA SINCE ONE AUGUST IF FURTHER DETAILS OR OTHER INFORMATION OF HIS STATUS ARE RECEIVED YOU WILL BE PROMPTLY NOTIFIED.

The telegram was signed in printed words, "Ulio, The Adjutant General." Below his name was the typed word, "BATTLE."

Nancy covered a muffled scream as her stepmother approached and took charge. Augusta immediately notified Dr. Franks in Vaughan, Mississippi, a small village in Yazoo County, thirty-two miles north of Jackson, where he was conducting a Baptist revival. Augusta did her best to soften the blow when she gave him the news. At first he did not comprehend the words, "missing in action." It was not the phrase, "killed in action," he feared most. An instant later he instinctively reacted and Dr. Franks reached out for a chair, gripped by an overpowering sense of unreality. He tried to steady himself and regain composure, but he was struck by a sorrow more profound than any he had ever experienced before. Years afterward Nancy Lee remembered him saying that was the worst day of his life.

"Why? Why?" he pleaded to his God. He had dreamed in his sleep that Red would be lost and anticipated in his waking hours that awful moment when a telegram might arrive at the front door. He had quickly shut these thoughts from his mind. Now Dr. Franks was flooded by memories of Red as an infant and a child, as a boy and a young man. He wanted to scold him for being so silly as to go to war when he was exempt, yet he was proud of his patriotism in a just cause. He wanted to curse the Air Corps for sending Red and all the other young men on such a deadly mission, yet he knew such missions were part of war.

Dr. Franks sobbed privately and violently and let the anguish and sorrow flow from his body. It was evening in Vaughn and he looked out over the flatness of the Mississippi delta country to the setting sun and wondered where Red might be at this moment. He was listed as missing, and Dr. Franks steadfastly refused to believe that Red had been harmed, yet he had lived too long to know that all stories don't end happily. He vowed that he would find him; that was his duty as a father.

Dr. Franks had pleaded in his quiet way for Red not to enlist, saying "You don't have to go." He explained that by staying the three-year course in seminary and completing his ministerial studies, he would be more useful in the war effort. The world needed the guidance and strength of men of God, Dr. Franks had said.

Red discussed his desire to enlist with friend and fellow seminarian, Herbert Gabhart, when the two got together to shoot hoops in the seminary gym or when they walked to class. Gabhart was a few years older and Red thought him wise for his years. "You have to do what you think is right," Gabhart had counseled, and in the end Red's combative instincts won out and he decided in January 1942 to leave the seminary and join the Air Corps after completing only one semester. His aim was to become a fighter pilot.

Dr. Franks recalled Red telling him, "Dad, all my buddies are going to war, and I don't want them to fight it for me." Red didn't want to hide behind a pastoral draft deferment, and Dr. Franks recognized that his son was now an adult and had always followed his instincts. Reluctantly he accepted Red's decision to join the military. But now, a year and a half later, he implored his God in despair. "It was so unnecessary."

When Dr. Franks wept for Red, it was in private, for no one except his wife and daughter ever saw him shed tears. He counseled strength to all his parishioners in the face of adversity, and he tried to live by that dictum. He had bombarded Red with lists of biblical passages from which his son could find solace and strength while in the Air Corps. But if there was ever a time in Dr. Franks's life when he himself needed strength, that time was now.

The people of Columbus learned that Red was missing from a front-page news report on August 17 in the *Commercial Dispatch* that ran under the headline, "MISSING IN ACTION—LT. J.D. FRANKS, JR." On August 19 Bernie Imes, the newspaper's owner and editor and a longtime friend of Dr. Franks, ran a piece on the editorial page under the headline: "Red Franks Missing."

The disturbing and distressing news has come that J.D. (Red) Franks, Jr., son of Dr. and Mrs. J.D. Franks, is missing in the European war theater. "Red," as he was affectionately known was a bombardier in a Flying Fortress [sic].

... Red was in there fighting for his country, for you and for me and for the freedom and liberty of the world.

Now he is missing in action and we can't help but believe that he is safe somewhere, either in enemy territory or in some out-of-the-way place.

"Red" was ready for whatever fate awaited him, brave, gallant, eager and fired with patriotism.

He was with the brave and gallant fighters in the sky over Italy and the Balkans.

He was on many dangerous missions, and now he is missing.

Somehow we feel that Red is safe somewhere and that when it is all over he will come back home to friends and loved ones.

This is the sincere hope and prayer of loved ones and all who admire and esteem him for his many fine qualities of character, gallantry and spirit of patriotism and devotion to his country.

Friends rallied to Dr. Franks's side. An old friend, Frank Milley, wrote, "My heart bleeds for you after the sad news from abroad. Since you told me he was making bombing missions I have been exceedingly uneasy. Red is such a wonderful boy. It is hard to realize he is 'missing.' A dear friend in Atlanta had a message that his aviator son was missing in action. Soon after, he had a message that he was a prisoner. I hope that you will get the same good news. God give you courage."

Dr. Franks hoped and prayed as well that Red was safe somewhere. He had experienced so much loss in his life that the thought of losing Red was more than he could bear. His own life seemed sandwiched between wars. He had grown up in Geeville, Mississippi, about twenty-five miles north of Tupelo in northern Mississippi. He was a boy in the 1880s and 1890s when the Confederate veterans of Gettysburg and Vicksburg were middle-aged men recounting their old war stories. They were proud, heroic men, but their scars, both physical and psychological, remained throughout their lives. The South had been shattered by the deaths of so many young men in battle, and the old Confederacy had been impoverished for decades after the war.

The yearly ceremony in Columbus's Friendship Cemetery a mile or so from the Frankses' house, where the nation's first Memorial Day observances were held in 1866, was a constant reminder of the cost of war. Columbus's grand dames and the Daughters of the Confederacy commemorated the dead of the Civil War annually by laying wreaths on the graves of the several thousand Confederate soldiers buried in the cemetery. The dead were laid out in neat rows under uniform headstones on which was inscribed the military unit to which they had been attached and the date and place of their deaths. There were many unknown dead. The neatness of the burial ground and its soothing calmness belied the messiness and the horror of their deaths. In the spring with the magnolias in bloom, the ground around where the Confederate soldiers were buried was almost a place of serene beauty. It was a noble gesture for the women of Columbus to honor the dead, and it was said that Friendship was the place "where flowers healed a nation" after the war. But Dr. Franks knew that there had been many families who had mourned those fallen soldiers for the rest of their lives. One needed only to recall a few lines from the poem, "The Blue and the Gray," that immortalized the yearly event in Friendship Cemetery:

From the silence of sorrowful hours

The desolate mourners go,

There was something so sad in the stories of young men whose lives are cut short in the violence of war in distant lands. They were forever young and so full of untested promise. Their fate brought to mind the prescient words of Paul Baumer, reflected in Erich Maria Remarque's *All Quiet on the Western Front*: "We stood on the threshold of life. . . . We had as yet taken no root. The war swept us away." Dr. Franks visualized all these young men as children when struck down. Many had certainly cried out for home and their mothers as they lay dying.

Dr. Franks was in his thirties when the United States entered the First World War, and he watched as millions of boys had rushed to join the army just as Red and countless others had enlisted in the military after Pearl Harbor in 1941. As a young minister with two parishes in Versailles and Osgood, Indiana, Dr. Franks had seen the recruits march away in 1917, smiling and stepping sprightly to the beat of martial music and cheering crowds. Later, he had prayed for the souls of those who did not return and he shared the grief of their families.

In his own life, he had lost his infant daughter, Graham Elizabeth in

1918 and his beloved Sallie in 1927. It had taken him years to overcome both losses, and now he would need all the strength he could gather to search for Red. Like Job, the Lord was severely testing Jesse Franks.

Dr. Franks prayed fervently that Red had survived at Ploeşti, but now his son was like a ghost inhabiting his every moment. He dreamed about Red in his troubled sleep and could not banish him from his mind during the day. Was his son alive or dead, and if he was alive, what was his condition? Was he badly burned and maimed? Was he suffering from amnesia after a traumatic bailout? Worse, Dr. Franks saw his son as a slave laborer sent to work for the enemy in the cruelest of conditions. Dr. Franks knew what the Germans were capable of doing to prisoners, and he remembered accounts of atrocities during the First World War as the "Huns" invaded the Low Countries and France and shot innocent nurses and civilians. Now he feared that Nazi brutes were torturing his son.

Dr. Franks vowed he would not succumb to despair; he needed to project strength not only for his family, but also for himself and his parishioners. There were other bereaved parents in Columbus, some in his own parish. The number of young men going to war grew daily. The First Baptist Church alone had sent 149 young men to war by the summer of 1943. One had already been killed and others would surely die, and their families would look to him for solace.

Dr. Franks also had to counsel and support Dottie Turner, whose life had been shattered by the news about Red. Dr. Franks had informed Dottie that Red was reported missing soon after he had received word, and she also believed that Red was alive, that it was not God's will that he should die so young. She stayed in constant touch with Dr. Franks as they prayed for Red's salvation and return.

As long as Red was listed as missing, Dr. Franks would never give up hope that Red was alive, and he would search to the ends of the earth if necessary. He would not allow his son to wander lost and aimless in this life or in the next. He would find Red.

8

Hope from Benghazi

The letter immediately caught Dr. Franks's eye; the handwriting was unmistakably Red's scrawl. It was the end of August 1943, four weeks after the Tidal Wave attack and a week after the Franks family had received word that Red was missing in action. Dr. Franks picked up the mail in the front hall of the parsonage and shuffled through the letters. He came to one with the distinguishing handwriting and yanked it from the day's stack of mail and turned it over. It was from Red! The envelope bore his name and his overseas address was on the back: "Lt. J. D. Franks, Jr., 0–734444, 93rd Bomb Group—328th Squadron, O.P.A. 634 . . ."

"It's from Red!" Dr. Franks threw up his hands in triumph and exclaimed aloud as he turned the letter over once again to examine the postal mark. It was dated August 3, 1943.

"Red's safe! He's safe!" Dr. Franks shouted as he turned and bounded up the stairs to show it to Nancy Lee who was in her bedroom with her friend Maud Yow.

"Nancy Lee! Nancy Lee!" Dr. Franks cried, his normal, quiet, and elegant southern drawl much louder than normal. He reached the landing and darted triumphantly into his daughter's room waving the envelope. "Red's safe and alive!" It was the first time since he had received the War Department telegram that he smiled. He held the letter out for the girls to see. "Look at the handwriting. It's Red's. Look at the postmark. It's dated August 3. They said Red was shot down on the first."

Nancy Lee and Maud were speechless and wide eyed as Dr. Franks danced about the room like an expectant child on Christmas morning, his normally taciturn face alight with joy, his conservative minister's gray suit and demeanor seemingly out of place. He stopped and opened the envelope with uncharacteristic force, his eyes sparkling with delight. Nancy Lee watched in anticipation and then noticed her father's expression change, imperceptibly at first, then fall into a mask of profound depression, the same look she had seen when he arrived home from Vaughn after being informed that Red was missing. She watched as her father bowed his head in silence and his shoulders sagged as he held out the letter for Nancy and Maud to read. Nancy Lee gingerly took it with shaking hands and read: "I want to write you a little note before our big raid tomorrow. It will be the biggest and toughest we have had yet. Our target is the oil fields . . ." She could read no more and slowly put the letter down as tears came to her eyes and she looked away from her father.

Dr. Franks turned in silence and went back downstairs, oppressed by the heavy reality that Red's fate remained uncertain and that he might have been killed. Maud and Nancy Lee heard his footsteps descend the stairs and fade as he entered his book-lined study. Later he would read the full contents of his son's last letter in private and weep until he thought he might die. The letter revealed a level of maturity, devotion to duty, and courage that few men possessed, and through his grief and sorrow Dr. Franks felt a sense of affirmation that Red had been so brave and fearless. He was a Christian martyr in the true sense of the word.

Dr. Franks had known all along that Red had been on bombing raids, and he had tried to steel himself against the awful day that he hoped would never come, when word would come that his son was reported killed or missing. Red could not be specific about *Euroclydon*'s missions such as the targets, the length of the flights, the number of planes involved, or the number of men killed or wounded; the Air Corps wouldn't allow that kind of information to be released for fear it could fall into enemy hands. Military censors reviewed every letter sent home by military personnel and blacked out words and sentences that they believed could help the enemy in any way.

But Red was able to say that he had experienced aerial combat, and he had even sent home a small souvenir from one mission, a cotter pin that he had removed from a bomb fuse shortly before *Euroclydon* attacked an Italian target. The pin was inserted in the fuse of a bomb to prevent it from accidentally detonating during flight. It was the fuse that determined when a bomb would explode, above, on, or below the ground. The pin that Red sent home came attached to a heavy paper tag with instructions printed on one side: "to be removed after bomb has been placed in dropping gear and arming wire inserted." Red had scribbled a note on the reverse side of the tag: "2nd raid—San Pancrazio, Italy—July 2, 1943—12 Bombs, 500 lbs."

In one letter Red sent to his father from the war zone, he wrote cryptically, "We have a rough raid ahead as you will find out in the newspapers. We are working hard and I hope and pray all works out fine." Red probably was referring to the Ploeşti mission.

Every airman flying against Germany in 1943 knew his chances of survival were poor. Antiaircraft fire over the target was intense and accurate even against planes at twenty-five thousand feet, and German fighters were decimating armadas of B-17s and B-24s as they flew on raids deep into enemy territory.

Red could not reveal to friends and family back home the name or location of Hardwick. He datelined his letters home, "Somewhere in England," and wrote that he was doing fine. "I'm in a good group of swell officers and all of us in combat operations live together and all is well." But the war was taking its toll. He ended his letter, "I just will be glad when it is all over and so will all the rest."

A few days later Red flew a harrowing first mission on May 29, 1943. He and Jack Warner volunteered to fly with another B-24 crew in need of a bombardier and navigator. Red and Jack had become fast friends in the four months *Euroclydon's* crew had been together. They had been a bit standoffish at first. Both were devout Baptists and from the South where one's religion was like a badge of social rank. Back in Columbus the way many people got to know one another was by asking what church they attended. It was assumed that all were Christians. When Red and Jack first met, they each thought the other was a heathen, and a generalized antipathy to the other's suspected religious beliefs held them back from immediately becoming friends. But once over that hurdle they were nearly inseparable, particularly since they both inhabited the confined nose section of the plane, scrunched in just in front of the pilot's platform where there was barely enough room for a man to stand, let alone room to move back and forth. The fact that both had wanted to be pilots but had washed out of flight school helped bond the two men. The tie was further strengthened by the knowledge that they were sitting ducks in the front of the plane where their chances of survival were less than for the rest of the crew.

A native of Lexington, Kentucky, Jack Warner was a skinny young man of twenty-six, but he looked younger than the huskier Red who was two year's his junior. Jack had kicked around for a few years after high school working as an auto body repairman to pay his way through the University of Kentucky's engineering program. He yearned to fly and applied to the Army's Aviation Cadet Program when war seemed inevitable, but was turned away because he was underweight.

He left college before completing the full four-year course and took a job with an Alabama shipyard building Liberty ships, but lost his draft deferment in the process. He was conscripted into the army in July 1941, and after completing basic infantry training he was assigned to the Fourth Engineer Training Battalion at Fort Belvoir, Virginia, constructing bridges and tank traps. It was tedious and unexciting work. He reapplied for flight school and was accepted into the Aviation Cadet program in January 1942. This time he made sure he weighed enough to make the cut.

Jack learned to solo in PT-17 Stearman biplane trainers, but failed pilot training; the army claimed he had not met all the requirements and washed him out. He applied to become a navigator, passed the course, and was commissioned a second lieutenant and received his navigator's wings. He realized later that if he had waited six months to take flight training, he would have become a pilot. By 1943 bomber losses in combat were severe, and the Air Corps needed all the pilots it could train.

The targets on Red and Jack's first bombing mission were the submarine pens at La Pallice on France's Atlantic coast near the port of Rochelle. To reach the objective the planes had to fly westward across England and well beyond France's Breton peninsula and down through the Bay of Biscay. It was an uneventful flight until the formation was within a few miles of the target when the plane's four engines abruptly cut out and the crew was enveloped in a sudden, terrifying quiet. The flight engineer had mismanaged the transfer of fuel by reversing the flow of gasoline to the engines, and every crew member scrambled as the plane went into a dive from an altitude of twenty-three thousand feet. The pilot jettisoned the bombs and Jack Warner frantically issued a M'Aidez call for help as the crew snapped on parachutes, checked survival gear, and readied escape hatches as the plane plummeted to earth, picking up speed as it fell. The whistle of wind rushing over the fuselage as the pilot struggled to restart the engines accentuated the strange silence within the B-24. The engines coughed and wheezed and the propellers barely rotated. Finally the engines sprang back to life in a throaty roar that seemed more deafening than usual. Red Franks and Jack Warner could only look at each other in relief as they realized they had come within seconds of bailing out on their first mission, prepared to squeeze out through the nosewheel hatch in the bottom of the plane just behind their position. The plane regained altitude and limped home without further incident, but thereafter Red and Jack had a pact that should one of them be wounded, the other would help him to bail out.

At Hardwick, a few days later, the aircrews were startled to find the Norden bombsights removed from the nose of the aircraft and replaced by simple reticule-type sights, useable only at very low altitude. *Euroclydon* and the Ninety-third were then ordered to conduct mysterious training flights over southern England. Instead of high-altitude practice bomb runs, the planes were sent in at heights of a hundred feet or less, and every crewman realized that there was no margin of error. One bad lurch and a bomber would hurtle into the ground. On one flight *Euroclydon* flew so low that its tail section scraped the treetops as Lieutenant Porter began a climb out. Everyone surmised that the upcoming mission was going to be rougher than any they had ever experienced. Red and his crewmates had heard talk of Ploeşti, but the refineries were just one of many targets mentioned in scuttlebutt about a low-level raid.

The Ninety-third was assigned to North Africa in late June and flew to Oran in Algeria in early July before flying on to its base at Terria, Libya, eighteen miles south of Benghazi. As *Euroclydon* hugged the North African coast, her crew saw the detritus of war. Wrecked German vehicles of all sorts littered the landscape just beyond the water's edge, and the crew passed by German air bases where Luftwaffe aircraft were lined up in neat rows, too badly shot up to ever fly again.

The base at Terria had literally been carved from the desert with a runway of hardened sand and pebbles. As *Euroclydon* taxied to a halt spewing great clouds of dust, the men looked out on an ageless North African scene of swirling sand, tents, camels, bleating goats, and Arabs in all manner of garb.

The crew was served snacks that included "grimy sandwiches and synthetic lemonade," and then went to work pitching their own tents. Later they trooped to a dinner that often consisted of powdered eggs scrambled with desert dust, bread, and canned sausage. The sweet for the day might be apple butter. Then it was back to their tents as night descended in a powerful, enveloping blackness never before experienced by most of the men.

Red wrote home that living conditions at Terria were spartan compared to Hardwick. On July 4, 1943, Red wrote a friend about his squadron's new assignment in Libya: "Hot, dusty and dry, live in tents and are getting a taste of combat in the raw. Quite a contrast to England. Things weren't so bad there. Well, it makes me want to end this war all the quicker." Red then mentioned his fantasy of swimming in the cool lake waters at Camp Ridgecrest in the billowing mountains of North Carolina, and he allowed himself to dream: "Maybe someday not too far off we will all come home again."

The other bomb groups assigned to the Ploeşti raid were also stationed at various airfields around the city, and when all were at full strength, the low-level training missions were resumed over the desert. But the bombers were also diverted to combat missions against targets in Italy. *Euroclydon* was among the planes assigned to destroy bridges and roads to cut off the German retreat through Sicily after the Allies landed on the island in July 1943. For the first time, the crew experienced flak and fighter attacks and suffered flak damage. On a mission to Messina, elements of the Ninety-third flew into heavy antiaircraft fire manifesting itself in big black, oily bursts from 88 mm guns that dispersed the tight bomber formation, and the crews watched helplessly as one straggling B-24 was unmercifully set upon by enemy Me 109s. On another attack over Reggio Calabria, Red saw the sky in front of the greenhouse fill with the menacing bursts from 88s as the formation began its bomb run.

Even when not flying combat missions, the crews were reminded of the war. B-24s from other bomb groups often came limping home to Benghazi trailing smoke after raids against Italy. Each attack usually cost the Americans several planes and their crews.

The Ninety-third was also assigned to bomb the Benedictine monastery atop Monte Cassino, north of Naples. The mission was flown in support of ground forces trying to take the objective and open the road to Rome. The bombs destroyed the ancient abbey, but to no avail. The Germans used the rubble to better defend their positions on the mountaintop.

The outskirts of Rome were the next target when *Euroclydon* and the Ninety-third struck railroad-marshaling yards. The mission was what the crews called a virgin target since Rome had never before been bombed by the Americans. *Hadley's Harem* and the 376th Bomb Group were also assigned to the raid, and the group's commander allowed any crew member to withdraw for religious concerns or convictions. The Ninety-third Bomb Group's chaplain was assigned to *Euroclydon* and observed the attack in the nose with

Red and Jack with instructions to report to headquarters and Washington if the planes accidentally hit the Vatican. U.S. intelligence reported that the Holy See had been spared but that bombs had partially destroyed the church of San Lorenzo fuori le Mura, one of the seven basilicas of Rome where several popes were buried. Italian authorities complained, however, that the damage was much more severe and that a workers' district along the Tiber River had been badly hit.

On the flight back to Benghazi, *Euroclydon* ran low on fuel and was forced to land on the island of Malta. The crew spent the night roaming the city of Valetta before takeoff the next morning from a runway that was not designed for heavy bombers. It was too short and ended abruptly in a fifty-foot drop to the sea. *Euroclydon* began her run and picked up speed. For the crew it was like being launched from an aircraft carrier; suddenly there was nothing but air beneath the plane when the runway ended. Red and Jack moved to the flight deck behind the pilots, as they often did on takeoff, and watched wide eyed as the sea rose up at them and *Euroclydon* sank below the land before her propellers tugged her upward.

Back at Terria, training for the raid against Ploești was intense and in earnest. The five participating bomb groups were ordered to undertake the "uncompromising, highly intensive, low-level training program," and they all flew daily practice missions against the mock refineries laid out in the desert. By the time *Euroclydon* flew on the Tidal Wave raid, the crew had flown ten combat missions, and Dr. Franks prayed every day that Red would survive the magic number of twenty-five. For Red, the war would then be over and he would be sent home.

9

Dad, Please Stay the Same

"Officers and Men of the Ninth U.S. Bomber Command."

The salutation came in a letter from Gen. Henry H. "Hap" Arnold, commanding general of the Army air forces, that was addressed to Dr. Franks in late August 1943 commending the men who participated in the Ploeşti raid for a job well done. Certainly, Dr. Franks was proud of Red's involvement in Tidal Wave, but the letter brought home the cruel fate of those who had become casualties of war by making only passing reference to the dead and missing from the raid. Their loss was quickly rationalized and General Arnold seemed to justify the reported loss of 446 young men when he wrote, "Those who gave their lives did so that others might live." These were noble words and sentiments, but they could not express the horror of loss to hundreds of families whose sons were killed over Ploeşti. The world had come to accept the terrible toll of war; 446 men for whom every living hope was now extinguished. Many of the missing had undoubtedly died and would later be listed as killed in action.

Dr. Franks also found himself among the thousands of Americans who were expected to be proud of their sacrifice even as they struggled to live with unending grief because of the war. Their ranks would multiply before the conflict was over, and most would never overcome the loss of those who were so young and who had died on foreign soil so far from home.

Dr. Franks received a rain of letters and telegrams, most from the War Department, in the weeks and months that followed Ploeşti. He shared many with Dottie and he kept her informed of his efforts to find Red. The notice he would remember most throughout his life was the telegram that arrived in late September 1943. He had not expected it, and when it came, it was the cruelest blow he had ever experienced. On September 23, 1943, the War Department inexplicably changed Red's status from missing to killed in action. The news was delivered to the Frankses' front door. Once again the letters were printed in uppercase almost as if to insure no one would miss their import:

REPORT RECEIVED THROUGH THE INTERNATIONAL RED CROSS STATES YOUR SON FIRST LIEUTENANT JESSE D FRANKS JR WHO WAS PREVIOUSLY REPORTED MISSING SINCE ONE AUGUST WAS KILLED IN ACTION ON ONE AUGUST IN MIDDLE EASTERN AREA THE SECRETARY OF WAR EXTENDS HIS DEEP SYMPATHY LETTER FOLLOWS.

The telegram was again signed, "Ulio, The Adjutant General," and, as before, the world "BATTLE" was printed at the bottom of the page.

Why the change in status? Whatever the reason, Dr. Franks adamantly refused to accept the War Department's conclusion. He struggled to contain his anger that the military would declare an American soldier deceased without explanation, and he was determined that the War Department should be made to exhaust every lead before declaring Red killed in action. Had Red's body been recovered? Had his grave been located? The War Department didn't say. Dr. Franks believed that Red could be a prisoner of war, and the government's lack of thoroughness in Red's case seemed almost criminal. The only thing the War Department had gotten right, as far as Dr.

Franks was concerned, was in referring to Red as "First Lieutenant." He had been promoted from second lieutenant shortly before the Ploeşti raid.

It is the natural order of things that a son should outlive his father, and Dr. Franks would never give up hope of finding his son alive, but every day the uncertainty sapped his strength and tortured his soul. Yet he stoically pressed on. "Blessed are those who mourn, for they shall be comforted," but these words from Matthew 5:4 offered little consolation.

Hopes that Red had survived were dashed again in October with the return of a letter Dr. Franks had mailed to his son on August 3 before news had arrived that Red was missing. Dr. Franks's note had been chatty, about life in Columbus that sent a touch of home. He was stunned when he held his own letter in his hands; it defied his belief that Red was alive. The envelope was returned to the Frankses' doorstep with the address penciled out and a large X slashed across the front. The symbol of a hand with a pointing forefinger and the wording "Return to Sender" was stamped on the left side.

Dr. Franks turned the letter over and paled at what he read. The backside had been marked by a stamped legend filled in, somewhere in the war zone, by a clerk's handwriting: "War Dept., A.G.O.—Status Changed To: Killed in Action." The insensitivity of the inscription left Dr. Franks momentarily breathless, but the words merely symbolized the heartlessness of a world at war and brought to mind the writings of Wilfred Owens about his experiences in the First World War: "My senses are charred. I don't take the cigarette out of my mouth when I write Deceased over their letters."

Grim, depressing news about Red continued to invade the Franks household like an ill wind that infiltrated every seam. On October 26, Dr. Franks received a letter from the Army Effects Bureau in Kansas City, Missouri, listing Red's personal belongings that he had left behind. The army sent the effects of every soldier killed in World War II to a large warehouse in Kansas City where the material was processed prior to shipment to their families. But before Dr. Franks could receive them, he had to fill out an application form and sign an affidavit that he was Lt. Franks's father. "Your local Red Cross representative will be glad to assist you if you desire," the letter stated.

Accompanying the letter was a sheet listing Red's personal items: "I Insignia, I Blouse, 2 Pr. Trousers Pink, 3 Shirts, Khaki, I Flight Cap, I T Shirt, 2 Bath Towels, 2 Pr. Shorts, 3 Handkerchiefs, I Sweatshirt, 2 Pr Athletic Shorts, I Shoulder Holster, 2 Ties, I Shaving Kit, I tropical Gar. Cap, I Pr Shoes, I Pr Tennis Shoes, 7 Pr Socks, I Bible with Pictures, I Pen & Pencil Set, I Pen, 3 Wallets, I Picture, I Trench Coat." Dr. Franks was deeply pained by the thought that his son's life had been reduced to a list of bath towels, handkerchiefs, and socks.

In early November Dr. Franks received another communication from the Kansas City quartermaster personnel effects depot that included a check for $182.76 that represented money Red had set aside while with the 328th Squadron. The army requested, "Some responsible person receive them [the effects] so that distribution may be made in accordance with the laws of the state of your son's legal residence." Was he not Red Franks's father? Did they expect him to steal the money?

Not long thereafter the American Red Cross confirmed the War Department's change of status of Red from missing to killed in action. The Red Cross had sent the letter to John E. Rankin, the Mississippi congressman to whom Dr. Franks had written for help in finding his son. Representative Rankin was a veteran congressman from Tupelo in north Mississippi who chaired the House Veterans Affairs Committee, and he had served in World War I. Congressman Rankin forwarded the letter to Dr. Franks.

> Lieutenant Franks has been officially declared deceased. . . . Before this notification was sent to the family every possible effort was made to properly identify this officer, and the fact that the report was sent to the family indicates that the War Department is satisfied that the report from the International Red Cross is official. The War Department is reluctant to change the status of a serviceman from "missing" to "deceased" until conclusive evidence of his death is received. If the family should find tangible evidence that this officer is still alive, they may request clarification from the War Department.

The Red Cross bluntly stated that as of that date, there was not enough evidence to retract the classification of killed in action. But what evidence did they offer that Red had been killed. There was none, as far as Dr. Franks was concerned.

Congressman Rankin expressed his regrets to Dr. Franks. In a letter with the salutation, "My Dear Friend," Rankin stated, "I regret more than I can express to you that the Red Cross report is not more encouraging."

There were further communications from the War Department in which the army stated that Lieutenant Franks had been listed as killed in action because of "authentic" information received from the Romanian government. Maj. Gen. J. A. Ulio, the adjutant general, wrote to Dr. Franks: "I regret that he [Red] must be officially recorded as having been killed in action on 1 August 1943." General Ulio ended by writing: "Permit me to extend again my most heartfelt sympathy."

But Dr. Franks still refused to believe that the War Department had sufficient information to declare that Red was dead, and if the War Department wouldn't search for his son, he would do it himself. He began making plans to travel to Romania, but such a journey could take months of preparation.

In November 1943, he memorialized Red in a service at the First Baptist Church and titled his eulogy, "The Christian Courage of Bombardier Jesse D. "Red" Franks." Dr. Franks expressed his unending grief and sorrow in the day's program in which he wrote in bold capital letters.

EXCEPT FOR THE GRACE OF GOD AND FOR THE LOVE AND SYMPATHY OF FRIENDS AND FOR THE ABIDING CONVICTION THAT THE CAUSE IS JUST FOR WHICH OUR NOBLE YOUTH ARE MAKING THE SUPREME SACRIFICE AND FOR THE SWEET MEMORIES OF THEM THERE WOULD BE NO COMFORT FOR US BACK ON THE HOME FRONT WHO HAVE RECEIVED THE COLD, HEARTLESS MESSAGE "KILLED IN ACTION."

His eulogy was prefaced by a quotation from I Corinthians 16:13 that was meant as much for himself as for the congregation. "Be alert; stand firm in the faith; acquit yourselves like men; be strong. Let all that you do be done from love." He would memorialize Red as though he had been killed, but in his heart and soul he knew that Red had to be alive.

His memorial began:

Lieutenant Jesse D. Franks, Jr., my son, gave up his life in the raid on the Ploeşti oil refineries on August 1, 1943. On the night before that fateful raid he wrote his last letter to me, which I have no doubt was the last message he ever wrote. When he wrote this letter, he had no thought that any others would see it, except his dad and his immediate family group.

I am giving it to you in full as he wrote it. It is too rich to keep for ourselves alone. It is a piece of literature that deserves to live because of the simplicity and naturalness of its style. Better still, it has a message of triumphant Christian faith which the whole world needs at this crucial time—a message that should inspire and challenge to highest courage and to noblest and most self-sacrificing patriotism, both on the home front and on our many battlefronts.

My son was a student for the Christian ministry in the Southern Baptist Theological Seminary, Louisville, Kentucky, when Pearl Harbor was raided. In the less than two weeks following he had volunteered for service in the Army Air Corps, not choosing to take advantage of his deferred classification, which was his right as a ministerial student.

Red Franks had made an enviable record at Mississippi College, Clinton, Mississippi, from which he graduated in June 1941. He was an outstanding student leader and athlete, having received many honors in those capacities, but he was appreciated most for his wholesome Christian character. His clean, vigorous manhood gave him great influence among his fellow students on the campus.

My son was formerly endorsed as a candidate for the Christian ministry by his home church, the church which I have had the honor to serve as pastor for more than twenty years, First Baptist Church, Columbus, Mississippi, just a few days before he entered the seminary in the fall of 1941. He died without having preached a formal sermon from the pulpit. I like to think of his last letter to me as his first and, as it now must be, his last sermon, though I am sure he never thought of it as a sermon.

With that thought in mind I am happy to share it with you and with the public in general, despite the embarrassment which I feel because of the extravagant personal references it makes to me. I consider it a choice bit of Christian witnessing, coming spontaneously out of the heart of a noble young man who was able to face a grave crisis in his life supported by a triumphant Christian faith. Through its instrumentality, as it goes to you and through me, I trust, to others, I pray that God may bring sweet spiritual comfort and encouragement to multiplied thousands who may read it, renewing their Christian faith and revitalizing their Christian patriotism. Through this means may God be pleased to round out for my son, a young preacher who never preached, a rich and fruitful gospel ministry.

Red Franks's last letter to his father on August 1, 1943, was so simple and so direct that it was later entered into the Congressional Record. Dr. Franks read it from the pulpit from which he had looked out for so many years to see his redheaded son seated among the worshipers. The First Baptist Church was absolutely silent that Sunday morning as Dr. Franks began to read:

Dearest Dad:

I want to write you a little note before our big raid tomorrow. It will be the biggest and toughest we have had yet. Our target is the oil fields, which supply Germany with three-fourths of her oil. We will get our target at any cost, and on a raid we can never foresee all that will happen.

Our planes are made for high-altitude bombing, but this time we are going in at 50 feet above our target, so there will be no second trip to complete the job. We will destroy the oil refineries in one blow. Hitler cannot run his planes, tanks and trucks without this oil, and the war will be shortened, they tell us, by a year after the raid, and may knock Italy clear out of the picture.

Dad, if anything happens—don't feel bitter at all. Please stay the same. I remember how happy you were when I decided to go to the Seminary, and then again, when I joined the Air Corps in preference to staying at the Seminary.

You are the best Dad in the world, and always too good to a boy who was a pretty bad little redhead at times.

I am glad I am in this group, and will get a chance at this important target. I know that it will save many lives from the results, so at any cost it is worth it. So, Dad, remember that, and the cost, whatever it may be, will not be in vain.

I don't want you to think that I gave up before I got into the air. No, that is not the reason I am writing this at all. We are fully aware of the danger of this raid, and I always want you to know that I love you, and am so proud to be your son, and can do this, even though my part is little.

Remember me to all the folks back home. Everyone has always gone out of their way to be nice to me. I love Columbus—everything about it—the people, town, and the spirit behind what makes it such a wonderful place to live. I love everything there.

Take good care of yourself, little Sis, and don't let this get you down, because I would never want it that way. Never change—be the same swell Dad always. Remember, you are doing the best job in the world now, and you always have done the best one.

Hope you don't get this letter, but one never knows what tomorrow may bring.

Your devoted son.

Dr. Franks struggled to hold his emotions in check as he read the last line of his son's letter: "My favorite chapter is the 91st Psalm."

1 0

The Gold Star

The Western Union deliveryman was the angel of death during World War II. Hundreds of thousands of mothers, fathers, and wives saw his figure framed in the front doorway just as Nancy Lee did in the early afternoon of August 16, 1943, two and a half weeks after the Ploești attack. By the time World War II ended in August 1945, around 406,000 American families had been informed that a son, a brother, a fiancé, or a husband had been killed in action or had died of wounds or disease or by accident in the war.

Some families received devastating news more than once. Lt. Gen. Leslie McNair, commander of Army ground forces, was killed in Normandy in July 1944 by American bombs falling short of the target. His son was also killed in action a few days later fighting the Japanese on the Pacific island of Guam. Brothers Daniel and Henry Unger of Tower City, Pennsylvania, were also killed in July 1944, six days and a few hundred yards apart in France while serving with the Second Infantry Division. The five Sullivan brothers of Waterloo, Iowa, were lost when the cruiser USS *Juneau*, on which they all served, was sunk in the South Pacific on November 13, 1942.

Ellie Pope Dodwell was six when her brother, William Leonard Pope, was killed in France in the summer of 1944. She remembers vividly the Western Union boy arriving late one summer morning at her family's duplex in Easton, Pennsylvania, a small industrial city at the confluence of the Delaware and Lehigh rivers eighty miles west of Manhattan. "To this day I can see him coming," Ellie said. She was bouncing a rubber ball off the front of their house, a game that angered the neighbor and that her parents had forbidden her to play. As the messenger rode up and rested his bicycle against a tree, Ellie noticed that he wore metal clips around the ankles to keep his pants from getting caught in the bike chain. He approached and asked Ellie where he could find her mother, and she pointed to the back porch where Mrs. Pope was hanging the wash. Ellie continued to bounce the ball until she was jolted by her mother's piercing scream. Mrs. Pope had opened the telegram and learned that her oldest son, Billy, had been killed in action. The Western Union boy had done his job. He strode back to his bicycle, picked it up, and rode away.

Ellie's father was at work at the sprawling steel plant in nearby Bethlehem, Pennsylvania, and Ellie and her brother were left to deal with their stricken mother, who lay collapsed on the back porch. They ran to a neighbor to summon the family doctor and the minister, who rushed to the Pope's house to offer aid and comfort. But Ellie's mother refused to be consoled, and she lay listless and crying for weeks while her six-year-old daughter hovered nearby in fear and wonder. "As a child I couldn't understand the crying all the time," Ellie said. Nor could she understand her mother's rage as she sobbed and mourned for Billy.

One salient feature of that day, which stands out in Ellie's memory more than a half century later, is the manner in which families were informed of battle death during World War II. "When I see how families of soldiers are notified today, they don't know how easy they have it. It's still horrible, but today if it happens, a representative from the military comes to your door, not some Western Union boy with a telegram."

During World War II most families were notified by a Western Union representative that a son or a husband had been killed in action, wounded, or was missing. The mother of one flyer shot down in the August 1 Tidal Wave attack on Ploești received the news from a cabdriver. The family lived on a farm, and she was puzzled in mid-August 1943 as the cab drove up the long driveway to the homestead. The driver got out, handed her a telegram, and, after asking her to sign for it, got back in and drove away. Her son was listed as missing in action.

During the Viet Nam War and the Gulf War, military delegations that often included a chaplain along with personnel trained in grief management delivered the news of death. But seeing a group of uniformed soldiers on the front steps was as devastating to families in later wars as was the Western Union boy in World War II. The mother of a young marine lieutenant serving with a rifle company in Viet Nam returned home from a ladies' bridge group in Princeton, New Jersey, in the summer of 1967, to find three uniformed men waiting on her front porch. She knew immediately that her son had been killed.

Elizabeth Teass was new to her job as a Western Union Teletype operator at Green's Drugstore in Bedford, Virginia, when she received nine telegrams on July 17, 1944, notifying families in Bedford that sons, brothers, or husbands had been killed during the D-day invasion in Normandy on June 6, 1944. The main Western Union office for central Virginia, located in Roanoke, began sending the notices at 8:30 A.M., and the transmission began with the cheery greeting, "Good morning," and concluded with the grim news, "We have casualties."

Teass fed her machine with a spool of yellow paper tape that was imprinted with words as it ran through the machine. She then pasted the tape onto yellow Western Union stationery and placed the telegram in a yellow envelope that was to be delivered to the recipient. In other parts of the country the telegrams were handwritten. Teass's main concern was confidentiality; she had to ensure that no one but the family would be the first to learn of the death. If the telegrams were delivered in town, Teass used the drugstore's delivery boy to convey the message. If the family lived on a farm or in the country, she called the undertaker, the sheriff, the doctor, or the cabdriver to deliver the news. She knew these men and trusted their discretion.

To Teass, handling telegrammed death notices was a job she took seriously, if unemotionally. For the people who received the news, however, it was the most devastating moment of their lives. "It was a sad thing just to think of those boys killed and then think of their mothers and fathers, wives, and brothers and sisters who received messages that they'd been killed in action. Your heart goes out to people like that," Teass said. "And to think that those boys had no choice. They were just gone."

During World War II the survivors often had to fend for themselves once they received death notices. If they were known in their community, friends and family rallied round them to help deal with the loss. Bedford was one such close-knit community where residents went to the aid of their bereaved neighbors.

Pontotoc, Mississippi, where Sarah Carter Schaen grew up with Dottie Turner and the Anderson sisters, was a similar community in which most of the families knew each other. Sarah graduated from MSCW in 1944 and was acquainted with Dr. Franks through her association with the college's Baptist Student Union and because of her regular attendance at Sunday services at the First Baptist Church. She met her future husband, Lt. Jim Schaen, in Columbus in 1942 when he was assigned to the Columbus air base. His dream was to become a bomber pilot and return to Columbus after the war and go into commercial aviation. He and Sarah courted for a year and were married on Christmas Eve, 1943, when Jim was a B-24 pilot. A short time later he was assigned to the Eighth Air Force in England and flew bombing missions over Germany. He was killed when his plane was shot down over Kassel on September 27, 1944.

Sarah vividly recalls the day in February 1945, when Mr. Calloway, the Western Union deliveryman in Pontotoc, arrived at her parents' front door with the telegram informing her that Jim had been killed in action. Mr. Calloway was accompanied by one of Sarah's best friends, Margaret, whose husband had also been shot down over Germany and was a prisoner of war.

Margaret held Sarah as she read the telegram and burst into tears; she had never dreamed that Jim would be killed.

Sarah's family and the entire Pontotoc community rallied around her, offering comfort until she could carry on. She also found strength in her religious faith. Sarah is a strong woman who plunged back into life, but she has never forgotten.

Families whose sons, husbands, and brothers were killed in World War II received a small fabric banner with a gold star centered on a silver-white background and trimmed with a red band to signify their sacrifice. The gold star that hung in the front window derived from a practice begun during World War I when families with men in service displayed similar banners with blue stars at the center. As the war progressed and more men were killed, families began superimposing a gold star over the blue.

The gold star came into being in 1918, when President Woodrow Wilson approved a suggestion that, instead of wearing conventional mourning black, American women should wear a black band on the left arm embossed with a gilt star for each member of the family who had been killed in service of the nation. Mothers who wore the gold star formed the Gold Star Mothers in 1929, and the organization has been active ever since. Grace Darling Seibold, of Washington, DC, founded the organization to remember her own son and the young men who were killed in World War I and to perpetuate the ideals for which they had died.

Mrs. Seibold's son, George Vaughn Seibold, 23, volunteered for military service in 1917 and was assigned to the flying corps. He was sent to Canada to fly British planes because the United States had no air force at the time. George was deployed to England and was assigned to the British Royal Flying Corps, the 148th Aero Squadron that was shipped to combat duty in France.

George corresponded regularly with his family, but his letters stopped coming in August 1918. Because he was serving under British command, American officials could not provide the Seibold family with information about his loss. They learned of their son's death on Christmas Eve 1918, six weeks after the armistice, when the postman delivered a package to the family's Washington, DC, residence marked "Effects of Deceased Officer, First Lieutenant George Vaughn Seibold, Attached to the 148th Squadron, BRFC." No other information was provided.

Grace Seibold continued to visit hospitalized veterans in the Washington area, clinging to the hope that her son might have been wounded and returned to the United States alive without any identification, suffering from amnesia. While working through her sorrow, she helped ease the pain of the many badly wounded servicemen and extended a hand to mothers whose sons also had been killed in military service.

After months of inquiry, the family received official notice. "George was killed in aerial combat during the heaviest fighting over Baupaume, France, August 26, 1918." His body was never recovered.

The honor of displaying a gold star was far from the minds of the Pope family of Easton in the summer of 1944. Like thousands of families whose sons were killed in World War II, the Popes were desperate to know the circumstances surrounding Billy's fate. Had he died quickly? Had he been with comrades? Did he have any last words for his family? Most important of all, the family wanted to know if Billy actually had been killed or whether he might still be alive.

"Tell me about my boy" was the request most frequently sent to the army's quartermaster general by families when they learned of a son's death, the army reported in 1946. It reflected the parents' need to know and to understand their sons' last moments that affected even the mightiest of men who suffered loss during the war. Gen. George C. Marshall, chief of staff of the armed forces during World War II, visited the grave of his stepson, 1st Lt. Allen Brown, at a temporary cemetery in Anzio, Italy, shortly after Allen was killed in action in May 1944. Marshall wanted to know the details surrounding his stepson's death and interviewed men who had been with Allen when he died. A lieutenant gave Marshall a memento of his dead stepson, the crumpled, marked-up road map that Allen had been using when he was killed. Allen commanded a tank and was shot by a sniper as he sat exposed from the waist up in the turret.

Marshall also interviewed Allen's tank driver and gunner and then boarded a small observation plane to fly over the site where his stepson had been killed in the Alban Hills north of Rome. Marshall biographer, Forest Pogue, noted, "These facts, noted calmly and precisely, made his stepson's last hours a part of his own experience, softening the pain of his death."

Few Americans were able to retrace the last hours and steps of their sons in combat. During World War II, the War Department released little or no information about casualties, which led some families that received death notices to believe that the military was in error and that a son or husband might still be alive. But too many soldiers were being killed for the armed forces to take the time to chronicle the last moments of each man and report back to their families. To do so would have required thousands of men to investigate all of the deaths.

Another grim fact of modern warfare is that many men simply vanish in combat; they are blown apart by shell bursts or bomb blasts, or their bodies are pulverized into fragments when their planes crash, or they are lost at sea when their ship is sunk. Paul Fussell recalled seeing a human liver lying by itself on the battlefield. Little remained of the body of Lieutenant General McNair, killed by American bombs during the fighting in Normandy, France. He had gone to the front to observe Operation Cobra, in which hundreds of bombers blasted holes in the enemy's defenses prior to an American break out from the Normandy bridgehead. Some of the bombs fell short and General McNair died along with several hundred other American troops. The army took great pains during and after the war to identify men badly mutilated by modern munitions, and General McNair was identified by a finger that still bore his West Point ring and by a scrap of material from his lapel that bore three stars.

During World War II the War Department also withheld information about how, when, and where a soldier or sailor was killed because it did not wish to reveal information that might benefit the enemy. The Nemeth family of Bethlehem, Pennsylvania, received word that their son, electrician's mate John Joseph Nemeth, had been killed in action in the Pacific aboard the Coast Guard cutter *Calloway*. The Navy Department and the ship's commander wrote letters of condolence to the family expressing their regrets.

The captain concluded his letter by writing, "You are requested not to divulge the name of the ship."

The family was informed, however, that John was "buried at sea with full military honors and religious services. The exact location of his burial was listed as "16° 51' north latitude, 119° 35' 15' east longitude." This was in the vicinity of the Lingayen Gulf in the Philippines.

There would have been little information to offer many families regardless. Ken Mooney, who served in Europe as a lieutenant in the Twenty-eighth Infantry Division, lost his brother, Hugh, to enemy action in France in 1944. Ken was in Normandy at the time and visited Hugh's infantry company to inquire about his brother's death but discovered little. Hugh had been killed in the heat of combat while his comrades kept their heads down and clung to the earth to stay alive. He became just another statistic to be wrapped in a mattress cover, unceremoniously carried away in the back of a truck to a temporary cemetery. His comrades would have wasted little time and emotion over his death, not because they didn't care, but because death was so commonplace.

The Popes went to see their congressman, Francis E. Walter from Easton, Pennsylvania, who in later years became the powerful chairman of the House Un-American Activities Committee. They begged him for information about how Billy had died, but the only news that Walters could obtain was that William Pope had died a hero and he had been awarded the Silver Star. Congressman Walters also tried unsuccessfully to locate comrades who had been with Billy when he was killed.

The War Department was so sparing with information about casualties that some families were never informed about how a brother or son had died until many years later. Donald McClusky, a retired professor of history at Lafayette College in Pennsylvania, did not learn how his brother, Edward, died in August 1943 until a half century later. Edward, a naval officer, was killed in the South Pacific, and his father, a former district attorney and judge, sought information about his son through every possible channel, but the government would release nothing.

In 1994, Donald received a telephone call from an amateur historian doing research on Edward's ship. Donald explained that he had no information and the surprised caller later sent him declassified documents, which revealed that Edward had died when his LST (landing ship tank) was torpedoed by a Japanese submarine. Edward's body was never found and he was believed to have gone down with the vessel.

Ellie Pope Dodwell remembers the innumerable correspondences her parents received from the War Department that always renewed the family's grief. "It seemed as though these letters and packages kept coming for years," Ellie said. The government sent the flag that had draped their son's coffin when he was buried in Normandy, and her mother once again collapsed. "Things would quiet down and then something else would come," Ellie said. The family received Billy's personal effects, and again, they had to deal with more sorrow and the pitiful reminders of their son.

Vera Brittain, in her memoir, *Chronicle of Youth*, described that "awful moment" when she received the personal effects of her fiancé, Roland Leighton, an officer in the British army, after he had been killed in France in 1915. The package contained his clothing, including the uniform he had worn when he had last come home from the front. It also contained the uniform he had worn while in combat. "Everything was damp & worn & simply caked with mud. All the sepulchers and catacombs of Rome could not make me realize mortality & decay & corruption as vividly as did the smell of those clothes. Even all the little things had the faint smell & were damp and moldy," Brittain wrote.

The Popes received an invitation to Washington to accept their son's medals in a special ceremony at the War Department. But they were too angry to attend. They believed the government had taken their son; why should they honor that travesty with an appearance. "I remember the crying going on in our house. My parents didn't want his medals; they wanted Billy."

Ellie has few memories of her brother except photographs. He went to war when she was four, and he was killed when she was six. After his death, however, he was virtually canonized by her parents. "Billy became perfect," Ellie said. "There was never a time that my parents said he had done something wrong."

Such veneration is common in families of war dead and is expressed in different ways. Vera Brittain, as did other grieving survivors, honored the dead by capitalizing the personal pronoun when referring to the deceased as though he had become deified. Brittain referred to Roland Leighton as "Him" or "He."

The Popes, like many families, erected a shrine to their son on a small table in the living room that consisted of two photographs of Billy. One was a flag-draped picture of him in uniform and combat boots taken when he was in basic training. The other was a portrait of Billy when he was a young man before entering the service.

The shrine to Billy was continuously decorated with flowers. Every week, until she died thirty-six years later, Mrs. Pope lovingly placed a new bouquet alongside the photographs. "On Saturdays, regular as clockwork, we took the bus downtown to buy flowers, and we brought them back and put them next to Billy's pictures, and this went on until my mother could no longer leave the house," Ellie says. "I don't think there was a Saturday in my life when we didn't go down and buy flowers."

The Popes chose to have their son buried among his comrades at the permanent Normandy American Cemetery overlooking Omaha Beach in France. They took him at his word when he said before he left for war, "If something happens, leave me lay where I fall." Ellie believes, however, that by not having his body returned home for burial, her parents made a mistake and contributed to their never-ending grief. They didn't have the resources to make a pilgrimage to France to visit his grave, and they had no remains to bury at home. They erected a tombstone, inscribed with Billy's name, in a local cemetery, next to the plot where the Popes are now buried, but they always knew he was not there. They mourned in a vacuum.

Ken and Hugh Mooney's mother also blamed the government for her son's death, but she asked that his body be returned to their hometown of Succasunna, New Jersey, for burial. "My mother memorialized Hugh on many, many occasions," Ken said. "She felt more at peace with having him back where she could go and tend to his grave."

The news of her husband's death in November 1944 was no less devastating for Alita Howard who lived in Spokane, Washington. Lt. Col. Clarence "Cory" Howard was a tall, handsome, twenty-six-year-old bomber pilot flying missions over Europe when his plane was shot down over Germany's Heurtgen Forest in November 1944. Alita and Cory had been high school sweethearts and were married in 1937. Cory joined the Washington State National Guard and volunteered for active duty in 1941, just before the war began. He jumped at the opportunity to become a pilot and trained in B-26s. He was flying missions over Europe from England in 1944 when his plane was shot down and he was killed.

"I absolutely knew he was coming back from the war and that he was all right," Alita said. "When he died, my faith was completely shattered." When she received news that Cory was missing in action, she stood in prayer with her parents and the family minister. But the roar of bombers overhead drowned out their voices. The noise vanished as they finished their prayers, and Alita realized the planes were in her imagination. She later believed that the racket was from Cory trying to communicate from another dimension.

The news of Cory's loss didn't seem to affect Alita for several days. Then, she suddenly burst into tears and was put to bed where she sobbed for a week. Even though she was in her early twenties, Alita suffered what her doctors diagnosed as severe angina and was ordered back to bed to recuperate. "Why? Why?" she asked over and over. "You've left me here, and by golly why did you leave me here?"

Alita's manner of healing was not unique; she retreated into the world of spirtualism and says she broke through the death barrier and began to communicate with her husband. Others who suffered loss in war also report communicating with the dead. "People write to people who died. They talk with them. They have dreams. They feel a real presence," says Dr. Donna Schuurman, executive director of the Dougy Center for Grieving Children and Families in Portland, Oregon. "Our society tends to say 'put it behind you,' but people can't put it behind them. People want to maintain a relationship with the dead."

Sarah Schaen experienced an event that in retrospect she believes may have been some form of extrasensory communication with her husband,

Jim, as he was dying in battle. It began sometime around 3 A.M. on September 27, 1944, when Sarah awoke with a start as her bedroom was spinning violently around her. She sat up in bed and turned on the light and the spinning stopped. Sarah was four months pregnant, but she had been healthy up to this point. She waited a few minutes before turning out the light and trying again to fall asleep. But the same violent spinning reoccurred, and she stayed upright in bed with the light until daylight came.

The next day Sarah caught a glimpse of the headline in the local newspaper: "40 B-24s Shot Down over Kassel." She had never worried about her husband, Jim, before; he was so confident he would survive the war, but she couldn't get the headline out of her mind. Jim was flying B-24s on bombing missions over Germany. Two weeks later Sarah received word that Jim had been shot down. He was listed as missing in action, but was later reported as killed in action. His plane was one of the Liberators shot down over Kassel.

Only after the war when she learned how Jim had died did Sarah associate the spinning room with his death. Several crew members on Jim's plane bailed out and later reported that they had last seen him working his way back through the fuselage to make sure all his men had jumped. By the time he got to the rear, the plane was plunging to earth. The big bombers frequently went down in a spiral that created so much centrifugal force that any men inside were pinned helplessly against the sides of the aircraft. Several thousand airmen lost their lives that way. Sarah had never believed in spiritualism or ESP, but to this day she cannot explain the events that she experienced that night in 1944, the violent spinning at the exact moment that Jim's plane was going down.

Vera Brittain alluded to similar ESP experiences when she wrote about Roland after his death: "I wonder where He is—and if He is at all; I wonder if He sees me writing this now."

The prominent British physicist, Sir Oliver Lodge, wrote a book about communicating with his son, Raymond, who was killed on the western front in 1915 during World War I. Lodge's work, *Raymond, Or Life and Death*, was published twelve times between 1916 and 1919 and again in 1922 and reflected the rise of spiritualism in belligerent countries like Great Britain and the profound suffering of the bereaved during and after the war. Sir Oliver's book chronicles his communications with his son and provides what he says is evidence of existence beyond this life. Sir Oliver noted, for example, that he was informed through a medium about a photograph of Raymond and a group of officers taken near the front the week before Raymond's death. Sir Oliver had previously been unaware of the photograph's existence.

Alita Howard experienced daytime visions and nighttime dreams of Cory but nothing that would be considered communication with him. The visions and dreams were passed off as the result of severe depression. "I wasn't good company for anyone, not even myself," Alita said, and her friends avoided her. Another friend introduced her to a Ouija board as a way to divert her attention away from morbid thoughts of her husband.

The two began to play, and immediately the Ouija board spelled out the words, "Kate—Kate, Cory deep shock—Heurtgenforestaachen." They separated the words—"Heurtgen Forest Aachen." Alita consulted an atlas and discovered that Aachen and the Heurtgen Forest were in Germany. She was too frightened to continue, and she put the Ouija board away.

In April 1945, she received confirmation that Cory had been killed when his plane had been shot down over Germany. She even was given a photograph of Cory's B-26 as it plunged toward the earth after being hit by antiaircraft fire. The news of his death came in a black-bordered telegram from the War Department:

I AM DEEPLY DISTRESSED TO INFORM YOU CORRECTED REPORT JUST RE-
CEIVED STATES YOUR HUSBAND LIEUTENANT CLARENCE H. HOWARD
WHO WAS PREVIOUSLY REPORTED MISSING IN ACTION WAS KILLED IN
ACTION ON EIGHTEEN NOVEMBER FORTY FOUR IN GERMANY PERIOD
THE SECRETARY OF WAR ASKS THAT I EXPRESS HIS DEEP SYMPATHY IN
YOUR LOSS AND REGRET THAT UNAVOIDABLE CIRCUMSTANCE MADE
NECESSARY THE UNUSUAL LAPSE OF TIME IN REPORTING YOUR HUS-
BAND'S DEATH TO YOU CONFIRMING LETTER FOLLOWS.

Alita could barely speak or move. "My wits seemed numbed—drugged. Several days later all I could do was mumble, "Why death, why death." My logical mind was in a confused battle with my heart, for during those bleak, dark months of uncertainty—of waiting to hear—I knew that I had *seen* Cory," Alita wrote. "It was in visions and dreams, and I had no way of understanding, no way of interpreting, but I had *seen* him and I had *heard* his deep resonant voice—unmistakable and clear. . . . He had told me, his voice directly in my ear, of his great love for me. . . . I had not been asleep. I had not been dreaming. I had been wide awake when I'd heard his voice."

Shortly after getting confirmation of Cory's death, Alita received a letter from the commanding officer of his bomb squadron in which he revealed how Cory had died. "His bomber was hit by flak over enemy territory, and we didn't locate the wreckage until just recently," the officer wrote. "It crashed over the Heurtgen Forest, which you will find in your atlas to be located about twenty miles east of Aachen, Germany. You've probably never heard of the place."

Alita said she realized later that the Ouija board's reference to Kate was to a "discarnate entity" communicating news about Cory from the other side. Initially she dismissed "the mystifying incident," but it began a lifelong communication and relationship with her dead husband. "You don't ask a psychiatrist about this. I know it's real," Alita said.

Hazel Minium had a premonition that she would hear from her husband, Daniel Unger, the day the Western Union boy arrived with the telegram notifying her he had been killed. Like Alita and Cory, Daniel and Hazel were high school sweethearts growing up in Tower City, Pennsylvania, in the 1930s. They were married in 1941, and shortly afterward, Daniel was drafted into the army. After basic training he was assigned to the Second Infantry Division that remained in the United States until 1943 when it was transferred to Northern Ireland to prepare for the invasion of France.

Hazel moved to Fort Sam Houston, Texas, to be near her husband. She lived off base and grabbed at the moments when Daniel had leave time. Every hour they were together was precious because they never knew when the division would be shipped overseas to war. That day came without warning, and Hazel rushed to the base just as the men were marching off to board trains for the trip to an embarkation port. Frantically, she searched for Daniel and found him in the marching ranks. He could not stop and step out of formation, so she said goodbye as she hurried alongside his company and blew him her last kiss.

June 7, 1944, the day after the D-day invasion of Normandy, France, the Second Division went into action among the hedgerows, and Daniel was killed on July 13, 1944. Hazel was notified a few days later by telegram. For Hazel, there was nothing left in her life but faith. She remarried, but her second husband died. She remarried, but her third marriage was unsuccessful and ended in divorce.

Daniel's body was returned in December 1947, and he is buried in his hometown in Pennsylvania's hard coal region alongside his brother, also killed in World War II. The only remnants of Daniel's life that the army returned to Hazel after his death were his identification bracelet, which she had given him when they were first married, and her gold high school class ring, which Daniel always wore. The ring was still caked with dirt from the spot where Daniel had died in France. She keeps the flag that draped his coffin when his body was reburied at home and also has the fateful telegram, dated August 3, 1944, notifying her of Daniel's death.

The emotional pain suffered by these men and women, and millions of others who experienced loss during World War II, is obscured by the magnitude of the U.S. victory in World War II, which included the destruction of Nazi Germany and the emergence of the United States as the world's leading power. While the losses were shared collectively during the war, afterward grief became a solitary experience. A French woman, widowed in World War I, once reflected on this isolation:

War widow! They should hail in me He who gave his life for them. They should admire the greatness and beauty of his gesture and bow before me, living Grief that I am. But it is pity that I see in their eyes, and also, selfishness: "She's the widow, not me, fortunately!" They approach mental suffering with a thousand precautions, like others approach a contagious disease with rubber gloves.

The mother of a soldier killed in battle wrote, "No matter how proud . . . we poor mothers may be of our sons, we nevertheless carry wounds in our hearts that nothing can heal. It is strongly contrary to nature for our children to depart before us since God gave them to us so they would shut our eyes."

After all the years, the loss experienced by Americans in World War II is still deeply felt by those who experienced it, but the pain remains hidden behind tapestries that depict only glory.

11

Christmas without Red

"Do not believe the government report. Your son is alive. I saw him get out of the plane and saw his parachute open."

Dr. Franks was stunned at the news that came from Lt. Jack Warner in November 1943. The letter contradicted the War Department reports that Red had been killed and confirmed his belief that Red was alive. It was the hope Dr. Franks so desperately needed. Jack Warner was in a better position to know what happened to Red than anyone else.

The news was exhilarating and added much needed joy to the approaching holiday season. Dr. Franks summoned Nancy Lee home from college to celebrate and placed Lieutenant Warner's letter on her breakfast plate the next morning. He beamed as she read it several times, and Nancy Lee has never forgotten the words and the hope that it gave her father—"your son is alive." She saw immediately her father's revived spirits expressed in the sparkle that returned to his eyes, his relaxed face, and the softer tone of his voice. He was smiling again. At Thanksgiving Dr. Franks allowed himself to believe that Red might be safe.

But he remained cautious. Lieutenant Warner was a prisoner of war and his information could be inaccurate or even planted by the Romanians. The War Department had not changed his son's status.

Red's plight was always on Dr. Franks's mind, and despite the good news he felt violated, as though Red had been ripped from his life. And the war raged on, seemingly with no end in sight. His powerlessness frustrated him, and like a man possessed, it drove him to search even more arduously for Red.

Dr. Franks carried on during the holidays, the same dedicated and caring pastor he'd always been, but his sense of goodwill came with effort as he attended to his parishioners' needs in these troubled times as Thanksgiving feasts gave way to preparations for Christmas. One of his duties was to supervise the annual church concert, *In Judea's Hills*, that was performed by the First Baptist choir on December 19 and broadcast on the Columbus radio station, WCBI. The performance brought a measure of Christmas spirit to Columbus. The city had curtailed its usual display of lights in the downtown because of the war, particularly along the parkway through town that had traditionally been a blaze of lights. To add to the dampened spirits, the weather was the worst it had been in decades, freezing and bleak.

The adjutant general, General Ulio, had notified Dr. Franks in November that the Air Corps would award Red the Distinguished Flying Cross (DFC) on December 22 for his participation in the Ploeşti raid. Red was one of 548 airmen receiving the medal, and Dr. Franks would proudly accept it on behalf of his son in ceremonies at the Columbus air base, but the DFC seemed insignificant compared to the life it represented.

The weather in December, however, precluded the award ceremony until January because ice storms paralyzed the community and even kept the planes at CAAF grounded. Temperatures dropped to fifteen degrees and brought icy rain, frozen pipes, and declining morale throughout a Columbus unused to such bleak winters. The cold was particularly unwelcome in the Frankses' parsonage where there was no central heat. The floors in the old house were notorious for being cold in winter anyway, but now they felt like ice and Dr. Franks lit fires in the bedrooms and in living areas to ward off the chill. Only the brightly lit Christmas tree in the living room seemed to provide a semblance of warmth in the world.

Dr. Franks gave his annual Yuletide message the week before Christmas, and his friend Bernie Imes printed it in the *Columbus Commercial Dispatch* as an expression of "the feelings and sentiments of all peace-loving Christian people of a disturbed, war-torn world." It also reflected Dr. Franks's sorrow and loss. As usual he had jotted down his thoughts on pieces of scrap paper as the anguish in his life and of the times came to him:

Not since the Christ child was born in Bethlehem in Judea has there been another Christmas like this.

Christmas 1943 is different

More sons and daughters away from home

More lovers dreaming, vaguely dreaming

More miles of separation from dear ones

More mothers and fathers longing and praying

More vacant chairs at the dinner table

More anxiety

More sorrow

More suffering from war's desolation

More pride

More hatred

More destruction

More disappointment

More dependence on war's achievements

More millions of earth's inhabitants demanding more relief and more emancipation from more conditions of distress caused by political misrule of more nations

More need for the counsel of the Prince of Peace

More need for the Gospel of Peace on Earth, Good Will among Men

More responsibility upon world leaders
God bless you, everyone.

On Christmas Eve Dr. Franks wrote Bernie Imes a letter thanking him for using his influence and the power of the *Commercial Dispatch* in trying to learn of Red's fate.

Let me take this occasion to thank you again for the many kindnesses you have shown us during the year now closing, particularly during the last five months. You have been so sympathetic, thoughtful, and helpful in many ways. I have greatly appreciated every reference you have made in the *Commercial Dispatch* to my son. It was through the *Commercial Dispatch* that his last letter was released to the world and that letter has brought great spiritual inspiration and blessing to multiplied thousands who have read it. It continues to be reproduced in other ways throughout the country and in other countries. God is using it in wonderful ways as a high testimony to a triumphant Christian faith. I wish you could see some of the many letters I have received regarding it from every part of the country. . . . I want to thank you for what you have done and are doing about running down facts concerning the last reports of my son's fate. Through you, Mr. Whittington has taken up the matter with the War Department. He assures me he will do everything possible to trace down the facts and will keep me informed about progress made. No happier message could ever come to us than that Red is alive and well.

The Christmas services at the First Baptist Church in Columbus had particular poignancy in 1943. The church was shrouded in the mysteries and wonder of the birth of Christ with all its religious rituals and ceremonies, decorations, and carols. Dr. Franks heightened the spirit with his sermons and readings about the nativity that he gave in the hush that settled on the congregation on Christmas Eve, when his voice seemed to echo more loudly through the decorated interior. It always reminded him of his children when they were young.

Dr. Franks looked out on his parishioners arranged in a wide semicircle around the pulpit. He knew them all and remembered them from more than a score of Christmases past when they had come to services with their own children, many who were now the young men fighting for the nation. The three Noland boys were at war. Howard was a pilot flying B-26s on missions over Europe. His brother Frank was in a marine aviation unit, and Riley was in an Aviation Cadet Program training to become a fighter pilot. Among those also on military duty was Nannie Kate Smith's brother, Rufus Ward, a childhood pal of Red, who was flying bombing missions over Germany. Jake Propst was a fighter pilot, and Shield Sims, Red's fellow student at Lee High and at Mississippi College, was piloting a B-24 in the Pacific. Dr. Franks prayed for all these young men in military service especially those from his congregation—350 by war's end—and for their families.

He also prayed for Dottie Turner. She was living in New Orleans and attended Christmas services at the Presbyterian Church on St. Charles Street, which also included prayers for the congregation's men in military service. Their names were not familiar to her, but she prayed for them as earnestly as though she knew them all. For Red, she prayed that he had survived the crash of *Euroclydon* and that he was well cared for by his captors, or that he was safe somewhere in Eastern Europe with a band of partisans. She hardly dared think that he had been killed; she hoped that a merciful God would guard the man she loved. She placed that day's church bulletin in her Bible as a reminder of Red. It would remain there and with her for the rest of her life.

After learning that Red was missing, Dottie wrote the Mississippi Red Cross asking them for information about her fiancé. The state chapter forwarded her letter to the Romanian Red Cross in Bucharest, which responded with a letter in contorted English that only heightened her sense of despair:

In further reference to our letter of 26.8.1943, we have the honor to inform you: Miss Dorothy Grace Turner, 413 Pecan Avenue, Philadelphia, Mississippi, U.S.A., that Lieutenant Jesse Dee Franks died in Rumania on 1.8.1943. The aviator was burned and his identification tag was found among the ruins of the plane.

The image of Red incinerated in the twisted wreckage of the plane was unbearable and drove her to find any shred of evidence that Red was alive. But wherever she turned, the reports stated that Red had been killed. Only her contacts with Dr. Franks kept her hopes and spirit alive.

The war now approached its third year, and America waited expectantly for the climactic battles that would bring it to an end. But they would cost the lives of hundreds of thousands of young American men. Casualty figures to date were listed as 131,098, and thousands of young Americans had already died in battle or had been wounded or were listed as missing in action. The carnage was unrelenting. Already, four members of the congregation had become casualties and were listed on the honor roll of war: Joe Creed, missing in action, William Thomas Crouse, wounded in action, James A. Lucas, wounded in action, and the pastor's own son, Jesse D. Franks, Jr.

Dr. Franks knew that others among his parishioners would experience the loss of a son, a husband, or a boyfriend, before next Christmas came to pass, just as other families around the country would suffer the same terrible loss. How then would they justify and rationalize that death? He knew they couldn't. They would sum up the few years that their sons had lived and try to give their lives meaning. But they would mourn forever over the lost promise of youth.

In his eulogy to Red in the Baptist Church, Dr. Franks had preached that the war was just. And earlier in the conflict he had defended the struggle. "We dedicate ourselves to the cause for which these, our members and friends, are giving themselves in the danger zones of war. To the glory of God and the honor of our nation," he had preached in September 1942. But back then he had not imagined that the sacrifices required of the nation's citizens would affect him so directly. Even when he rode the bus for two days from Columbus to Victorville, California, to attend Red's graduation from bombardier school in 1942, he found it difficult to believe that his son could actually become a casualty of war. How vain he had been. How vain was the world in this cruel war that saw thousands of young men and boys dying every day all over the world. Was there no way to stop the slaughter? Did the lessons of Christmas have any meaning?

Dr. Franks was as diligent about the needs of these parishioners at war as he was about his home congregation. Just after Christmas he printed the first issue of a newsletter, which was sent to all church members serving in the armed forces. He greeted the young men by telling them they were remembered in prayers:

> Last Wednesday night at the midweek prayer service we called out about fifty names on the service roll of our church. Members of the families represented in the list answered for the boys. We had special prayers for them, calling them by name. Next Wednesday night we shall continue the roll call, beginning with names *G* through *L*. Let no name be called that some dear one in the family or close friend does not answer for. These boys answer for their own names on the battlefront. We will not fail to answer for them in home prayer.

The Newsletter was meant to bring a whiff of home and holiday cheer to those at war and Dr. Franks tried to be chatty. "It was good to see Frank Noland this week on a home visit, Howard the week before. They're both looking fine. Howard now has his wings. How handsome he looks in that officer's uniform. Riley Noland, the youngest of the three brothers, is now trying out for his wings. Lavert McGahey gets his wings at the CAAF next week."

While the boys in his congregation were in distant lands and bases, he gave comfort to many soldiers stationed in Columbus at special Christmas and New Year's services and events offered at a canteen on the first floor of the church's education building. The army had begun building an airfield outside the city in 1941 as a pilot training base, and thousands of young men passed through it every year and flew all kinds of training planes that buzzed around Columbus day and night. They referred to their aircraft as AT-6s, AT-8s, AT-9s, and AT-10s, but to the folks of Columbus, they were just airplanes. Many of the men did not have holiday leave, and the weekly social events in the church's education building were well attended. Nancy Lee was home from college for Christmas and was enlisted to play the piano and lead the men in singing carols.

Dr. Franks's ministerial attentions were not focused solely on lonely airmen. Every afternoon, particularly after the holidays, he set out to visit parishioners, some who were sick, some who had suffered the loss of a loved one, and others experiencing one crisis or another in their lives. The war had made him a familiar figure on the sidewalks of Columbus. Before Pearl Harbor, he had made daily rounds in his old Franklin touring car and later in a tan and black-trimmed Buick where he was seated rather stiffly behind the wheel.

Gas rationing, imposed early in the war, now precluded automobile trips. About the only time that Dr. Franks used his car was on his trips to his cabin, and now the townsfolk frequently saw him walking everywhere, his familiar, slim figure impeccably dressed in a dark blue or gray suit, with starched, removable collar, and wearing one of his beloved homburgs. Everyone knew he was on his afternoon rounds.

Dr. Franks lived his life day to day, buffeted by his efforts to find his son. A photograph of Red would trip a string of images in his mind. So too would a familiar sound, the school bell or the noise of playing children. He often wondered how he got through each day. Struggle as he might against self-indulgence, it was difficult not to personalize the war and magnify his own loss above that of all others. Red had been special, but so was every man and woman's son serving in the nation's armed services. When Dr. Franks heard of other families whose sons had been killed or were missing, it often brought tears and refreshed all the anguish that gripped his own life.

The constant stream of letters and telegrams to and from the War Department was also a reminder of Red. Like the Pope family of Easton, Pennsylvania, Dr. Franks could be cast into a deep depression by a short, terse note from a general or a congressman repeating the now familiar information that the government listed Red as killed in action, but offering no proof that he was dead. Dr. Franks responded to each letter, asking over and over for evidence to support the government's claim. It had found no remains and until it did, Dr. Franks would not give up hope that Red was alive. Lieutenant Warner's letter had renewed his hope. His task now was to discover where his son was imprisoned and to begin communicating with him and his Romanian captors. That was his responsibility as a father.

12

Status Notation in Error—
Red Is Alive

The new year, 1944, brought news that Dr. Franks wouldn't have dared to dream. In January the adjutant of Red's 328th Bomb Squadron, Ninety-third Bomb Group, responded to Dr. Frank's September note asking why his letters to Red had been returned stamped "Killed In Action."

The 93rd BG had been reassigned to Hardwick in England after the Ploești raid, and the squadron adjutant, Lt. Frank H. George, wrote Dr. Franks that the 328th had recently received intelligence reports that Lieutenant Warner was alive and being treated for his wounds in a Romanian hospital. "There is also evidence to believe that several members of the crew are alive. An eyewitness attests that several parachutes opened as the plane went down," Lieutenant George wrote. He added: "In your letter you state that your returned letter bore the notation 'killed in action.' This is definitely incorrect as he (Red) is officially carried as 'missing in action.' If the letter was marked 'killed in action,' the status notation is in error and you have my apology." Lieutenant George also included the addresses of other families of *Euroclydon* crew members. "Perhaps they have received some official information or news through other sources, which I have not received. If you receive any information, please pass it on to us, as we think of him often. May I share your hopes that 'Red' is safe."

Lieutenant George's letter offered a glimmer of hope, and additional positive information came from Congressman Rankin confirming that Lieutenant Warner was a prisoner of war. Rankin wrote that the War Department was trying to discover whether Lieutenant Warner had information about Red.

Dr. Franks also received a letter from Congressman W. M. Whittington questioning the veracity of previous Air Corps intelligence reports of Red's death that Dr. Franks had long believed to be suspect. "I am advised that while the War Department must accept the report from the Romanian government as being official, they often wonder if statements such as that made by Lieutenant Warner when he was questioned by the Romanian government as to the fate of your son are not sometimes different from what the statements would be if the boys were not perhaps under duress at the time of the questioning."

The days dragged on, but in March Dr. Franks received another letter from Lieutenant George. Dr. Franks prayed it again would bring good news as he tore it open. Lieutenant George wrote: "I recently received your letter requesting information concerning your son, 1st Lt. Jesse D. Franks, Jr. Lieutenant Franks was reported missing in action on August 1, 1943, and since that date we have received no further official information in regard to his status, but unofficial sources lead us to believe he is alive."

Red is alive! Dr. Frank literally stood up at the news. He held the letter out with trembling hands. Was it true? Could he believe what he was reading?

Lieutenant George added: "I am sorry that the War Department reported him 'killed in action.' It must have caused you great sorrow. This is

definitely an incorrect status. He has been carried as missing in action in
this squadron since August 1, 1943."

This was the news Dr. Franks had so desperately wanted to hear. He
could barely recall any other emotions over the past eight months other than
anguish and sorrow.

Lieutenant George's letter continued:

> In January 1944 we received an intelligence letter, which reported that the
> crew navigator, 2nd Lt. Raymond P. (Jack) Warner is "reportedly in a Ro-
> manian hospital." Since then Mrs. Ray Warner, mother, has written us
> that she has received several cards from her son. In one of these cards he
> said, "All the officers are safe except Enoch [Lieutenant Porter, pilot] and
> Joe [F/Q Boswell, copilot]," implying that Jesse is safe. I know this will
> make you happy. Let us pray it is correct.

Dr. Franks had received a recent letter from the wife of the *Euroclydon*
crew member, Mrs. Frank C. Farrell, that added weight to reports that Red
was alive and a prisoner of war in Romania. "A friend of mine was able to
see the files of the 328th Squadron, which is in England now, and discovered that in addition to the known P.O.W. Warner, Reed, and Vest, one
other gunner and Franks are reported as prisoners, although the government
has not confirmed it." T.Sgt. Frank Farrell was the flight engineer and one of
the plane's gunners as well, who also was reported missing. Mrs. Farrell
asked Dr. Franks: "Has Jack [Warner] ever written you telling who the gunner might be. There are only two that it might be, my husband, Farrell, or
his assistant, Corn." Dr. Franks had the deepest empathy for Mrs. Farrell.
She too was seeking to learn the fate of a loved one.

The news that Red was alive was clouded, however, as other letters continued to arrive with conflicting information, from the War Department, from
the Red Cross, from the 328th Bomb Squadron, and from Lieutenant Warner.
In April Dr. Franks received a correspondence from Lieutenant Warner cau-
tioning him not to raise his hopes that Red was alive. Lieutenant Warner

was aware that Dr. Franks had received reports from his mother that Red was safe. He wrote:

> I received your letter this week inquiring about your son, and my friend, Red. It is with deepest regret that I must inform you that my mother has misconstrued something I have said in my letters to her. It would be unfair and unkind of me to let you, Nancy Lee, and Dot Turner go on thinking that Red is safe and will someday be with you again. In spite of all my hopes and prayers, Red is now listed as among the dead at Ploeşti; his place of burial was not listed.

Dr. Franks was perplexed. Lieutenant Warner had written Dottie Turner as well as the Franks to say that he had seen Red bail out of the plane. "I saw his chute open and then he was carried from my view."

Dr. Franks realized that Lieutenant Warner did not know whether Red was alive or dead and was merely transmitting information he had picked up from the Romanians. But he believed Lieutenant Warner's original statement to be true, that Red had gotten out of the plane before it crashed, and it refuted the Romanian Red Cross's report to Dottie, and War Department reports to him, that Red had been incinerated when he went down with the plane. If Red had died in the crash, the Romanians would have recovered his body.

Dr. Franks wrote the War Department asking for an explanation about Lieutenant George's letter. Why was it, he asked, that the 328th Squadron believed Red to be alive while the government insisted, without verifiable facts, that he was dead? Dr. Franks tried to couch his anger and frustration in his letters. The military responded by saying it could not confirm any of the information that Dr. Franks had received from Lieutenant Warner and from Mrs. Farrell, and it refuted Lieutenant George's statement. The War Department reiterated that Red had been killed in action, and the Romanian government and the International Red Cross had confirmed his death.

Dr. Franks also received a letter from General Ulio stating that Lieutenant George had no authority to offer information regarding Red's status and the general apologized for "the added sorrow, which you have been caused in receiving this conflicting information." General Ulio stated that Lieutenant George would face disciplinary action for going around channels and suggesting to Dr. Franks that his son was alive.

Despite the War Department's claim that Red was dead, Dr. Franks continued to receive correspondences that held out hope for his son's survival. On April 8, Congressman Whittington wrote to him stating that the American Red Cross would never give up an investigation relating to the status of a missing American soldier "unless a boy is positively identified, even though he may be officially pronounced dead, the search goes on. The report of the Rumanian government is officially accepted, but the search goes on until actual proof is obtained." The statement confirmed Dr. Franks's conviction that unless the U.S. government could produce Red's remains, there was no proof that he had been killed. To accept a claim of death from a foreign, belligerent government and to cease searching for a lost American soldier would be criminal.

The barrage of conflicting reports and evidence continued, and Dr. Franks began seeking clearance for a trip to Romania to search for Red himself. He had previously made inquiries about Red through various non-government Romanian sources and friends, and they reported back that no one knew of a burial site containing Red's remains.

On March 27, 1944, Dr. Franks received a package containing Red's personal belongings. It was another cruel blow; they came back in a package from the Quartermaster Corps's personnel effects bureau in Kansas City. He removed each item separately and lovingly. They were reminders of his son and the closest thing to Red he had touched since his departure nearly a year before. They seemed forlorn and lost. Included among the effects was Red's gray Harris Tweed jacket that Dr. Franks gave to Nancy Lee. In these lean times she could cut it down and make a sporty outfit.

But not all Red's belongings had been returned, and the next day Dr. Franks wrote to the Quartermaster Depot in Kansas City:

Checking through them I do not find his watch, his Air Medal, which he
received while overseas, or any of the official record of his services after
he left the States for England. I am sure he must have had some letters,
papers, pictures, and other personal possessions, which he was keeping
somewhere. There is nothing at all to indicate that he had heard from
home in the package I received. I wonder if what you sent represents all
he is supposed to have had with him.

Dr. Franks added a postscript that reflected the depth of his sorrow.

Nothing he had would represent very much intrinsic value, but everything
he had would have great sentimental value for us. Anything you can do to
help trace down all of his personal belongings would be greatly appreciated by us who loved him dearer than life itself.

On April 16, Dr. Franks received a letter from the Army's effects depot
stating that when, and if, more personnel effects arrived, they would be forwarded to him. Lt. R. E. Rodgers added, "As you no doubt understand,
conditions in theaters of operation, together with the distances involved,
make it not only difficult to receive property, but also, to obtain any specific
information regarding missing items."

It took many months for the Army to respond to Dr. Franks's request
for Red's watch. In November 1944 the effects depot wrote again to state
that Lieutenant George had searched for the missing items and had responded: "The missing wristwatch was not placed in safekeeping in this
squadron when Lieutenant Franks departed on detached service. It is the
opinion of the undersigned that Lieutenant Franks would naturally have
been wearing his watch on the date of the accident, and that in all proba-
bility it was never recovered." Dr. Franks acknowledged receipt of his son's
Air Medal in November and thanked Capt. F. A. Eckhardt for helping to
"trace down every item of his personal effects."

As 1944 progressed, the war casualties from Columbus and the First
Baptist Church began to mount. In the spring came word that Rufus Ward,

Nannie Kate's brother, was missing in action over Germany after bailing out of his B-17. In June James Burnett, another member of the congregation, was reported killed on an air combat mission after first being reported as missing in action in April. "Jimmy" Burnett was a year behind Red at Lee High and had gone to Mississippi College for several semesters when Red was enrolled there. He had left college to help with his family's grocery store before joining the Air Corps after Pearl Harbor. In August another parishioner, Jesse Dodson, died of his wounds in France.

In the fall the Howard Nolands, next-door neighbors to the Frankses on Second Avenue North, received notification that their eldest son, Howard, a second lieutenant and a flyer like Red and one of Red's boyhood pals, was killed on September 24, 1944, while returning from a mission over Europe. Howard was piloting a B-26 medium bomber when it crashed while attempting to land at his base in England. The war had come on the quiet, peaceful life in Columbus like a sudden, terrible storm, and Dr. Franks could feel only a grim consolation that he was not alone in his grief.

The summer of 1944 brought revived hope that Red might be found alive. The Romanians withdrew from the Axis alliance and joined the Allied cause. In September they released all the American POWs in their custody, including those from the Tidal Wave raid, and assisted in their evacuation to Italy. Dr. Franks was anxious to learn whether Red was among them. Lieutenant Warner was released and interrogated prior to being sent back to the States. The Air Corps wanted to know as much as possible about the many U.S. airmen who had been shot down over Ploeşti and who remained unaccounted for, including Red. As Dr. Franks expected, some men who had been reported missing or killed in action over the refineries turned up alive. One was Lt. Irving Fish, Jr., a Williams College graduate whose father had been informed by the War Department that his son had been missing after an attack in 1944.

Lieutenant Fish was shot down on August 18, 1944, and was imprisoned before being released when the Romanians capitulated. The POWs literally walked out of their camps, and Lieutenant Fish, and his fellow POWs, made their way on foot to Bucharest where he had a chance encounter with a former professor at Williams:

I decided we'd try to go to the largest hotel in Bucharest, the so-called Waldorf Astoria of Bucharest, The Athenée Palace. And we arrived in rags and tatters. My gracious if you could have ever seen us. Uniforms all torn and dirty. No showers, no baths, no teeth brushed, etc. . . . As I walked across that lobby, the whole lobby was being dominated by one man in his Second Lieutenant's pink full dress uniform, and I thought my gracious what have we come to. This contrast! And I got up closer and I recognized that the man standing on that box trying to get our attention was Lieutenant Philip Coombs from whom I had taken freshman economics at Williams and I was floored by that extraordinary, I thought, incredible, coincidence. So I walked up to him and reached up with my right arm because he was of course above me, and introduced myself and I said, "I took freshman economics with you, Professor, and I think you gave me a 'D', I'm not sure." And then we could only chitchat then for 30 seconds. . . .

I should say that my father, a loving father if there ever was one, was casting about in every direction he could think of for somebody who might know something about the situation in prisoner-of-war camps, which is where I had been. . . . He knew I was missing in action. They had received the MIA telegram, which all families in those days dreaded: the little boy on the Western Union bicycle. God, I can't believe that they used to exist. Anyhow, when Coombs got back to Washington, he had a lunch date with Phinney Baxter, who of course was president of Williams before the war and who now had a high job in the OSS, now known to us as the CIA, and Coombs was reporting on what he had just seen in Bucharest, and as sort of an afterthought apparently, and I got this from both men, he said, "Oh, incidentally, I bumped into a Williams student of mine." "Oh really?," says Phinney Baxter. "Yes, Irving Fish." And Phinney of course bolted out of the chair running for the telephone to call my father, and that's how my father first learned that I was alive and well.

Dr. Franks was not so lucky. Red was not among the POWs, and the mantralike statements from the Air Corps that Red was dead infuriated him. On December 9, 1944, he fired off a series of questions to the acting adjutant general, Edward F. Witsell, in Washington:

I should like to ask two simple questions? (1) Does the War Department have any evidence at all beyond the bare statement issued by the Romanian government "killed in action" upon which to base its conclusion? The War Department has not furnished me any further evidence than that. Your second telegram, which included those three fateful words, is all the evidence, if indeed it should be called evidence, I have received from the War Department. The Romanian people, as you no doubt know, are somewhat noted for their graft, duplicity, and double-dealing. I would never take their bare unsupported word for anything.

(2) Do you not think that parents and other loved ones here at home are entitled to know the facts concerning their men who are reported killed, when such information does not give aid to the enemy? What point is there in withholding the facts? Certainly you cannot think that it makes it easier on the loved ones at home. It only makes their burden of sorrow harder to bear. Besides you do give details to some, even the families whose sons were in this same raid and were reported as casualties. Why withhold the details from others who are as much entitled to them?

Besides that, General Witsell, other families whose boys were in that same raid and were reported killed have received detailed information concerning the circumstances of their death, including families who are good friends of ours. I cannot understand the discrimination, if you have the "conclusive evidence" of my son's death you say you have.

After all, with all the care the War Department must take in matters of this kind, it sometimes is in error in its death messages. We have had two such cases in this little community, and I know of others nearby. Until you supply me with the details, which I think I am entitled to have as a loyal American citizen, if and when those details can be disclosed without aiding the enemy, I shall continue to believe that it is possible for the War Department to have been mistaken concerning my son's status, and hope that he may still be alive. And I shall continue through every possible channel that offers any hope that I may learn the facts to make investigations. I would be unworthy to be the father of my noble son if I did less. I sincerely trust and pray that I may have the continued interest of the War Department and its official cooperation in my quest for the facts, and that the department will not strike my son's name off the list as a closed case.

One of the two cases referred to by Dr. Franks involved a young flyer from Columbus, Sgt. Joe McCrary, a waist gunner on a B-24 shot down on mission over Germany on January 29, 1944. McCrary bailed out and his family received word on February 12 that he was missing. On March 9, his family was informed that he had been killed.

Three months later, however, they received a strange and cryptic note: "We are all in good health and Stuff. Everything is fine. Sweet kisses from stuff and us." The McCrarys were astounded and hopeful. It had to be a message from their son. His nickname was Stuff, and only his family and close friends knew him by that name. On August 8, 1944, came another message: "We are having a better time than you think. Stuff." Finally, in September the McCrary family received word from the International Red Cross that Joe was alive. He had bailed out over Belgium and had been harbored by members of the underground. Sargeant McCrary came out of hiding when the Allies liberated the country, and U.S. military authorities sent him home. He arrived in Columbus in October 1944.

The other case he referred to was that of Lt. Elbert DuKate from Biloxi, Mississippi, who was shot down over Ploeşti on the Tidal Wave raid and listed as missing in action for more than a year. He escaped from an Italian POW camp and later from a German compound and was rescued by American forces on June 5, 1944, when Rome fell. His mother assumed Elbert had been killed, and her first inkling that he was alive came just after his release when a local Biloxi bank notified her that a check, signed by Elbert, had cleared. He had drawn cash from his account before authorities notified Mrs. DuKate that her son was alive. Dr. Franks had clipped a lengthy article about Lieutenant DuKate's story and saved it in his files.

Dr. Franks also knew that Rufus Ward had been listed as missing in action for about six weeks in May and June of 1944. He had counseled and prayed with the family in their grief before word came that Rufus was alive and a POW. Even then his family had no proof that he was alive, and it wasn't until September 2, 1944, when they received a card from him, mailed in June, that the Ward family knew for certain that Rufus had survived.

Dr. Franks referred General Witsell to the saga of the mother of Sgt. Charles Bridges, a gunner on the B-24 *Porky Two* that was shot down over Ploeşti on the Tidal Wave attack. A Roman Catholic priest had found Bridges covered with blood, delirious, and babbling in Latin as he pulled him from the burning wreckage. Sargeant Bridges asked the priest to notify his mother in Andersonville, Indiana, that he had survived. The priest sent word to Mrs. Bridges, via the Vatican's network, that her son was alive, but two days after she received the Vatican cable, the War Department sent the Bridges family notification that their son was missing in action. It was months before Mrs. Bridges knew that her son was a prisoner of war of the Romanians.

But the hopeful stories of other young men who turned up alive after going missing for months did not bring Red back and could not lessen Dr. Franks's pain. The Franks family of 705 Second Avenue North, Columbus, Mississippi, celebrated Christmas of 1944 without Red. Dr. Franks put on his game face for family and congregation. But alone in his study and alone in his thoughts, he wept.

1 3

Tell Me How My Boy Died

Four hundred and six thousand Americans died in World War II, and it is difficult to imagine today how the American people accepted the relentless carnage. A July 5, 1943, *Life Magazine* article romanticized and rationalized death in war just as most cultures have done throughout history. America's sons died gloriously, thinking of home, mom, and apple pie, so *Life* suggested. In the editorial entitled, "The American Purpose," about "the boys who have gone over the Big Hill," *Life's* euphemism for being killed, the magazine wrote that in the instant that a boy knew he was dying, "he would see home, and he would see Mom bending over the stove and hear the kid brother in the yard; he would see his whole town and the movie theater and the baseball diamond and the cars, and hear the voices of the girls, and remember the first girl he kissed, and even more the last one; he would all in an instant relive that life and know that it was a good life."

The military was less maudlin, but still couched combat death in heroic terms. The Nemeth family of Bethlehem, Pennsylvania, received a letter from a navy chaplain offering solace for the death of their son, John Joseph, in January 1945. John Joseph was a crew member on the USS *Callaway*, a Coast Guard vessel serving near the Philippines.

"While I realize there is little anyone can say or do to soften this blow or lessen your grief, still I know you will be in great measure consoled by the knowledge that he was fully prepared to meet his God, and to receive from Him a hero's eternal reward."

The truth about soldiers who died in battle was far less romantic or heroic. It was wrenching.

Medics were the ones who saw young Americans die; often, they were the only ones who did. One medic was assigned to every rifle platoon of about forty men and was often overwhelmed by the number of casualties. Medics became father figure, priest, or friend who helped a soldier in his last moments. Being a medic was a lonely, helpless, and terrifying experience. Former World War II combat medics Jack Davis and Dr. John Kerner remember firsthand the trauma of battlefield death as they tended to the wounded and fought desperately to keep men alive. Their descriptions of death are unsentimental, unheroic, and often horrific.

"If a soldier is conscious and he knows he's not going to make it, he's probably thinking of his family," Davis said. But most of the dying men Davis treated were unconscious and often gasping for breath. "I would have been thinking about my family, but I never heard the dying express this." Foreign battlefields are alienating, and Davis was always moved by the fact that most men killed in combat died in a strange country and didn't even know where they were, just somewhere in France or in Germany.

"In the movies they always have guys lying there saying, 'Tell Mary I love her,'" said Dr. Kerner, a combat medic with the Thirty-fifth Infantry Division in Europe during World War II. "Most men who are dying are usually in deep shock and unconscious."

Life Magazine reflected that it was God's will when a young man died in battle and philosophized, "The great light of America is rekindled in the breasts" of those who have been informed of the death of a loved one. Most who experienced loss during World War II would suggest that this was nonsense.

Many men in the front lines didn't see it that way either. "I have never adjusted to all that death," Davis says. "I can't live with it yet; it's always with me. It's been almost sixty years, but when I go to bed, I see those guys' faces all the time." He remembers the dying as though he were still tending to their wounds. He can see his hands, scarlet and sticky, feverishly working to staunch their blood and restore their breath, which came in wrenching gasps as life dissipated like wisps of vapor.

Davis was a combat medic with the Fifth Infantry Division that fought from the hedgerows of Normandy just after D-day in 1944, through eastern France, to the Battle of the Bulge, and into Germany in the spring of 1945. He learned to respond instinctively to the cry "Medic," as he hauled two large shoulder bags containing medicines, morphine syrettes, and compresses and crawled out to men screaming from wounds or hovering near death. The first soldier who died in Davis's care was an infantryman shot through the chest in the fighting in Normandy in 1944.

"He had been hit by small arms and was pretty well riddled. He was unconscious, his mouth was opening and shutting, and blood was running out of his mouth and nose. I saw him expiring, but there was nothing I could do."

Davis trained as a medic for the mayhem of the battlefield by learning to deal mechanically with the shattered limbs and disfigured faces, the sucking chest wounds and gaping abdomens. He became inured to the sight and smell of blood. "Blood didn't bother me at all. I had so much blood on my clothes, my pants stood up by themselves."

But Davis was hardly prepared for the emotional impact of the battlefront. "The noise, the shooting, the shelling, the popping of machine gun bullets overhead—you weren't sure where the front was. I was so scared I really didn't have any feeling of anything at all." An additional concern of American medics was that they were often unintended targets of the enemy. "In World War II American aidmen (always medics to the troops) wore four red crosses painted on their helmets and a red cross armband on the left arm—and as they learned the facts of battlefield life, on the right arm as well. They were still underidentified in contrast to their German counterparts, who wore armbands and also a very visible white body tabard with large, two-foot-square red crosses on both front and back. Especially, once they got dirty, the American red crosses were seldom visible enough in snow, rain, and dust storms, and then the only protection for the wounded was the shout, 'Medic at work!' from the (as it were) sidelines," Paul Fussell writes.

Many medics broke under the strain. Davis reports they had one of the highest casualty rates of any group in the Army, they faced constant death under fire, and they were terrified. Many medics were wounded. Davis once looked down at his own legs and realized he had been hit when he saw blood in the snow around his feet. He had been so focused on treating the wounded that he had not felt the wounds. Davis became a highly decorated medic who won the Silver Star, the Bronze Star, the Purple Heart, and campaign medals for combat service in Normandy, northern France, the Ardennes, the Rhineland, and Central Europe.

Most of the men who died in Davis's care were anonymous; they all looked alike in their olive drab uniforms. But he remembers the names of some. "I ran across a field exposed to fire to get to Calvi. There was no infantry in front of me, just Germans. This poor guy took a bullet through his chest. He lay there unconscious, on his back. He was gasping. He went pale and all the blood drained from his face. I couldn't get a heartbeat. I tried to patch his wound, but to no avail. We carried him back to our lines. I watched him die."

Davis was once startled to see a soldier sit down and take off his boots after being shot through the mouth. He was choking in his own blood. What prompted the man to take off his boot? Davis wondered. He later read that some dying people instinctively take off their shoes. Their notion, Davis said, is that "they came into the world with no shoes and they will go out with no shoes." Crewmen on *Euroclydon* witnessed a similar phenomenon of a soldier taking off his boots before dying in the seconds just before the plane went down at Ploeşti. The radio operator, Tech Sergeant Lucas, was hit in the back by fragments from a large-caliber antiaircraft shell. In an Individual Casualty Questionnaire completed for the *Missing Air Crew Report* after the war, one of the surviving waist gunners reported: "Technical Sergeant Lucas was standing beside me at the waist window when he was hit by a shell.

I believe he was dying. He asked me to remove his boots. This I did and then had to jump for my life."

There were no medics on the bombers and fighters on their missions over enemy territory. Bomber crews fended for themselves and used basic medical training to keep wounded alive. Lt. Walter Stuart remembers using first aid training he learned in the Boy Scouts to revive a gunner who had gone loco when his oxygen line froze and he began singing over the inter-com as the plane approached the target. Lieutenant Stuart said the Air Corps offered little or no first aid and medical training for bomber crews. At twenty-five thousand feet and under fire, men easily bled to death or died of the cold, and those tending to the wounded in aircraft often slipped and skidded on blood that froze instantly on walkways at high-altitude temper-atures of sixty degrees below zero. In at least one case, crew members of a B-17 allegedly strapped a critically wounded airman who was bleeding to death into a parachute and pushed him out of the plane over Germany with the hope that he would be rescued and saved by the Germans; he would never have survived the long flight back to England.

In the aftermath of the Ploeşti raid, the Germans and Romanians had to deal with scores of badly burned and wounded American flyers, includ-ing Jack Warner. In one case, Romanian peasants reportedly killed an Amer-ican pilot to put him out of his misery after his chute failed to open and he was still alive after he hit the ground. Triage points were established around the refineries and the city. A school in Ploeşti was a collection point for thirty American flyers who lay "burned and broken, naked and dying." A flak battery barracks was used as another aid station where several other Americans were laid out, unconscious. All were beyond medical help and were being administered morphine to ease their deaths. So many of the men who had bailed out over Ploeşti or crashed with their planes were so badly wounded that the enemy found only twelve flyers in a condition to be inter-rogated immediately after the raid.

All battlefields produced horrendous wound cases. The worst that Davis experienced was a soldier whose abdomen had been ripped open by shellfire in the battle for Metz, France. "His intestines were hanging out and

I stuffed them back in as best I could. He was conscious and in terrible pain. We tried to get him on a litter and place him on a jeep for evacuation, but he jumped off and his feet got tangled in his intestines in the blood, mud, and snow. When you're in that kind of pain, you have inordinate strength, and it took four of us to tie him down. He was pleading with me, 'shoot me! shoot me!' We strapped him on the litter. He died later at an aid station."

Davis also ministered to dying Germans. During the Battle of the Bulge, his unit repulsed an enemy attack that left clumps of dead and dying Germans in the snow in front of the American positions. As night descended over the pine forest in southern Belgium, a wounded enemy soldier pleaded for help from the American line. "I never heard such screaming in all my life; it echoed all through the woods, and I finally couldn't stand it any longer. I asked my men to cover me and I crawled out to him and hit him with three or four syrettes of morphine." The narcotic eased the pain and the screaming ended. But at first light Davis saw that the enemy soldier had died; his arms were raised up in frozen supplication.

Davis developed a kind of kinship with the dead, an envy for their state of peace and grace. "After a while being dead didn't seem so bad because you knew they were out of it," Davis said.

Still, the life force is potent, and one of Davis's greatest fears was that he didn't do enough to save a dying man. He once crawled out to a soldier who had no vital signs. Davis checked for a heartbeat and turned the man over to look for wounds and was sure the soldier was dead. Orders came down to retreat and leave the dead behind, and Davis pulled out with the rest of his rifle company. He worried for years that the man may actually have still been alive. His fears were heightened after the war when a former comrade mentioned that the soldier had survived and had returned home to become a minister. Davis was in anguish thinking that he had left a man for dead who had eventually recovered. He was relieved to learn that the minister was the brother of the soldier who had been killed.

Dr. Kerner experienced a different kind of guilt, the guilt of the survivor. "He got killed; why not me?" he remembered wondering. Dr. Kerner was a medical doctor, trained at the University of California School of Medicine,

San Francisco, in gynecology before going to war. He took charge of a battalion aid station in the Thirty-fifth Infantry Division and was usually stationed within yards of the front lines. "I was not prepared for what I experienced even as a doctor. I saw things that even medical students didn't see. In medical school, most of the people you see die, die of old age." In war they are young, some not even out of adolescence.

Years after the war Dr. Kerner sat down to write about his experiences during World War II in his book, *Combat Medic.* The memories came flooding back in such vivid, horrid detail that he had to confine his writing to the mornings; otherwise his sleep was interrupted by recurring nightmares of war.

"You never get over those experiences," Dr. Kerner said. "It's still so vivid, amazingly so. Some of the details I didn't realize I remembered came out. It was like psychoanalysis."

Like Davis, Dr. Kerner still sees the faces of the dying and their wrecked bodies. "In my mind the sight of the dead is still so shocking. I can see the handsome young man, dead and leaning against the side of his foxhole in the sunlight. I can see men killed with whom I'd been talking just an hour before."

Dr. Kerner's division had a particularly difficult time dealing with the horror of war. The Thirty-fifth was a National Guard division from Nebraska and was made up of units from small towns where the guard was more social club than military unit. The men trained together, drank together, worshiped together, and raised their families together. Suddenly in France these inexperienced, former weekend warriors met face to face with Wehrmacht veterans who had been fighting all over Europe for years. The Thirty-fifth was cut to pieces in its first combat encounters.

"We had a tremendous number of casualties when we first went into France, and it was devastating for these guys to see an old drinking buddy from Omaha come in mortally wounded. It was the next thing to having a relative killed."

Dr. Kerner went to war in Normandy with a footlocker crammed with whiskey. "All the money I had I spent on booze, and it was one of the best investments I ever made." Overwhelmed by casualties pouring into the aid station from the front, the medical personnel were exhausted and disheartened by the end of each day. "I'd pass around the booze because everyone was so damned depressed. At least it did something for the survivors."

But alcohol wasn't a complete palliative. On several occasions Dr. Kerner passed out from exhaustion. "The guys would pick me up and put me away somewhere until I came to. Some guys couldn't take it. I found a fellow doctor curled up in a foxhole crying uncontrollably. We sent him to the rear and he never came back to the front."

As the fighting moved on toward Germany, the death toll increased. "By the time we got to the Ardennes, they were sending us recruits who were young kids mostly in their teens. They'd come up with clean, fresh uniforms, and they were sort of bewildered. They be given an assignment and you'd either pick them up wounded or see them killed in the course of the next forty-eight hours. It was terrible."

Dr. Kerner would often sit with a dying soldier and tell him he would do everything he could to pull him through. "I would always give them a shot of morphine and a cigarette. Usually they would ask for a cigarette, if they were conscious. I always had a pack of cigarettes in one pocket and a batch of morphine syrettes in the other." Luckily, most of the dying were in shock and unconscious or only semiconscious and not aware of impending death. "The body does protect you when you're mortally wounded," Dr. Kerner said.

Dr. Kerner tried to follow the progress of some patients to evacuation stations or to hospitals in England, and he was often surprised to hear that men had survived who he thought had little chance of making it. "If anyone got back to England, their chance of survival was around ninety percent."

Jack Davis often wonders how many of the men he cared for died after they were sent back to aid stations and hospitals. He too tried to follow up on some of the men to check their progress, and he once received a letter from a soldier thanking him for helping to save his life. But the rest of those who survived, like the dead, remained anonymous and became faces to be recalled three score years later in the middle of a restless night.

During his sleepless nights when he recalls the war, Dr. Kerner thinks about the need for nations to strive for peace. "I've become so antiwar ever since then," he said. "I just couldn't believe there was such enthusiasm about going to war in Iraq. I felt that when we were over there during World War II, the war seemed reasonable because of what had gone before. But we might have been able to prevent that war by being more active against it. War is such a horrible and wasteful thing."

Jack Davis harbors similar sentiments against war. "I am more antiwar because of the foolish things we have done since World War II. Viet Nam, how foolish that was? This country has never been an aggressive country and we shouldn't be. We are a country that ends wars. We don't start them."

1 4

To the Ends of the Earth

As the war neared an end in Europe in the spring of 1945, Dr. Franks kept a watchful eye on the names and photographs of American prisoners of war being liberated by Allied forces from POW camps in Germany. Many were emaciated from months of starvation and were dressed in a welter of tattered uniforms and caps. The man who had planned Tidal Wave was among them, Col. Jacob Smart, weak from malnutrition and wounds. Even if Red were among the prisoners, as Dr. Franks fervently hoped, there was no certainty that he would recognize his son after nearly two years in captivity. But he would keep looking.

The sliver of hope that Red might still be alive prompted Dr. Franks once again to write the War Department for new information about Red once the POWs started coming home. He communicated his fear that his son could be suffering from amnesia and could even be in a Russian slave labor camp, picked up by the Soviets as their armies swept through Romania.

The Russians might not know that Red was an American, or they might not care to know, and he would languish without hope.

Dr. Franks received a letter in reply from Brig. Gen. Leon Johnson, a Tidal Wave veteran who had won the Medal of Honor for leading the Forty-fourth Bomb Group, the Eight Balls, over Ploeşti. General Johnson had witnessed the planes and men falling from the sky as he piloted his B-24 at thirty feet through a wall of fire that leapt from the blazing refineries and blackened his plane. The Forty-fourth had bombed the target after *Euroclydon* and the 93rd BG had made their runs, and ironically, General Johnson's plane could have flown directly over the downed *Euroclydon.*

General Johnson wrote Dr. Franks: "A careful check of all available files reveals that there is no record of any unidentified amnesia case. Victims of amnesia remain unidentified for only a few days as fingerprints, dental charts, etc. . . . afford means of identification." Dr. Franks knew, of course, that General Johnson was referring to U.S. soldiers who had been found and were in American custody.

Dr. Franks received a lengthy letter from Major General Witsell, the acting adjutant general, in which Witsell wrote, "Captured enemy records are being carefully checked, and you may be assured that in the event further information is received in this office concerning Lieutenant Franks, it will be conveyed to you promptly." The admission that the military was searching enemy records to locate missing servicemen was tacit admission to Dr. Franks by the War Department that it had not recovered Red's body and had no idea whether he was alive or dead.

General Witsell also assured Dr. Franks that any serviceman found to be suffering from amnesia "with no identity paper in his possession or an unidentified wounded American soldier is admitted to an army hospital, it would require only that he be fingerprinted and these prints compared with the files in Washington, DC, to establish his identity." But the letters failed to mollify Dr. Franks. He wrote General Johnson a letter and included newspaper clippings about an amnesia patient in the military who went unidentified for two years.

Dr. Franks also demanded to know why some of the families of Tidal

Wave dead had received positive identification of the bodies of sons and husbands and proof of burial.

> I do know that other families affected by the casualties of that raid on Ploeşti have received definite and positive reports concerning their sons, reports from the Romanian government, giving photographs showing funerals, graves, etc., with markers identifying individuals. I wrote the department concerning one such case, the case of Lieutenant Little, a good friend of my son, who also lost his life in that battle. The department has not yet explained how or why that evidence was given to his wife, Mrs. Lucille Little, of Memphis, Tennessee, and that similar evidence could not be furnished to others similarly affected.

There was no forthcoming explanation from the War Department.

In addition to the hours he devoted to searching for Red, Dr. Franks was kept busy with church affairs. Foremost among his ministerial duties was to the families of sixteen young parishioners who had been killed. He offered solace and understanding to the grieving parents. To Howard Noland's parents he wrote a quick note when he learned that Howard's name would appear on a memorial plaque to American Air Corps dead to be erected in a memorial chapel in St. Paul's Cathedral in London. "It will be a source of comfort to you to know that Howard's name will be on that immortal list. St. Paul's is one of the most famous cathedrals of the world. Have thought of you and prayed for you daily since the tragic news of Howard's death finally came." He ended his letter wistfully: "How I wish I knew where, or if, Red is buried."

Dr. Franks presided over the usual funerals and weddings, and he took a keen interest in the Baptist Student Union at nearby MSCW. Many of the students regularly attended Sunday services at his church. He also organized Baptist revivals at First Baptist and at other churches around the state. As a pastor Dr. Franks could mesmerize a congregation with his quiet and persuasive presentations. "He could paint a picture with words," remembers Bob Fuqua, a member of the congregation. Dr. Franks was also elected to chair the Lowndes County chapter of the American Red Cross and devoted many hours in organizing relief operations to the families displaced by a devastating series of floods that struck the area.

Dr. Franks again sat down at his typewriter and wrote to General Johnson that he intended to visit Romania to locate Red's body. "I shall continue to hope that every effort possible will be made to ascertain definitely what happened to my son, and I shall continue my personal efforts in every way possible to learn the facts. I could never be so satisfied to leave the matter as it stands today, with all the uncertainties, contradictions, and confusion, which the reports I have received have left with me. I hope to visit Rumania myself personally as soon as the permission is granted by the government." The War Department was silent for months.

On August 15, 1945, World War II finally ended with the Japanese surrender and most everyone rejoiced at the news. For Americans VJ Day represented a new beginning, but for Dr. Franks it meant continued struggle with the past. The war, and those who died in it, would soon be forgotten. Red would become a statistic that no one cared to notice.

"Thank God It's Over!" the *Commercial Dispatch* proclaimed when the news finally came. Spontaneous celebrations took place in cities and towns around the county and around the world with the word of the final Japanese surrender. The people of Columbus poured from their homes and flocked into the downtown to exult. The *Commercial Dispatch* recorded the event.

Usually conservative Columbus flung off its wartime restraint and exploded in its greatest, wildest celebration in history here. Boisterous, happy crowds sang, danced, and cheered late into the evening. Space was roped off on Market Street. Veterans were toasted, praised, and wept over. The crowd began gathering uptown just after 6 pm and by 8 they were at their height. The cool atmosphere was punctured for hours by the din of horns as motorists burned gasoline they had carefully hoarded for this occasion. Many of them sat on the horn. Streets soon were littered with crepe paper and tissue paper. Never had there been a celebration equal to it here.

The next day the city's residents marched to the Magnolia Bowl, the high school stadium where Red and the Lee Generals had celebrated so many other victories. The Lee High band, members of the state's National Guard, and veterans from this and previous wars led the parade of citizens as planes from the CAAF flew over in formation. The stadium reverberated to the strains of "America The Beautiful," and ministers from the various faiths led the people in prayer and thanksgiving. Then the Magnolia Bowl became strangely silent as the names of all the young men from Columbus who had given their lives in the war were read aloud. The ceremonies brought to mind the words of President Franklin Roosevelt's prayer as American troops fought their way ashore at Normandy on June 6, 1944, when he prayed for America's youth at war.

> Almighty God: Our sons, pride of our nation, have this day set upon a mighty endeavor. . . . They will be sore tired, by night and by day, without rest. . . . The darkness will be rent by noise and flame. Men's souls will be shaken with the violence of war. . . . Let our hearts be stout, to wait out the long travail, to bear sorrows that may come, to impart our courage unto our sons wheresoever they may be. . . . These men are lately drawn from the ways of peace. . . . They yearn for the end of battle, for their return to the haven of home. . . . Some will never return. Embrace these, Father, and receive them, Thy heroic servants, into Thy kingdom.

As the name of each Gold Star soldier was read, a family member stood in his place of honor. Dr. Franks stood proud yet humbled when Red's name was called.

Wheresoever they may be! Dr. Franks still could not believe that Red was dead. Just weeks before he had insisted in a letter to Lt. Col. Mayo Darling in the Office of the Quartermaster General that the report of the Romanian government that Red had been killed still did not "fit the picture of what happened. . . . Please do not take that report as final. All the facts evidently are not accounted for."

At the end of the roll call in the Magnolia Bowl, a bugler sounded taps that echoed hauntingly through the stadium and out across the prairie. The landscape in August was haze covered as it was on the day Red had been shot down two years before.

When the joyous celebrations ended and the crowds dissipated, Dr. Franks returned to the quiet of his office and contemplated the end of the war with mixed emotions. He struggled to feel the same sense of joy as his fellow countrymen, but he was too weary from anguish and a sense of loss. It seemed so simple a request—to know where Red was. Years later, his friend, Birney Imes, Jr., editor of the *Commercial Disptach*, wrote: "With Dr. Franks there was absolutely no compromise with his convictions." He was convinced that Red could still be alive and he would never cease his searching.

Dr. Franks longed to visualize Red somewhere overseas, or in the United States, celebrating along with his comrades and thanking God that he had survived the war. Red would have returned home, dashing looking in his officer's uniform, with Dottie rushing to greet him. The two of them would still be young and standing at the gateway to life. He could recall the heady days of his own youth when he and Sallie embarked on their life together.

Dr. Franks looked out the window of the parsonage to Second Avenue North, the street on which Red had returned home so many times. What chance was there now that Red would come back? Dr. Franks did not answer his own question. He knew the answer and was overcome by sadness. The war was won but he had paid a terrible price for victory, and only his faith in God would see him through his ordeal.

Always a light sleeper and plagued by painful arthritis in his spine that made sleep difficult, Dr. Franks frequently rose in the middle of the night, dressed in his preacher's best, and walked the three blocks to downtown Columbus where he visited the police station or the firehouse and chatted with the men on duty. His nocturnal ramblings had increased after Red's disappearance. And at the height of a Mississippi summer, nighttime diminished the stultifying heat of the day and the air was softer and fragrant. Sometimes he carried pen and paper and settled into a desk at the Gilmer Hotel, where he wrote the many letters he sent to family, to parishioners, and to government and military officials involved in the search for Red. Nancy Lee received many correspondences from her father penned at the Gilmer in the predawn hours. In the summer of 1945 she had just graduated from Shorter College and was teaching music at a college in Arkansas, prior to taking graduate courses in music at the University of Michigan. Dr. Franks also wrote Dottie Turner who was much on his mind.

In November 1945 Dr. Franks sought help from the army's Graves Registration Service and asked for information regarding Red's "death or burial." He suggested that if Graves Registration did not know of Red's whereabouts, they could turn the matter over to the State Department, which might be able to obtain information from Romanian authorities about his son. A month later he received a reply: "Up to the present time no further information concerning the place of burial of your son has been received in this office. However, you may be assured that the American Graves Registration Service is endeavoring to locate the graves of our deceased military personnel. This practice will continue until every effort to locate the graves has been exhausted."

In 1946 Dr. Franks wrote to Congressman Whittington inquiring about the prospect of finding employment in Romania. Whittington offered little hope that such opportunities existed. "I have contacted UNRRA [United Nations Relief and Rescue Administration] for the purpose of securing employment for you in Romania to find that they do not have offices in Romania at this time but that they do have offices in surrounding countries. They tell me they only need people of highly professional and technical skills, agriculture rehabilitation work, as well as biological specialists." The congressman suggested that Dr. Franks fill out an application form that would be passed on to the appropriate authorities but noted that the United States would not issue him a passport to travel to Romania because it was under the domination of the Soviet Union. "You would go at your own peril. Generally it is difficult, if not impossible, to enter Romania."

Congressman Whittington also sent Dr. Franks a copy of Public Law 383 that provided for the return of the war dead to national or private cemeteries in the United States at government expense. The bill also covered the burial of American dead in military cemeteries abroad. The irony was not lost on Dr. Franks. He had no remains to bury.

On July 7, 1946, the church elders honored Dr. Franks on the twenty-fifth anniversary of his appointment as pastor to the First Baptist Church with special ceremonies. The praise was effusive and the accomplishments listed were many. During his twenty-five years Dr. Franks had preached 5,177 sermons, conducted 1,400 prayer meetings, taught more than 975 Sunday school lessons, conducted 671 funeral services, officiated at 500 marriages, and conducted a total of 100 revival meetings in Columbus and in various parts of Mississippi. Most important of all, the church had grown nearly sevenfold under his ministry. In 1921 church membership stood at 541. There were now more than 3,300 parishioners.

All the accolades could not distract Dr. Franks from his mission. Later that summer he received a startling report that Red's body had been found buried near Ploeşti with his identification tag attached to the grave marker. The information, from the Red Cross, was confirmed by Congressman Whittington, who had been verbally informed of the same finding by a high-ranking officer in the army's casualty branch. Dr. Franks quickly replied that "since the International Red Cross has reported that my son's body was discovered with identification tags, it ought not to be difficult to locate the place of burial."

Congressman Whittington immediately asked the army for written confirmation of the report. He noted that he had been advised that Red Franks "was buried in Romania and that one identification tag was buried with his body and one attached to the grave marker."

General Witsell replied, "You were informed that a report had been received from the International Red Cross which revealed that Lieutenant Franks's body had been charred by flames and his identification tag found in the wreckage of the plane. The records of this office do not show specifically that he was interred in Romania with one identification tag buried with the body and the other attached to the grave marker."

In September 1946, Dr. Franks asked the War Department for further clarification about additional conflicting reports about Red's body when he noted that he had been advised "that the official report of interment has been received in this office from the Romanian government though the International Red Cross which shows that the remains of your son were recovered, but due to the nature of the accident could not be individually identified."

In October Dr. Franks received another letter from General Johnson stating that the Air Corps still believed Lieutenant Franks had been killed during the raid and that the information it had received from the battle site was irrefutable. General Johnson added, however, "the Quartermaster General has assured this headquarters that a special investigation has been requested of the Graves Registration Service operating in the area where your son's aircraft crashed."

After that no word came for several months. In January 1947, Dr. Franks requested permission from the U.S. government to visit the Romanian battlefield sites around Ploeşti to search the area himself for evidence of Red's body. His request was side stepped by War Department officials who stated that nothing new had been found, but that a radiogram had been sent to graves registration units "in theater" requesting any available evidence.

Dr. Franks and Augusta had been planning for several years to travel to Europe to search for their Red. Augusta noted in her diary that ever since the war's end they had sought permission to visit Romania but the Iron Curtain that had descended across Europe, kept them out. By 1947 Dr. Franks's plan to work in Europe was in earnest, and in February he realized his hopes when he was offered a position to work with the World Council of Churches in their relief and reconstruction program in Europe. He would be stationed in Geneva, but his work would take him throughout Europe. When Dr. Franks asked when he was expected to begin his new duties, he was surprised by the reply: "in three weeks."

They were shocked at the sudden turn of events. The assignment was for a year or more and Dr. Franks would be leaving the parish he had served for twenty-six years. But he and Augusta realized that it would offer them an opportunity to travel to Romania where there was a chance they could learn about Red's fate.

His parishioners knew why Dr. Franks was leaving. Those who remained in the congregation sixty years later still recall his anguish over Red's loss and his determination to find his son. One hundred-year-old Nannie Kate Smith, Dr. Franks's neighbor, remembered his silent pain. "He would not show his grief. He would bear his sorrow in private," Nannie Kate said. "It hurt him so badly he went overseas to find Red's grave," said Marietta Mc-Carter, a member of Dr. Franks's parish. "I just know he went over to Europe looking for Red. That was always on his mind," said Betty Holland, Nancy Lee's childhood friend.

On Saturday night of March 9, 1947, Dr. Franks remained in his office most of the night writing his letter of resignation and at the close of the Sunday morning service read the letter to the stunned congregation. Many in the church would lose the only preacher they had ever known. Dr. Franks bade them farewell:

Last summer on the first Sunday in July, this church sponsored a very beautiful occasion in celebration of the 25th anniversary of my services as your pastor. One outstanding feature of the celebration was the presenting of an anniversary love offering to the pastor in the amount of exactly $1,784.07. In addition to that, the church voted a three months leave of absence with full salary continued, suggesting that he use the time and money given to visit some of the foreign mission fields.

On that occasion which shall ever be a most memorable one in my life, I said in my heart "I know what I shall do with these three months and with this money. I shall spend them on a trip to our mission fields in the Balkan States, particularly in Romania. I shall hope to leave with the little Baptist Church in Ploesti, Romania, a sizable portion of this money, as a memorial to my noble preacher son, who was reported to have been killed in action in the first air raid on that city. August 1, 1943."

A few weeks ago . . . Mrs. Franks and I received appointment by the Church World Service to serve with that organization in its relief and rehabilitation program in the countries of Europe, representing Southern Baptists in their relief work in that area. Our headquarters will be in Geneva, Switzerland. The period of service requested of us calls for one year and will likely last much longer.

I love you too much to make any request of you of a personal nature that might cause you to slacken your hold on the noble work you have undertaken, or to "look back" even temporarily. The word for you is "Forward with Christ."

I am therefore offering my resignation as your pastor, to take effect when we leave for our work in Europe, which if our present plans work out satisfactorily, should be about the first of May.

I regret to think of leaving this field now. There are so many unfinished tasks that I should like to see accomplished before I leave. Outstanding among them are the Soldiers Memorial Endowment Fund, which must be raised, and the Baptist Student Center Building, which must be provided. But there are clearly enterprises of the Lord's own ordering.

We shall need and greatly covet an interest in your prayers.

On May 1, 1947, Dr. Franks and Augusta set off on a freighter bound for France. Ostensibly it was a journey to a new position with the World Council of Churches. In reality it was a mission to find his son. In the end it lasted more than eight years.

1 5

A Father's Nightmare

Lesser men would have given up their search, but not Dr. Franks. He pressed the army's quartermaster general to explain why he had not received the results of an investigation into Red's status that had been initiated in June 1946. General Witsell responded, "As you know, the report of his death submitted through the International Red Cross contained the distressing news that his body had been charred by flames and his identification tag found in the wreckage of the plane."

It was the War Department's well-worn version of events that Dr. Franks refused to accept. He had read and heard enough reports to know that Red had been seen bailing out of the plane by members of *Euroclydon*'s crew and from airmen in oncoming bombers. Lieutenant Warner had affirmed to Dr. Franks in writing that he had seen Red bail out.

If Red had gone down with the plane, his body and his dog tags would have been recovered, and he would have been buried somewhere in Romania, most likely around Ploeşti. But the army could find no grave, and in

January 1947 Dr. Franks received a letter from the quartermaster general re-
iterating that "no burial information concerning the remains of your son
has been received since our letter of 20 August 1946."

Dr. Franks's crusade had enlisted such strong support from the two
Mississippi congressmen, Rankin and Whittington, that the army now considered the Red Franks matter top priority. One interoffice memo relating
to Lieutenant Franks in the quartermaster general's office noted, "Hand
carry to F/C for Grave Location Letter. Please Expedite. This is a Congressional case."

Despite the congressional interest, the army still did not know Red's
fate and could not answer Dr. Franks's inquiries. In February 1947, he received a letter from the army's memorial division stating that it had dispatched a radiogram to graves registration teams operating in Romania to
forward all information about Lieutenant Franks. Graves Registration
replied a short time later:

> REFERENCE YOUR CABLE WILLIAM ABLE ROGER XRAY NINE ONE FIVE
> TWO ZERO DATED SEVEN FEBRUARY FOUR SEVEN REGARDING SECOND
> LIEUTENANT JESSE DOG FRANKS JUNIOR CMA ZERO SEVEN THREE FOUR
> FOUR FOUR PD CASE BEING INVESTIGATED PD NO REPORT OF REBURIAL
> RECEIVED TO DATE PD NO UNKNOWNS RECOVERED CAN BE ASSOCIATED
> PD REPORT SHOULD BE AVAILABLE BY ONE APRIL PD E D.

By January 1947, Graves Registration was in the final stages of a large-
scale body retrieval operation around Ploeşti to locate and identify the remains of an estimated six hundred American airmen who had been killed in
air raids over the refineries in 1943 and 1944. Ploeşti had remained a critical, strategic target long after Tidal Wave, and the raids continued to reduce
the flow of German gasoline and oil.

But it was nine months before new fleets of B-24s and B-17s, teamed
with hundreds of escorting P-38 fighters, came back. The August 1 raid
had produced more tears and heroes than damage, and while not a complete
failure, it was not deemed a strategic success. Battalions of slave laborers

quickly repaired the damaged facilities, and the output of oil was back to normal within weeks, and even increased.

The first post–Tidal Wave mission against Ploeşti came in early May 1944, when 485 Liberators and Fortresses bombed the refineries and adjacent railway yards. Nineteen U.S. planes were shot down and more U.S. airmen were killed, wounded, or taken prisoner. In mid-May the Fifteenth Air Force bombers struck again. The new attacks no longer came from distant North Africa, but from airfields in southern Italy where the Fifteenth was based after the Italians surrendered in 1943.

The air war between the Germans and the Americans over Ploeşti became personal and deadly. As the bombers approached the target, enemy pilots were waiting for them and often radioed personal greetings to individual pilots as they swooped down on the bomber formations with vengeance.

The Germans and Romanians continued to build up their antiaircraft defenses by adding more guns of all calibers. "The flak over the target was just god-awful," remembered Irving Fish, Jr., who was shot down over Ploeşti in August, 1944.

Colonel Smart also remembered the flak. He could not fly on the August 1, 1943, mission but later commanded missions against Ploeşti in B-17s as a bomb group commander. "I don't think I was ever more heavily shot at than at Ploeşti," Smart said. "They had flak over that target until hell wouldn't have it."

The Germans also installed two thousand smoke generators to obscure the refineries. To circumvent a thick smokescreen every time its planes bombed Ploeşti, the Air Corps sent in P-38 Lightnings, each laden with a thousand-pound bomb, to go in under the smoke. The strategy failed as German fighters caught the planes before they reached the target and shot down twenty-six.

The Fifteenth Air Force adopted still another strategy when it sent individual "master bombers" over Ploeşti in P-38s flying high above the target in advance of the bombers. This was a tactic borrowed from the Royal Air Force (RAF); the master bomber circled the refineries looking for holes in the smoke, and when the B-17s and B-24s arrived, he directed them to drop their ordnance through the openings. The Fifteenth Air Force continued to improvise its tactics, and by the summer of 1944 Ploeşti was being pulverized.

"Every day that God made, the attackers swept over," one German soldier remembered. He also recalled that black clouds from burning oil tanks hung over Ploeşti so heavily that enemy gunners were enveloped in darkness by day, and night never came because raging oil fires lit the darkness.

By July 1944 the Americans and British were sending formations totaling more than six hundred planes to Ploeşti, and the Luftwaffe no longer had the fighter planes to stop them. By August the bombers came with near impunity. The last raids came on the nights of August 17–19, 1944. Shortly thereafter, the Red Army closed in on the city and captured the oil fields.

When the campaign ended, the Allies had launched twenty-three heavy bombing missions against the refineries totaling 9,173 individual bomber and fighter sorties and had dropped 27 million pounds of bombs. But even with the constant pounding, the Germans had been able to keep some oil flowing. A postwar survey found that the refineries were operating at 20 percent capacity when the war ended. The price of Ploeşti had been high. The United States lost 286 heavy bombers, and more than 2,829 men were killed or captured.

The cost was worth the price. By some enemy accounts, the destruction of Ploeşti was the most powerful blow struck by the Air Corps against Nazi Germany in World War II.

The graves registration teams that searched the Ploeşti area began the painstaking task of retrieving the dead after the Germans were driven from Romania. The Romanians had collected the bodies of American known and unknown dead immediately after the Tidal Wave attack and buried them in local cemeteries or in mass graves where they were sometimes interred side by side with German and Romanian soldiers who had been killed in the battle. Many of the American flyers were buried with full military honors.

After the war Romanian nationals, hired as interpreters and for their knowledge of the country, assisted graves registration personnel in the search.

The teams also made use of intelligence information gathered from the aircrews that had made it safely back from previous Ploeşti missions. The flyers returning from Tidal Wave were questioned by Air Corps intelligence personnel shortly after landing in Libya for information about downed planes and flyers. They wanted to know as precisely as possible where the planes had crashed and the number of parachutes seen coming from them. As the bombers flew over the refineries, many airmen in the oncoming Liberator stream noted the number of chutes popping open from falling bombers ahead of them. That information could prove valuable in determining the number of men who had survived in a crew and the number of POWs being held by the enemy. It could also be used to pinpoint geographic areas where bodies might be found.

When the Tidal Wave POWs were released from Romanian prison camps, all were thoroughly questioned for information about missing comrades. Lieutenant Warner filled out a questionnaire relating to Red Franks.

"Did he [Franks] bail out?" Warner writes, "Yes, altitude approximately fifty feet."

"Where?" Warner responds, "Two miles northwest of target area."

"Last contact or conversation just prior to or at time of loss of plane?" Warner writes, "Surveyed the damage and extent of fire together and decided to abandon the plane."

"Was he [Franks] injured?" Warner responds, "Yes."

"Where was he when last seen?" Warner writes, "Leaving ship through nosewheel door."

"Any hearsay information?" Warner responds, "No."

In one interrogation, an unnamed surviving gunner from *Euroclydon* revealed that the last words he had heard from Red Franks were "bombs away," (over the intercom) as the plane released its bombs on the target. After that he knew nothing about what happened to Lieutenant Franks. An exploding antiaircraft shell severed communications between those in the front and the gunners in the rear of the plane.

Another *Euroclydon* crew member, gunner Charles Reed, reported that he had approached the plane's crash site shortly after bailing out at about one hundred feet. "I, under guard, visited our crashed airplane twenty minutes after it crashed. Plane was a total wreck as it struck houses. It was still burning, so close inspection was impossible. However, did see five bodies. All unidentified."

Lieutenant Warner was interrogated by German intelligence officers, but answered only the standard Geneva Convention questions and they did not press for more details. The enemy interrogators supplied Lieutenant Warner with more information than he gave them. They revealed the name of his plane, its serial number, which Lieutenant Warner himself did not remember, and they knew the route *Euroclydon* had flown from Benghazi, and finally they stated that only three men had survived the crash, Lieutenant Warner and gunners Charles Reed and James Vest.

The Romanians knew where the planes had crashed and where many of the airmen had been buried and passed this information to the Americans when they arrived to retrieve their dead. Graves registration teams also searched the countryside looking for additional unmarked burial sites and questioned local farmers, priests, and village officials about Americans who might have been buried where they fell or asked them if they had seen any bodies that had been removed by authorities to a local cemetery. The graves registration teams exhumed all of the remains they found and placed them in rubberized body pouches or mattress covers and shipped those whose names were unknown to an army laboratory for identification. Many of the Tidal Wave flyers, however, had been so badly burned that little was left of them except charred bones. The army described them as having been "carbonized."

Dimitrie "Jimmy" Siladie was an Albanian member of an American graves registration search team that worked around Ploeşti in 1946 and 1947 to locate American dead. Born in Romania in 1920, he had come with his parents to Akron, Ohio, in 1920 but returned to Romania at age fifteen to study. Caught in the maelstrom of war at the outbreak of World War II, he was unable to return to the United States until after the war. He was living in Ploeşti on August 1, 1943, and never forgot the sight of the endless stream of B-24s streaking over at fifty feet, some on fire, others struggling to stay aloft, while others had hardly been touched by antiaircraft fire. Siladie recalled the air armada: "They just kept coming and coming."

Siladie and his graves registration team looked for personal possessions found on the remains such as wallets, belts, ID cards, and photographs, or for military gear such as pieces of uniform, insignias, and rank badges, that would help identify them. "Some were burned beyond recognition," Siladie said. "It was creepy. You found bones; you found worms. Some were pretty advanced into putrefaction."

Body parts such as tufts of hair and segments of jaw with teeth were of critical importance. He placed the artifacts in marked boxes that could be examined later in the military laboratory to help establish identify. Siladie filed individual reports on each body recovered. The findings in one report stated:

I. Box 40, Row 2, Plot C, Section Hero, contained the following upon disinterment:
  a. One complete skull
  b. Remnants of a suntan shirt.
  c. A Lt. Bar was found on shirt collar.
  d. An Air Corps insignia was found on left sleeve.
2. The above findings show these to be remains of one airman who crashed on August 1st, 1943.

> J. Siladie
> Civ. Investigator

Siladie drew diagrams of the cemeteries where the teams exhumed bodies. Whole sections of graves were either marked by the words "Ostasi Americani Necunoscuti"—Unknown American Soldier—or they were numbered with the letter X, for unknown, listed before an identification number.

In the same Row 2, Plot C, Section Hero were forty other unknowns and one known American flyer, S. Sgt. Milford Spears. Overall there were 194 recovered remains of unknown flyers found interred around Ploeşti, and only fifteen had been identified by early 1947.

Two of Red's crewmates, Lt. Howard L. Dickson and Lt. Joe E. Boswell, were identified after their bodies were exhumed from a small village cemetery near Ploeşti. But the identity of these two men was tenuous. The graves registration report noted that the bodies of Dickson and Boswell were found on September 6, 1943, more than a month after Tidal Wave, when Romanian authorities sifted through the wreckage of the plane. "Two identification tags were found in the ashes and bones of what remained of airman." They were also badly charred.

The graves registration report concluded, "In summation, remains of two American airmen were buried in common grave . . . no individual identity having been found, and only few remains of bones made it impossible to separate or segregate into two bodies. Because of limited amount of information available on this crash, it is going to be necessary to continue the investigation in the months ahead, and when the airmen are disinterred from Bolovan Cemetery at Ploeşti."

Identification of many of the American dead was hampered because Romanian police and troops had removed the two dog tags that every American soldier carried and sent both to the Red Cross. The standard procedure used by American personnel was to leave one tag with the body while graves registration units or enemy authorities maintained the other to authenticate the death. Without their tags, the identity of many Tidal Wave airmen was unknown when their bodies were found scattered around Ploeşti. Civilians also scavenged bodies that had not been burned and removed all personal belongings that would have helped to identify them.

"We mapped all of Romania so no bodies were left there," Siladie said. The dead were exhumed and their remains were transferred for reburial in American military cemeteries in Western Europe. Red Franks was not listed among them, nor were any of the five *Euroclydon* crew members, other than Dickson and Boswell, who had gone down with the plane.

The question of what had happened to Red Franks remained a mystery. No one could say whether or not he was alive or dead. The Romanians reported him killed in action, but there were no identified remains and no definitive information to prove that Red had been killed. The answer to the secret might lie among the 179 or so American airmen killed over Ploeşti, whose names remained unknown.

By July 1947 Dr. Franks and Augusta were living in Geneva, Switzerland, where he was named secretary of the department overseeing Bulgaria for the World Council of Churches. He set out to learn everything possible about the country, particularly about the churches and their relief needs. Bulgaria's neighbor was Romania, and Dr. Franks realized the possibility of visiting the Ploeşti area on one of his trips to Sophia, the capital of Bulgaria. A month after assuming his new position, however, Dr. Franks was reassigned because of the deteriorating political situation in Bulgaria. He became the department secretary for Poland and once again tirelessly strove to understand the needs of the Polish people and their churches. He would come to greatly admire the Poles.

But his determination to find Red remained a near obsession. He continued to write congressmen and generals and he bared his soul to his new colleagues at the Council of Churches. Being in Geneva gave him the opportunity to examine prisoner of war records at the headquarters of the International Red Cross. He searched them for any clue to Red's fate and passed his thoughts to the quartermaster general: "To my way of thinking those records are very inconclusive as a basis upon which to report as final that my son was killed in action. I am positive in my own mind, from these records, that he was not in the plane when it crashed. The War Department's report is based on that theory. I am also positive in my conclusion based upon these records that he bailed out before the plane crashed."

In July, members of the World Council of Churches joined the quest to find Red. A council employee, Mrs. Ilse Beale, wrote the army's memorial division with a new request that "search parties in Romania could be made acquainted with this case and find out more news for us. We shall be most grateful."

Mrs. Beale concluded, "Pastor Dr. Franks works here with us in the World Council of Churches. He has acquainted me with the facts of his son. He seems to be very harried by the doubt of his son's disappearance. I would consider it a personal favor if you could find something definite about Lieutenant Franks's death in order to allay the nightmare of his father."

The memorial division took three months to reply and the response was the same. Red Franks had been killed in action on August 1, 1943. Lt. Col. R. M. Bauknight added, "An extensive investigation is currently in progress. . . . If it is determined that the remains of Lieutenant Franks are among those thus far recovered, his family will be advised without delay. If further search for his remains is necessary, you may be assured that it will be conducted."

The Army restated its certainty that Red Franks had perished over Ploeşti. In an internal memo relative to Mrs. Beale's letter, the army's adjutant general's office concluded, "Second Lieutenant Jesse D. Franks, Jr., 0734444, was killed in action on 1 August 1943, the date he was previously reported missing in action while on a mission to the Ploeşti oil fields." But Dr. Franks refused to concede.

His new position required extensive travel to Poland, and Dr. Franks was soon aware that his own personal sufferings were no worse and no more unbearable than those of millions of Poles and Europeans two years after the war. Entire families had been shattered, cities lay in ruins, and everywhere there was inadequate food and shelter. Dr. Franks and Augusta got their first glimpse of the condition of millions of Europeans when they visited a refugee camp in Copenhagen, Denmark, while attending the Baptist World Alliance meeting a month after their arrival in Europe.

Augusta sometimes traveled with her husband, and they were both shocked by the physical devastation of Poland and the poor condition of the people. The condition of Warsaw was even more devastating and was said to be the second worst destroyed city of the war. "The marks of man's inhumanity to man were still in evidence. We had difficulty in travel and in getting proper food. We spent a whole month in Poland this time and I can still hear the hunger cries of little children and see the apprehension in the faces of people," Augusta noted.

"Everywhere we went we saw little but the devastation of war and human misery—all the horrible aftermath of the scorched-earth policy of two invading armies which had swept over the country, first the Germans, then the Russians," Dr. Franks wrote as he traveled through the countryside around Warsaw and Gdańsk along the Baltic.

He was moved by the fact, however, that the devastating aftereffects of the war had removed many of the obstacles and barriers that divide churches in times of peace. "When hunger or great physical need is the common lot of Christians, they place little emphasis on the few points of theology which, under easier circumstances, would divide them. Real hunger makes it easier for them to find practical ways of working together."

The aftermath of war had spilled into neutral and undamaged Switzerland. The Franks had experienced shortages in the United States during the war, but were unprepared for the depravation in Europe. "Everything was rationed," Augusta wrote, and she and Dr. Franks had to learn how to deal with ration cards. To make matters more difficult, the ration cards were in French, a language that neither of them spoke. Luckily, the Swiss were helpful and guided Dr. Franks and Augusta through the details of their new life in Europe.

The Franks were also happy to see Nancy Lee, who visited from France where she was studying music at Fontainebleau. Dr. Franks had given Nancy all of Red's back pay, amounting to several thousand dollars, which she used to study piano for a year. Her parents' apartment in Geneva, small as it was, was a welcome relief from the bleak life of postwar France, where there was little food and virtually no heating fuel.

As Christmas approached, Dr. Franks remembered his old friends and parishioners in Columbus. In Christmas greetings to the First Baptist Church in Columbus, he related what he had seen and called upon his former congregation to share their good fortune with the many unfortunate peoples around the world.

The grim reality of a world unprepared for the birth of a savior will be understood best this year by the multiplied distress of millions of people around the world who have been rendered homeless by the war. They are

huddled in cellars and caves, in old outbuildings and in kinds of improvised shelters as refugees, displaced persons, orphans, helpless people of
every description with no place to call home. Again the words, "no room,"
are heard everywhere, everyway these unfortunate people turn as Mary
and Joseph heard them in the long ago. Millions have no room. For many
expectant mothers throughout the war-torn world today, the manger bed
is no imaginary crib, but is a stark reality. Many little ones will be cuddled
in straw with old rags and newspapers as their swaddling clothes. I greet
you in the name of the child of Bethlehem and on behalf of the millions
of children who have suffered and still suffer from the war's desolation.
We are calling these suffering millions in Europe to be brave and be men
of good will. But by the grace of God and in spite of their suffering, shall
we not also call upon you in the midst of your abundance to be men of
good will by sharing generously your good things with your helpless
neighbors around the world? Let us labor and share in his name the good
tidings that our Christmas greetings may be more than mere words.

The Frankses would spend another Christmas without Red and without knowing where he was. They had hoped to travel to Romania in late
1947 or early 1948 to continue the search on their own, but whatever hope
Dr. Franks and Augusta had of obtaining visas to visit Romania was dashed
by political realities of the Cold War. "In August of the first year we both
attended the Baptist World Congress meeting in Copenhagen, Denmark,"
Augusta wrote. "It was here that we learned that because the iron curtain
had fallen so hard, we could not get into Romania. This was a sad blow."

16

Retrieving the Dead

Assignment to a graves registration company was the most gruesome duty of the war. Tom Dowling was attached to one such unit that served just behind the front lines in France in 1944. He and his comrades landed at Normandy a few days after the June 6 invasion when the bodies of Americans still floated in the waters off Omaha Beach. Once ashore the team immediately went to work collecting and burying Americans killed in the fighting. Dowling described in a 1989 army magazine article the task in all its unspeakable horror, and it remained for him a never-ending reminder of the awful cost of World War II.

"It was the faces of these dead GIs . . . that hurt the most. Some stared wide eyed; others had died in the middle of a scream, and their mouths hung open. Others had no face at all."

The writer Paul Fussell, in his short history, *The Boys' Crusade*, described the hideous life of Graves Registration soldiers. " They were unlikely to have known any of those whose bodies they collected and so, if they were lucky, could do the heartbreaking work with little emotion. . . . Many of the bodies could be located only by smell, and most were days and weeks old and in what might be called poor condition. And they weren't laid out neatly, or even formed up into decent skirmish lines. One quartermaster body collector, who had been busy in a major battle area, had this to say: "Everywhere we searched we found bodies, floating in the rivers, trampled on the roads, bloated in the ditches, rotting in the bunkers, pretzeled into foxholes, burned in the tanks, buried in the snow, sprawled in doorways, splattered in gutters, dismembered in mine fields, and even literally blown up into trees."

Dowling and his comrades found the job so odious at times that they envied the dead who had found release from the war. "He is dead and going back. We are alive and going in," Dowling remembered thinking after an encounter with a dead American soldier floating in the surf off the Normandy beaches. "But it was not the sight of the dead and torn bodies that bothered us anymore," Dowling wrote. "It was that there had to be any dead at all."

Their work tormented the men. "We picked them up, began our burial details, and vomited our insides out. . . . Eventually, as the days dragged on, our loathing for our job increased." They cleaned, tagged, and fingerprinted the bodies and directed their transfer to nearby temporary burial grounds, generally just yards away, where the remains were interred to await removal after the war to cemeteries in the United States or to an American cemetery overseas.

Dowling's unit was also responsible for sorting and storing personal effects such as rings, wristwatches, wallets, and letters. These were sent to the Army Effects Bureau at the Kansas City Quartermaster Depot in Missouri, where they were carefully inventoried. Soiled garments were laundered, government-issue articles removed, foreign money converted to U.S. currency, and cash or negotiable checks deposited in a bank to the credit of the owner. The effects were then packed for storage prior to being sent to the families.

Dowling expressed the sorrow men felt at dealing with the once-living detritus of war.

It was horrifying to think of how life could be snuffed out on foreign soil, far from home. It was the thinking about the possessions we stuffed into bags. It was seeing them and knowing that even as we lowered young bodies into graves, there were people at home who did not yet know they were dead. Only we knew; only we gagged from the stench and the horror of seeing young guys who would never again play ball, chase girls, kiss their mothers and wives or girlfriends. . . .

There were times when I, in sorting possessions to be sent home to next of kin, had to read bits of letters the dead men carried about. Words of a loved one leapt off the pages and brought forth emotions that I had difficulty dealing with." The dead, most always, were young men. Their lives had been ahead of them. They had been compelled to fight and had died alone far from family and home.

The members of Dowling's unit instinctively felt the need for some form of spiritual relief. Not long after they went ashore at Normandy, the men fell to their knees in a spontaneous act of prayer for those whom they were burying. It happened one moonlit night in France as they could hear the pounding of the guns not far off at the front.

"The lieutenant stepped forward into the moonlight. He held his helmet at his side. His face was seemingly aged by many years. He dropped to one knee and bowed his head. As if on cue, the rest of us quietly slid down also. Not a word was spoken, but I was saying my first word for the dead who were buried there and for all of us who needed each other's prayers."

Not all the dead were picked up soon after battle. In some places they were left where they fell in enemy-held territory for months until American forces could retake the ground. In many cases retrieval operations had to await the end of the war, and one of the most challenging tasks for graves registration units was to locate the bodies of soldiers who had been left behind on contested battlefields. In February 1945, Maj. Gen. James Gavin, commander of the Eighty-second Airborne Division, recalled the ghastly sight of unburied Americans who still lay where they had been killed in

November 1944 in Germany's Heurtgen Forest. General Gavin was scouting the terrain around the village of Schmidt prior to launching an attack into Germany. The dead lay in an area from which the Twenty-eighth Division had retreated, and the Americans could not return to retrieve the bodies. Gavin wrote, "Many, many dead bodies, cadavers that had just emerged from the winter snow. Their gangrenous, broken, and torn bodies were rigid and grotesque, some of them with arms skyward, seemingly in supplication." The sight of American dead was so gruesome that only battle-hardened infantry were ordered to attack over the cadaver-littered ground for fear that less experienced troops would bolt in horror.

Medic Jack Davis remembers serving on the southern edge of the Battle of the Bulge in mid-January, 1945, on ground where scores of American dead littered the battlefield. They had been killed in early December when the Germans first attacked and drove the American army out of the area.

Richard Albera, a young army lieutenant, led a graves registration team searching battlegrounds in Bavaria in southern Germany to retrieve the unrecovered bodies of American soldiers as the war ended in Europe. His men were formed in picket lines and were ordered to cross bucolic pastures looking for bodies. Often they did not have to look far. Some of the dead whom they retrieved were downed flyers, but most had been ground troops whose remains were left behind after some local action with the enemy. The bodies were usually in an advanced state of decomposition, if there was any flesh on the bones at all. Some had been buried where they fell either by civilians or by comrades who could not carry the body with them. Many revealed the trauma of their deaths. "Bullet wounds were evident," Albera said. "Some were pretty badly burned. The tank cases were bad; the air crashes were bad. Many were mangled."

The men in Albera's unit lived daily with the sickening smell of putrefaction that collected on their clothing and filled their nostrils. Some of the men smoked incessantly to offset the smell of death while others wore surgical masks in a vain attempt to filter out the smell, but it lingered.

In Paul Fussell's memoir, *Doing Battle, The Making of a Skeptic,* he recalled observing soldiers in a graves registration unit in Europe. "They were hopelessly drunk, and they had been for many weeks. It was the only way, they explained, they could do their work."

Retrieving the dead was often dangerous work. Recovery operations on some battlefields were delayed because the search areas had to be cleared of mines and unexploded munitions before the remains could be removed. Bodies could be found with live munitions such as hand grenades, and sometimes they had been booby-trapped by the retreating Germans in efforts to slow the American advance.

Civilians often retrieved and buried American dead in village cemeteries and tended to their graves as they would for their own sons. When the American graves registration teams arrived to remove the bodies, the villagers sometimes objected. The graves were regarded as monuments and memorials to liberation from Nazi tyranny, and the locals wanted the bodies to remain.

Villagers in Eschweiler, Luxembourg, buried the body of an American soldier, Pvt. George Ottmar Mergenthaler, in the local cemetery after he was killed during the Battle of the Bulge. Mergenthaler, a Princeton University graduate and grandson of Otto Mergenthaler, a German immigrant to the United States who invented the linotype machine, had been billeted in Eschweiler for a month before the German attack and spoke French and German well enough to befriend many of the locals. When the Battle of the Bulge began on December 16, 1944, Mergenthaler was killed while manning a machine gun so that his Twenty-eighth Division unit could make its escape from the German onslaught.

Mergenthaler's unburied body was discovered in March 1945 near Eschweiler by a strolling villager. She first noticed a photograph of Mergenthaler's family lying near the body, and then she saw that the body was clad in a purple sweater showing underneath an army field jacket. It was the sweater Mergenthaler's family had sent to him while he was billeted with Father Bodson, the village priest.

To confirm that the body found near Eschweiler was that of Private Mergenthaler, graves registration personnel contacted members of his former unit that had been reassigned to the Sixth Army Group front in the Vo-

Second Lieutenant Jesse D. Franks, Jr. in late 1942, just prior
to assignment overseas with the 8th Air Force in England.
(courtesy of Nancy Lee Goodall)

Dr. Franks, wearing his customary Homburg, in Switzerland, 1948.
(courtesy of Nancy Lee Goodall)

Portrait of the Franks family –Red, Dr. Franks and Sallie—
around 1923 on the steps of the First Baptist Church parsonage,
Columbus, Mississippi.
(courtesy of First Baptist Church)

Red as bugler at Camp Ridgecrest at age 14, 10 years before Ploesti.
He sounded Taps every night at bedtime.
(courtesy of Darrell Richardson)

Red playing his favorite game, football, at Ridgecrest
in 1939. Red is the quarterback.
(courtesy of Darrell Richardson)

Red Franks, at right, with high school
buddies in Columbus in 1937.
(courtesy of Nancy Lee Goodall)

Dr. Franks and his second wife Augusta at the celebration of his
25th year as pastor of the First Baptist Church
(courtesy of First Baptist Church)

Portrait of Dottie Turner circa 1941
(courtesy of Dawn Gerakaris)

Red's wallet contained his calling card as well as two pictures of Red and Dottie. The photos were taken three months before Red went overseas and were in his wallet when he bailed out over Ploetsti. The wallet and its contents made its way back, through the years, to Nancy Lee Goodall, who gave it to the author. The photo is a typical WWII photo of young lovers made poignant by separation and loss.

(courtesy of the author)

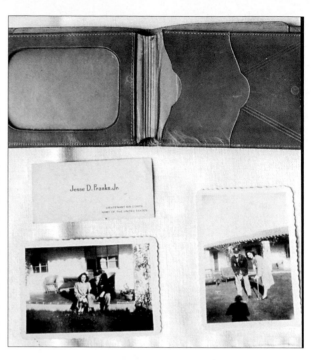

A booklet of prayers sent by Dr. Franks to Red in North Africa shortly before the Ploesti attack.

(courtesy of Nancy Lee Goodall)

Photo of the B-24D Strawberry Bitch, similar to Euroclydon. Strawberry Bitch
was assigned to the 376th BG, the Liberandos and flew out of Africa. She is
painted the putty color, desert camouflage, of the planes that were stationed there.
The photo clearly shows the greenhouse where the bombardier sat. Strawberry
Bitch is on display at the U.S. Air Force Museum in Dayton, Ohio.

(courtesy of United States Air Force Museum)

The crew of Euroclydon in the Libyan desert just days from the Ploesti
mission. Red Franks is 4th from left, kneeling in front row, wearing his officer's cap.
Lt. Jack Warner is 3rd from left, front row, without a shirt.
(courtesy of Karen Warner Pearce)

ges Mountains, many miles to the south. His former comrades remembered the purple sweater as being one of Mergenthaler's prized possessions.

Mergenthaler was given a full Christian burial in the church cemetery attended by the entire population of the village. When the Americans came to remove his body after the war, the villagers asked that Mergenthaler's body and grave be left undisturbed as a lasting memorial to the war and to the American soldiers who gave their lives liberating Luxembourg. But Mergenthaler's family wanted their son returned home, and in 1947 his body was removed for reburial in Rochester, New York. The villagers later erected a plaque in memory of Private Mergenthaler that was placed at the entrance to the church.

Formal graves registration units like Dowling's and Albera's have served in America's conflicts since the Spanish-American War in 1898. Their need, however, became apparent long before during the Mexican War of 1848, when American soldiers, killed in actions on Mexican territory, were buried in unmarked graves. Years later the Mexican government proposed a monument in Mexico City to honor the dead of both nations, and only 750 unidentified American dead could be found at the various battle sites.

The Mexican War did establish one precedent. In 1850, the U.S. Congress authorized the construction of an American cemetery in Mexico City for the remains of American soldiers killed in the war, the first such cemetery on foreign soil.

The Civil War again demonstrated the need for a military branch to properly care for America's war dead when tens of thousands of Union soldiers were left where they fell. It was only after the conflict the United States embarked on a massive campaign to exhume, identify, and bury the dead from battlefields where they had been hastily interred. Soldiers and civilians alike were disturbed by the callous treatment of those who fell.

In 1864 Union forces advancing into Virginia were shocked to see that many Union dead from the Battle of Chancellorsville, fought the summer before, remained unburied. One soldier with the 124th Infantry wrote, "Our dead were but partially buried, and the skulls and bones lay about in great profusion. . . . The Confederate dead, it would seem, had all been decently buried very near where they had fallen." The Union soldiers immediately began searching through the scattered remains in hopes of identifying friends. They sought marks on clothing and equipment, name tags, and even characteristics of tooth structure. "I saw where poor Captain Kirk lay," wrote one soldier from the 105th Pennsylvania Volunteer Infantry Regiment. "His skull was entirely exposed and lying on top of the grave. The fatal bullet that took his noble life was partly pushed out of the skull. We identified his remains by a peculiar mark on his shoulder strap, one of which adhered to his bones."

The Army never forgot the outrage of these Union troops. During World War II the War Department studied various plans for the final disposition of the dead and stated in one report, "The resentment expressed by officers and men of the Army of the Potomac, when they passed over the battlefield of Chancellorsville and witnessed the exposed remains of their comrades, offers convincing evidence that American citizen soldiers would not tolerate the burial methods that had sufficed in wars of the past."

It wasn't just that the bodies of Union dead were often left unburied. Their exposed bodies represented a form of sacrilege. In traditions dating back to the Egyptians and earlier, a nation's war dead achieve the status of mythical heroes and deserve proper burial and commemoration, and this has long been considered the duty of the state.

During the Civil War it was general practice to assign the retrieval of the dead to burial parties of soldiers who were untrained in proper graves registration practices. Nevertheless, many took great pains to identify the dead and to give their bodies proper care and burial. Capt. Warren H. Chudworth of the First Massachusetts Infantry recorded how men in the unit had worked: "Occasionally something would be found to identify the remains, but not often. One former member of the First, whose skull lay bleaching upon the top of the ground, was identified by some peculiarity connected with his teeth."

The only time a graves registration unit of sorts was employed during the Civil War was in 1864 when Confederate General Jubal Early's troops threatened the nation's capital. A Confederate reconnaissance force was repulsed outside Washington in a skirmish that resulted in the death of forty Union soldiers. An improvised unit was formed to retrieve the bodies of the dead, and every one of the forty men killed was identified.

Because there was no organized graves registration service during the Civil War, only 58 percent of the recovered remains of Union dead were identified. A vast reinterment program was begun at the war's end in 1865 and continued until 1870, when the bodies of an estimated 315,555 soldiers were exhumed from battlefield graves and reburied throughout the United States in newly established national cemeteries.

During the Spanish-American War of 1898, President McKinley instructed the Army to mark all graves with the name of the interred soldier, and by World War I, the Army had established the separate graves registration service whose sole purpose was to insure the proper identification and burial for each fallen soldier. Once World War I ended, graves registration troops were involved in the exhumation of the dead and the transfer of their remains either to cemeteries in the United States or to one of several American cemeteries in France. To facilitate the identification process during World War I, each soldier was required to wear a set of aluminum dog tags.

By World War II the army had a well-established graves registration service attached to the Quartermaster Corps, and its duties were spelled out in detail. The basic section included an officer in charge, one medical noncommissioned officer, a section chief, and three privates. Their equipment included mattress covers to wrap the body, a shovel and a pick, a pair of scissors, one fingerprint set, two litters, a personal effects bag, a grid map of the area where the team was working, and notebook and lead pencils.

Graves registration teams in World War II followed the American armies as they swept forward, and for the most part, retrieval of the dead was relatively uncomplicated during most actions. U.S. troops, more often than not, were moving forward and pushing back the enemy.

But in places like Ploeşti, graves registration teams came many months after the battle, and the trail of many flyers had been lost and few traces remained of many young men. But the military never ceased trying to find it lost soldiers. Even today the Department of Defense quickly dispatches teams around the world to exhume and identify the bodies of fallen Americans from World War II and bring them home.

17

Burying the Dead

Burial of the dead is the most solemn task in war. Families of those killed far from home are tormented by thoughts that their sons and husbands lie unburied on some distant battlefield, their flesh left to rot, and their bones left to scatter. Burial provides the living with some sense that loved ones are still whole and that they are at peace in consecrated ground.

It is sometimes difficult for the American government to treat the dead in a befitting manner. In modern warfare thousands of men are killed and their disposal requires large numbers of troops. And the dead are of no use against the enemy. One veteran combat soldier of World War II observed, "The dead were afforded no more status on a battlefield than a pile of manure."

But by World War II the military was making every effort to treat the dead with respect, and ordinary GIs did their best to sanctify their treatment and burial. James Strawder, a black American engineer, recalled collecting and burying the dead from the Normandy invasion. "There were thousands of them," Strawder said. "We didn't bag them or anything. We'd just wrap them in a blanket or in whatever else we had, carry them up to the cemetery, and put them down there all lined up. We were very honorable with those dead. You want to do the best job you can, and you're feeling sorry for all these fellows, yet thankful because by the grace of God, it's not me."

Every American soldier whose body was retrieved during World War II was buried near where he fell. None was returned to the United States during the conflict as was the case for those killed in Viet Nam when huge air force transport planes, filled with the dead, embalmed and in caskets, made regular flights from Saigon to the States. In World War II, the dead were buried in simple shrouds in makeshift, temporary cemeteries all over the world where their bodies would remain until the end of the war. Mounds of earth and wooden crosses marked the bodies. Then they were exhumed and transferred to larger cemeteries prior to shipment home or to interment in a permanent American cemetery in Europe or in the Pacific.

Col. Wallace Hale, an army chaplain serving in Italy during World War II, recalled the daily duty of burying the dead in isolated, temporary cemeteries near the fighting. He remembered one burial in particular. He watched a half squad of soldiers struggle towards him through the Italian mud in 1944 as they carried the body of a dead American GI to his grave.

Dead men are hard to carry. I looked into the mud that oozed and sloshed around my boot tops and could think only of the hurt and refuse and nastiness of real war. I was plain sick and tired of the whole business—not sick of burying these dead, just sick in heart and soul and gradually growing numb to everything that did not help me and my boys keep living.

Colonel Hale was division chaplain for the Eighty-eighth Infantry Division that fought its way up the rugged Italian peninsula in 1944 and 1945. He grew up in the cotton fields of east Texas and was raised in the Baptist faith. He decided after graduating from Baylor University in the mid-1930s to become a Baptist preacher, but not like the ones he'd known as an impressionable child. "I grew up in the hellfire, damnation days when the preacher told everyone how bad they were to try and get them to do good. It's a horrible way to approach religion. You went away with a headache." Colonel Hale wanted to soften his approach and chose to be a minister among soldiers. His first assignment as an army chaplain was in 1939 in remote Marfa, Texas, Big Bend Country in the desolate region along the Mexican border.

Little did Colonel Hale imagine that soon he would be ministering to GIs in combat, and nothing prepared him for the heartaches of being the head chaplain for an infantry division in the thick of the fighting. The Eighty-eighth went into action in early 1944, the first division comprised almost entirely of draftees to see combat. These were not the eager volunteers like Red Franks and his fellow Mississippians who rushed into the fray early in the war, but men who had been inducted into military service and compelled to fight and die. Colonel Hale buried as many as three thousand of them before the war ended. "So many of them I knew," he remembers.

Burial of the dead in temporary cemeteries was one of the main functions of an army combat chaplain in World War II. Capt. Russell Cartwright Stroup, an army combat chaplain in the Pacific, wrote to his family in 1944 of the many interments he presided over. The letters were collected in a memoir, *Letters from the Pacific: A Combat Chaplain in World War II.*[1] "Much of my time the past few days has been spent in a little field of white crosses beside the sea where the rows of graves have been growing as the bitter harvest is reaped. . . . It's heartbreaking business." Captain Stroup described how the bodies were brought to the cemetery on litters "tenderly wrapped in blankets, sometimes carried by details, sometimes carried by their dearest friends." He remembered one young soldier who drove up and down the road looking for the cemetery with his best friend dead in the jeep with him. "He drove like a man who was drunk, for the tears blinded his eyes."

Captain Stroup sometimes helped dig the graves and assisted in caring for the bodies, "and as often as I could, I have helped lower them into the graves, or to carry them to the graves, because I like to do that service for

[1]Letters from the Pacific is distributed at creeksidepress.com.

such men. It is a proud privilege. I am an honored pallbearer, as well as a priest."

Afterward Captain Stroup sorted through the dead men's personal effects. "It's not an easy thing to hold in your hand the smiling pictures of a sweet-faced mother, knowing that soon the word will come to her which above all she dreads to hear."

Both Captain Stroup and Colonel Hale wrote condolence letters to the families. Hale personalized them and related how each man had died, where he had died, and buddies who were with him. "I had a system whereby I knew how each man had been killed and gave his family the broadest type of information I could give them." It was a sorrowful task, but his letters brought the families closer to their sons, brothers, and husbands in their last moments and gave the families some sense that their dead had been well cared for by a chaplain. To the mother of one soldier killed in action, 2nd Lt. George Oertel Jr., Colonel Hale wrote: "He was a platoon leader of one of our weapons platoons and was moving his machine guns into position on the afternoon of that day. As he was leading his men around a building, an enemy shell scored a direct hit on the side of the building and he was killed instantly by shell fragments."

One mother wrote to thank the chaplain for his letter telling her of her son's burial. "Words can never express my gratitude to you for writing. I am so thankful that my son had a Christian burial. Even the smallest details mean all the world to me. . . . May God bless you and reward you according to His riches in glory. . . . I'd love to see that grave by the sea where my boy is sleeping now. My husband passed away in July 1943, and I have only one other son, a twin of Bernie's, also in the service. My heart is bleeding and broken, but I know God doeth all things well."

Another responded, "It means so much to know that my husband's body was found and properly laid to rest. Since the War Department notified me of his death, I've been tortured by visions of his body lying neglected under the sun."

In burial ceremonies Colonel Hale tried to restore some dignity to each man before he was committed like a stone to the earth to become part of the muck in which he had died. It was a Herculean task that brought mostly pathos.

> I immediately scanned the cold, cruel hunk of rock that raised its boasting head over the U.S. Military Cemetery, and I felt the driving wind pulling at my parka and peeking into my good old "long handles." Here they came with a body. Four Italian soldiers, one on each corner of a litter, staggering through the mud and mire trying to walk reverently, but almost deterred from their purpose by the slippery, heavy mud and dead weight of their precious cargo.
>
> Oh God, how precious! "An American soldier saying good-bye to a world, dressed in a shroud," as the Army called it, but actually no more than a cotton sack tied at the top. Everyone was "dressed" that way— generals, colonels, lieutenants, sergeants, and privates. That was the way a "combat soldier" went through.

Colonel Hale had heard of a few "high rankers" who were buried in makeshift coffins. But he would never allow himself to be buried that way in a combat zone where soldiers were dying every day. "I'd hate to try to explain to the dead all around me why I was different."

But how does a chaplain, or any man of faith, rationalize the daily killing in war? Colonel Hale believes that all the men who died in World War II gave their lives for a noble and higher purpose. "Hitler was such a problem that if he had not been conquered, this world would have been a heck of a lot different for all of us. Theologians talk about a just war and I believe World War II was a just war."

Colonel Hale also believed that the soldiers who died recognized this higher purpose and realized how important their mission was. "The men I knew who fought well were the husbands and the men who had a good home life and a good home to go back to and who wanted to keep it that way even if they lost their lives in the process. The sacrifice was justified, generally."

Captain Stroup was less certain, but he knew that America had little

choice in World War II. "While I believe with all my heart that freedom, de-
cency, and brotherhood are not secured through war, I do believe that their
destruction may be averted by opposing force with force. This seems to be
the only method we have had the wisdom to devise. I feel with all my heart
that this is a time of revolution when the whole world is divided between
antagonistic philosophies of life. Both cannot live in the same world."

Captain Stroup expressed concern that the men who were killed in
World War II died without any sense of the larger purpose of the war. He
had seen this in World War I. "So we accomplished the greatest tragedy of
this war: that men go out to die unsustained by any consciousness of fighting for ideals so great and worthy."

Colonel Hale's belief in the rightness and justice of the cause gave
meaning to the burials he presided over every day.

The quartet moved into the row and staggered into the narrow opening
between the graves. They set the litter down, and with an efficiency betray-
ing long and much practice, they placed the two ropes—one under the
armpits and one under the bend of the knees. Someone bailed water from
the grave. The soldiers tugged at the ropes, lifted the body clear, and let it
swing dizzily, but easily, into the tomb—a grave dug out of rock. There
was no easy digging in these mountains—even foxholes were hard to dig.

I stepped up to the grave with my New Testament, opening it at the
proper place as the soldiers on my left withdrew and folded their muddy,
sticky ropes. All activity became subdued and onlookers removed their
hats—in spite of the rain that had begun to blow through the passes, in
spite of the fact that the temperature was almost freezing. Suddenly, I
could hear the muffled, mountain-stifled booming of our artillery, as I
glanced toward the familiar rows of new graves to the knolls that hemmed
us in. A few days ago we were fighting on this very hill. The hell of crashing mortars, the disciplined condensed rat-a-tat-tat of the machine guns,
the booming, ground-shaking heavy stuff, the spat of the rifle, and the

groans and agony of wounded and dying. With their spilled blood they had made this valley as scared and hallowed as the ground on which Moses met God.

Chaplain Capt. Stroup heard the same dissonance of warfare thousands of miles away in the Pacific and worried that it conditioned the men he knew to an acceptance of violence and death. "A peaceful and helpful Sabbath day was marred a moment ago . . ." Captain Stroup wrote in May 1944, "by the snarling staccato of machine gun fire not far away. I don't like the sound that speaks so eloquently of pain and death. It's hard to get used to being where suffering and slaughter are the commonplace of every day."

As the war raged and men died within yards of his pulpit, Captain Stroup taught peace and understanding to the troops to prevent the brutality of war from hardening their souls. "I preached today on the Sermon on the Mount: 'Ye have heard that it was said by them of old time, Thou shalt not kill; and whosoever shall kill shall be in danger of judgment: But I say to you, That whosoever is angry with his brother without cause shall be in danger of the judgment.'"

Captain Stroup knew it was not an easy message to bring to combat soldiers who must kill or be killed. "But I thought it was needed and I made it as strong as I could. I want desperately that these men shall return home with as few spiritual scars as is possible under the circumstances—for their own sake in the days of peace, and for the future that they must build on a sure foundation. They will be better soldiers if they can hear this message, and certainly better men back home."

Colonel Hale sensed that many American soldiers felt the horror of having to kill and that the majority felt that war was "sinful." He said that most also believed that World War II represented a moment in history when war and killing were justified. To soldiers plagued by doubts about the need for so much killing, Colonel Hale reminded them "that the same Moses who brought down the law, 'Thou shalt not kill,' slew thousands of his own men with a sword when he came down from the holy mountain and found them dancing around the golden calf. . . . Moses could lead his men into combat; Joshua led his soldiers into war; David and most of the rest of the Jewish leaders were combat people, and they glorified in their military victories."

Even as the New Testament taught that we should live peaceably with all men, Colonel Hale pointed out "that at the end of 100 AD there were many Christians in the armed forces and that by 330 AD, Constantine had become a Christian and became the greatest Christian general of all Europe. Peter did not hesitate to take a sword and chop off one of the Roman soldier's ears after all the teaching and the time he had been with Jesus. I feel that 90 percent of all men are basically against war. They are against it in the depth of their hearts, and their mind and their body."

But the cost was unfathomable.

My heart hurt and my lips were so dry I had to moisten them. I was the one who was to say the last good-bye to this man who had died so far from where he had intended to die. I forgot the people as I looked into the grave at the shrouded form. How strong he must have been. There was scarcely room for his broad shoulders. He was tall too—a six-foot regulation grave was almost too short. Only a few days ago he was alive like I am now. He feared, he sang, he prayed, he dreamed. He wanted to go home and he loved his wife like I loved mine. He loved and was loved; he had hopes for tomorrow and yearned for the days he would be out of khaki and ODs. He didn't like war. But all that is finished now. He won't go back. He's dead.

Our Gracious Heavenly Father who made the world and all of us Thy children. Thou who understandeth our frailties, our mistakes, our problems. Wilt thou deal mercifully with this Thy son who has so abruptly come to Thee? Give him the best that Thy justice and mercy can offer and be with us who remain behind, and wilt Thou especially bless his loved ones who will be so saddened when they hear of his passing. Give them strength and courage to carry on. Give them wisdom and faith to live purposefully and sacrificially. They have given so much to their country but let all of us be content to give even more. In the name of our Savior who taught us thus to pray, we ask these things. Amen.

For Colonel Hale, however, the torments and pains of earthly life had their own reward. These dead spoke to the chaplain.

I finished the prayer and slowly opened my eyes. There was the mud, and the cold and the war, but there was the chorus of the men I had thought dead. "Chaplain, we have carried the torch this far. None of us were ready to cash in our chips but here we are. Few of us were gallantly patriotic, but we did love America.

We loved our homes and our way of life, and deep down we would rather have this than the slavery the enemy would have imposed upon us and our loved ones. We have done all we can. Here's the torch; we give to all who can bear it. May you never forget our beckoning and may you and America succeed where we and other tens of thousands have failed.

That happened a long time ago, Colonel Hale said, but he says the dead still speak to him.

I can still see the rows and lines of graves. I see the strained but jovial faces of these men as they lived and I see their shrouded forms as they lay dead. I never looked at a dead man's front or back that I did not put myself in his place. I thought about his unborn children, his unrealized hopes, and his earthly unfulfillment. He wanted to go home.

1 8

Identifying the Dead

W here was Red Franks? Was he dead? Could a graves registration unit have retrieved his unidentified body?

At the end of World War II, the remains of as many as 18,641 of the approximately 325,000 recovered American dead were unidentified either because they were too badly disfigured and decomposed or because dog tags and personal papers had been lost. The War Department was determined to identify as many of these unknowns as possible, and once the task of retrieving the dead from worldwide battlefields had been accomplished, identification of unknown remains became a major priority of the recovery program. The job was painstaking and began as the war ended and by 1947 required a force of more than eight thousand servicemen.

Even if Red were among the unknown dead, Dr. Franks faced another uncertainty. If his son's body were found, Dr. Franks might never be sure that the remains that came home were really those of Red. This was a dilemma faced by every American family who experienced loss during World War II as sons, brothers, and husbands came home in flag-draped caskets. The issue of identity troubled many families in every war of the twentieth century until DNA identifying techniques were employed.

Alita Howard was uncertain that the man whose body was returned to her in 1947 was her husband Cory. Most families accepted the military's conclusions as to the identity of remains. Some did not. The military honor guards that accompanied each casket during burials in the United States were expected to prevent families from opening the coffins. David Naugher, who returned to Pontotoc, Mississippi, after serving as an infantryman with the Fifth Division in the European theater, was a member of one such VFW honor guard that attended the burials of returned Pontotoc County war dead. On several occasions the men forcibly prevented relatives from opening the caskets.

Families would not have found much had they viewed the bodies. Most were little more than skeletal remains, maybe with the residue of some rotted flesh. For a family member to identify the remains would have been difficult, if not impossible, and would have been further traumatizing. Alita, however, asked her brother to secretly open Cory's casket. He said her husband's facial features were preserved, his hair turned white, and his legs missing while his body smelled of what was believed to be formaldehyde. But there was no question that the man buried in Spokane, Washington, was Lt. Col. Clarence Howard.

Hazel Minium wondered for more than a half century if the remains she buried in Tower City, Pennsylvania, in 1947, were those of her husband, Daniel, who had been killed in France in 1944. She had received his ring and identity bracelet after his burial, leading Hazel to believe that she buried another soldier. An accompanying member of the honor guard tried to assuage her fears by saying that regardless of who it was, she was burying one of America's honored war dead. What upset her most, however, was the fear that the man in the casket was a German soldier whose body somehow had gotten mixed up with the remains of American dead.

The military was aware of family concerns and understood that identification had to be 100 percent accurate. "The capital importance of this obligation was recognized at the outbreak of hostilities by adding the

Memorial Division . . . to process all burial reports of unknown dead and conduct such investigations as might be suggested by fingerprints, tooth charts, and personal effects," the Army reported. But no matter how hard the Army worked, it could never completely convince skeptical relatives.

Mistakes were made and while most were remedied, it would have been impossible to correct every one. There was at least one case of a tragic mix-up of bodies being shipped home for reburial. A crew member on the *Joseph V. Connolly* witnessed an accident that occurred while loading casketed remains of American merchant seamen in Reykjavik, Iceland, where the bodies had been temporarily interred during the war. A cargo sling snapped as it was being raised to convey the bodies into the ship's hold and dropped six coffins onto the pier below. They broke apart and the bodies were scattered on the pier and some fell into the water. No one knew which set of remains went where. The bodies were collected and placed back in new coffins, and everyone who witnessed the event was sworn to secrecy. Six families in the United States undoubtedly received a body marked as a son or husband who was neither.

"I can talk about that mishap today," the seaman said. "We were told to keep it a secret, but they can't do anything to me now."

The military often went to extraordinary lengths to identify the remains of fallen soldiers in an era before DNA testing made identification a virtual certainty. In one case, the Army found itself with a body marked "X-43," buried in Marigney, France. It had arrived at the cemetery with a medical tag marked, "KIA [killed in action], 8 –2, A. Co., 18th Inf., Driver, Herman Rosen."

The Army was uncertain whether Rosen was the deceased or the soldier who delivered the body to the cemetery, and graves registration personnel needed to resolve the issue before it could begin the process of identification. It set out to find Herman Rosen and discovered that he had survived the war. Rosen reported that it was he who had delivered the body to the cemetery but said he did not know the identity of the dead soldier. He suggested that the Army look for a Lieutenant Kaspar, who might be able to shed light on the matter. Graves registration investigators located the lieutenant who had been mustered out of the service and was now home in the United States.

Kaspar replied that the unknown body probably was a soldier from the Ninetieth Division who was with two other infantrymen on a reconnaissance mission when he was killed. Kaspar and Rosen had encountered the three on a road in Normandy, and all five men had taken cover together during an artillery barrage. Shell fire killed one of the men in the reconnaissance team, and Rosen later drove the body to the cemetery.

Graves registration investigators wrote another letter to Rosen, who replied that after the war his father had received a ring from the Army Effects Bureau in Kansas City, Missouri, because the Army believed his son, Herman Rosen, was X-43. Herman reported that the ring wasn't his and suggested that it may have belonged to the unknown soldier. He sent the ring to investigators who sent it to the FBI for further examination. The FBI discovered that the inside of the ring was engraved with the inscription, "SVHS, Spring Valley, 1944, D.T." Investigators believed the initials D.T. were probably those of a woman and located the ring manufacturer, the Josten Manufacturing Co. of Owatonna, Minnesota. Josten checked its files and found that the initials D.T. referred to Dorothy Thomas and that more information might be obtained by contacting the principal of the Spring Valley High School in Spring Valley, Wisconsin.

After writing to the high school principal, the Army finally obtained the information that it needed to identify the body. The principal reported that Dorothy Thomas had given her class ring to Don Peters, a soldier who served in the Ninetieth Division. Peters had been in Normandy at the time of X-43's death and was reported killed on August 2, 1944, which matched the date on the medical tag that accompanied the body. Peters also was from Spring Valley, Wisconsin. The matter was closed.

In another case, investigators had the partial remains of what they believed to be two soldiers. All that graves registration personnel could find of Lt. Walter B. Bidlack, who served with the 112th Engineer Combat Battalion when he was killed on D-day, June 6, 1944, was a left foot; the Army did not know what happened to the rest of his body. Another unidentified grave contained the body of a soldier marked with the name of Frank Nawakas. Investigators discovered, however, that Nawakas was still alive and had been discharged from the Army. They disinterred the body that was supposed to be Frank Nawakas and found that it was missing a left foot. The foot in Lieutenant Bidlack's grave matched the footless body, and Lieutenant Bidlack was finally laid to rest in his entirety, and his body remains in the Normandy American Cemetery in France.

Even the most thorough investigations, however, sometimes failed to convince families of the accuracy of the identification process. One woman whose son was reported killed near Hagenau, France, in December 1944 was certain that a soldier that she saw in a newspaper photograph of POWs released in Germany at the end of the war in April 1945 was her son. The image was fuzzy, the men's heads had been shaved, and they were emaciated from starvation and illness. But Mrs. Udya Podoloff of New Haven, Connecticut, was convinced that the "heavy browed youth," shown in an upper bunk, was Stephan Lautenbach, her son from a previous marriage. The Army was equally certain that the young man in the photo could not be Stephan because his body had been recovered immediately after his death with his dog tags. Graves registration personnel had also retrieved letters from his family in his pockets along with a fountain pen Mrs. Podoloff had given him.

Because of her persistence, however, the War Department reopened the case. Mrs. Podoloff traveled to France to identify the body that was twice exhumed. When she was shown the body, she claimed the young man in the grave was two and three-quarters inches taller than her son, his hair was too dark, and a dental filling was of "foreign origin."

The Army attempted to persuade Mrs. Podoloff that the height of a cadaver can change as much as two inches after death and that human hair frequently becomes darker. Furthermore, the Army was convinced the young man was Stephan Lautenbach because his dental chart was a perfect match with that of the body. The odds against a mistaken dental match, the Army stated, was 24,000,000,000,000,000,000,000,000,000 (an octillion) to one. The Army also took testimony from a sergeant in Lautenbach's unit who said he had seen Lautenbach killed on December 3, 1944, by a burst of German machine gun fire. Military authorities also located the POW who testified that it was he in the upper bunk in the prison hospital.

The Army considered the case closed. But Mrs. Podoloff did not. She claimed the Army had pressured the sergeant into testifying that he had witnessed Lautenbach's death, and she hired a lawyer to pursue her case and to find her son. The man whom the Army claims to be Pfc. Stephan C. Lautenbach, 314th Infantry Regiment, Seventy-Ninth Division, never came home from World War II. He was buried in the permanent Lorraine American Cemetery in Saint Avold, France.

As the efforts to identify the unknowns continued, the Army continuously improved its laboratory and investigating methods. It soon found that it needed better trained and more experienced analysts operating in the field with graves registration teams, particularly specialists in anatomy.

In 1946 the army called on Dr. Harry L. Shapiro, chairman and curator of physical anthropology at the American Museum of Natural History in New York, to study and recommend more advanced procedures and anatomical techniques in the identification process. Dr. Shapiro immediately recommended the creation of a central identification laboratory where the unknowns were to be sent. The recommendation was implemented, and the lab performed so well that two similar central labs were established in the Pacific, one located in Hawaii and the other in Manila in the Philippines, to process unknown dead from the Pacific war.

Dr. Shapiro also suggested that a greater range of lab specialists be employed, including a director, he recommended, who should be a physical anthropologist "with broad background and a high scientific attainment, familiar with various techniques that might aid in problems of identification, particularly the study of skeletal remains." Beneath a director would be a group of highly trained assistants and technicians. Among the assistants brought in was John Aievoli, a detective in the New York police department, who was experienced in the procedures and techniques of identifying murder victims.

The processing at the central lab in Strasbourg, France, began when a set of remains was laid out on a table where four technicians closely examined the body. They removed all clothing and equipment for analysis and looked for identifying clues such as laundry marks, clothing size, and name tags. They also made certain that the deceased was not clad in an enemy uniform.

The body was washed and examined and searched again, particularly the chest cavity and the abdomen; the team was looking for artifacts such as embedded dog tags. The remains were studied for gross abnormalities and surgical or accident scars. Finally, the team made a tooth chart and took fingerprints, if possible. Personal effects that were found on or with the body were also scrutinized. These frequently included letters or fragments of letters, rings, pens, watches, lockets, and bracelets, all of which were later sent to various specialists who examined them further.

An anatomical chart was drafted showing all the missing pieces of the body, and the height of the individual was estimated. If the skull was present, it was measured to determine age and race.

The body was then wrapped in a clean sheet and blanket and placed in a casket with the head resting on a pillow. If the identity of the body was still unknown, the letter X marked the casket. The final step came when the casket was removed to a shipping room and draped with the American flag.

The central lab prided itself on its accomplishments. Shortly after opening in August 1946, the lab received a shipment of forty unknown dead that had been previously interred at the Saint Avold cemetery in France. Various field teams had been unable to establish the identity of any of the men. The central lab was able to name eight of the soldiers while uncovering "substantial clues," about the possible identity of twenty others.

The lab operated at Strasbourg until the spring of 1947 when its functions were divided and removed to new sites. The section involved in analysis of personal effects and artifacts found with the remains was relocated to Fountainebleau, France, just outside Paris. The morgue section, which worked with the bodies, was transferred to the Neuville-en-Condroz Cemetery in Belgium.

Beginning in 1947, the Army sent sixteen hundred remains of unknown American servicemen from all over Europe to Neuville-en-Condroz, where they were processed. Central lab teams identified 348 of the men; 206 were "believed to be identified," 943 "possessed clues," and 103 had no clues. Those who remained unknown were buried in a special section at Neuville-en-Condroz, which later was renamed the Ardennes American Cemetery.

1 9

Missing in Action

At the end of World War II, Red Franks was among the ranks of an estimated ninety thousand American soldiers missing in action. Among these men were the 18,641 unknown dead whose bodies had been recovered but who remained unidentified as of early 1946. The rest were soldiers who had vanished during the war and their bodies were lost or unrecoverable.

Most of the missing went down with their ships or were in aircraft that crashed in remote jungles and into inaccessible mountain ranges, or they were lost over vast deserts. Many disappeared on open battlefields where their bodies were shattered and blown apart by the effects of modern munitions. Like Red, they went missing on or over crowded battlegrounds where thousands of men were engaged in combat. To this day, 78,000 are still missing, and among this number are some eight thousand whose remains were recovered but who are still "known but to God." The only identity all these men carry today is their name recorded on the lengthy roles of honor for the missing in American cemeteries around the world.

In light of today's focus on the nineteen hundred MIAs—missing in action—from the Viet Nam War, and about eighty-one hundred Americans still unaccounted for from the Korean War, it is difficult to comprehend why there is no similar outcry to recover the remains of the thousands still missing from World War II. But few Americans are aware of this vast army, and many are shocked to learn of the numbers.

Recovery efforts for the MIAs of Viet Nam and Korea have strong emotional and political backing, and the Department of Defense (DOD) is engaged in an active search program for the missing from these two wars. The Defense Prisoner of War/Missing Personnel Office has developed a detailed file on each missing man from Korea and Viet Nam to assist in finding his remains. Each file includes relevant information such as the serviceman's unit, when he was last seen, and whether he was believed to have been a prisoner of war. Search teams are regularly sent to Viet Nam and to North Korea to seek and locate remains, and the bodies of scores of men have been found and returned home for burial.

The missing from World War II, however, are all but forgotten. The DOD does not maintain individual files containing information that might lead to their recovery, and there is no ongoing program to seek and locate their remains. Recovery teams are sent to retrieve the bodies of World War II soldiers only when they are accidentally found. The government has neither the funding nor the manpower to maintain an active program for so many missing men. There is little chance that their remains will ever be found.

At one time, however, recovery efforts to find the missing from World War II were as extensive and as relentless as those conducted today for the Viet Nam MIAs. In the months immediately following the war, there was little distinction between retrieving the dead and the missing. By 1946, however, the search for American soldiers was a search for MIAs similar to today's mission to recover the missing from Viet Nam.

The search began even as World War II was being fought. Walter Stuart recalls searching for a B-24 in 1943 after the plane disappeared over the Libyan Desert following a bombing mission over Sicily. Stuart and his crew spent two days in *Utah Man* crisscrossing vast expanses of the Sahara until they spotted six of the lost plane's crew 350 miles southwest of Benghazi. They dropped water and alerted rescue teams that traveled overland in vehicles to pick up the downed flyers. Stuart believes some members of the crew were never found and their bodies remain unburied in the Libyan Desert.

Once the war ended, the military conducted an intensive, worldwide search program to find and identify as many MIAs as possible. The effort continued until 1951 when graves registration teams had exhausted every effort to find the missing.

As search teams scoured the countryside around Ploeşti, similar operations were conducted in remote locations all over the world, in the Philippines, on Halmaheras, in Indonesia, and in New Guinea until 1950. Teams traveled to the far provinces of China and to the barren islands such as Attu in the Alutians. Even on accessible islands like Okinawa, searches continued long after the war ended because some areas had not been completely cleared of mines and explosives.

Teams followed every lead. In one case they hacked their way through thick jungle on the island of Guam to locate the suspected remains of a missing American soldier. They found instead the bones of Brownie, a dog still bearing its name tag.

In another case a team followed up on a report from villagers on a battle-scarred Pacific island that an American soldier was buried high in the island's hills in a grave marked by a cross. Searchers crawled and struggled up to the site over sharp coral and found the inscribed cross: "Latrine, closed 1944."

In the summer of 1946 a team acted on reports from Chinese farmers that barbarous tribesmen were holding American airmen as slave laborers in western China. Monsignor Stanilas Baudry, the bishop of Hsichang, passed the information on to the American ambassador to China.

Searchers established a base camp in Hsichang in the area where the airmen were believed held prisoner. Leaflets about the missing airmen were published and circulated among the surrounding villages in hopes that some of the local people might come forward with pertinent information. Efforts to dispatch the team into the area were thwarted, however, by provincial authorities who were split by factional differences.

Finally two members of the team, Sgt. John C. Fox and Capt. Edward E. McAllister, disguised themselves as traders and entered the area. Instead of finding a fierce, warlike tribe, they found friendly people. The tribesmen welcomed the Americans and Fox and McAllister eventually concluded that the rumors were without foundation.

Other search parties operated around Hsichang to locate the many U.S. planes that had been lost there, and they found the graves of several American flyers. Another team moved into the rugged terrain northwest of Chengdu to look for remains but was forced to withdraw when ambushed by bandits.

One of the most celebrated search missions came fifteen years after the war during the hunt for the crewmen of the B-24 bomber, *Lady Be Good*, which disappeared after a bombing mission over Italy in April 1943. *Lady Be Good* was assigned to the 376th Bomb Group, the same Liberandos that led the Tidal Wave attack on Ploeşti four months later. She took off from an airfield near Benghazi to bomb Naples, and reports from accompanying planes indicated that she turned back to base about thirty minutes before reaching the target, possibly because of engine failure. *Lady Be Good* was never heard from again.

Immediately following the war, aerial search operations were conducted throughout the Mediterranean region to locate missing planes, including *Lady Be Good*, but she was never found. The Air Corps assumed that she had crashed into the sea on the return flight from Naples. In 1959, however, an oil-prospecting team flying over the Libyan Desert spotted the remains of a World War II B-24 that turned out to be *Lady Be Good*. Her crew had bailed out and the plane crash-landed.

The Air Force mounted a massive operation in 1960 to retrieve the bodies, and one by one, the *Lady Be Good*'s crewmen were recovered as searchers followed their paths northward towards the sea from the spot where the plane crashed. The men had bailed out over the Sahara several hundred miles from the coast and died of thirst and exhaustion on their trek to the sea. The bodies of all but one crewman were found in the desert sands.

The military reconstructed the final hours of the plane's last mission and surmised that in the dark *Lady Be Good* made a navigational error when she reached the North African coastline near Benghazi. Her crew believed she was still over the Mediterranean Sea. After the men bailed out, the plane continued its flight overland until it ran out of gas. Miraculously, the bomber came in for a near perfect crash landing with no one at the controls.

Today, when the remains of lost World War II aircraft are located, the military mounts similar expeditions to retrieve the bodies of crew members. One such effort began in 1987 when European tourists trekking over a mountain range in Mandang Province, New Guinea, observed the tail of a World War II bomber in the underbrush. The sighting, along with a serial number on the tail of the aircraft, was reported back to the army's Central Identification Laboratory in Hawaii (CILHI). The serial number matched that of the B-24D Liberator bomber, *Ready Willing and Able,* which disappeared in a thunderstorm on March 5, 1944, over Papua New Guinea. The plane, piloted by Lt. Raymond J. Dremelow of Waterloo, Iowa, and its crew of ten men had taken off on a bombing mission from an airfield at Nadzab. The bomber never reached its target and was later believed to have crashed into a mountainside. *Ready Willing and Able* remained unaccounted for, and the crewmen were declared dead on January 25, 1946.

After the war the Air Corps conducted searches over New Guinea to locate the several hundred military planes that had gone down over the island during the war. *Ready Willing and Able* was on the list of missing aircraft, but the plane was never found. The jungles of New Guinea are so thick that they immediately consume a crash site, and planes are discovered only by chance by passing hikers or native tribesmen.

CILHI dispatched three teams between 1989 and 1990 to investigate and to recover the remains of the airmen, which were shipped to Hawaii. Eventually DNA testing confirmed the identity of each crew member. One officer, 2nd Lt. Edward Sparks, twenty-seven, of Alton, Kansas, was buried separately, while the fragmented remains of the other men were buried together in a common grave at Arlington National Cemetery in Virginia.

CILHI is the descendent of the military's identification laboratories established at the end of World War II. These labs eventually were closed but were reopened during the Korean and Viet Nam wars. Following the Viet Nam conflict, the labs were consolidated in Hawaii at CILHI, where it has operated ever since, charged with identifying the remains of American dead from all previous wars, as well as victims of recent disasters, including the destruction of the World Trade Center. In the past decade the importance and workload of CILHI has increased dramatically, and its staff has grown from forty in 1992 to a force of 247 today that includes personnel from the Army, Navy, Air Force, and Marines and civilians.

The recovery of remains is as painstaking and time consuming today as it was after World War II, and CILHI maintains eighteen teams to retrieve the bodies of missing Americans. A typical team consists of between ten and fourteen specialists who are anthropologists, photographers, explosives experts, medics, morticians, linguists, and radio operators.

Discoveries of remains of World War II servicemen, mostly flyers, occur every year. In January 2001, a French farmer installing a drainage system in a field near the town of Longueville, 155 miles northeast of Paris, uncovered the wreckage of an American P-51 Mustang fighter that crashed in boggy ground on January 15, 1945. Still inside the cockpit were the remains of pilot Lt. William Wyatt Patton, twenty-seven, from Stark City, Missouri. Patton was a veteran combat flyer and had entered the Army in 1934 at age sixteen after graduating from high school. He was stationed at Pearl Harbor during the Japanese attack in December 1941 and later earned his wings and flew missions against the Japanese in the Pacific before being transferred to the European theater in 1944. He was flying a scouting mission for Eighth Air Force bombers to check weather conditions over proposed target areas in Germany when he went down. His fighter group initially believed he had experienced mechanical problems and had landed at an airfield behind American lines in France, intending to return to Wormingford, England. Later, the Air Corps surmised he had probably tried to make it back to his home base and had crashed into the English Channel.

Older residents around the crash site in France remembered the wreck, and some even had scavenged metal from the Mustang's tail fin. But the plane was soon covered by soil and forgotten for the next fifty-six years.

Once rediscovered, Patton's remains were returned to the United States, and he was buried with full military honors in the Springfield National Cemetery in Missouri. Patton was awarded the Purple Heart, the Distinguished Flying Cross, the Air Medal, and four Bronze Stars for his actions in Normandy, northern France, the Rhineland, and the Ardennes.

In another operation, a CILHI team searched Butaritari, a western Pacific island, formerly Makin atoll, to retrieve the remains of nineteen missing marines killed during a raid on the Japanese-held island in August 1942. The marines were members of the Second Raider Battalion, organized and trained to conduct commando and guerrilla-style attacks behind enemy lines. Lt. Col. Evans Carlson commanded the unit, and Maj. James Roosevelt, son of President Franklin D. Roosevelt, was his deputy. Sgt. Clyde Thomason, whose remains were among those recovered, was the first enlisted marine to earn the Medal of Honor in World War II. During the two-day battle, the raiders killed an estimated eighty-three Japanese soldiers, but their attempts to leave the island were impeded by high surf, and they were unable to evacuate the bodies of dead comrades.

The CILHI team at first tried to locate the bodies with a magnetometer that detects anomalies in the earth's magnetic field. When modern technology failed, they reverted to the old-fashioned technique of interviewing the local inhabitants. An elderly man, who was sixteen at the time of the raid and who had helped Japanese troops bury the marines, led the searchers directly to the grave site.

The CILHI team began the retrieval process like archeologists in an ancient ruin, digging one-meter wide trenches in the burial site and sifting the coral, sand, and dirt that was removed. The screening process is designed to find body parts and artifacts such as pieces of uniform and equipment that might help identify the men. When the bodies were finally exposed, they were slowly removed to keep the remains intact. The bodies were flown to the CILHI labs in Hawaii to establish their identities.

CILHI maintains the largest group of forensic anthropologists in the world and employs more than thirty anthropologists and four forensic odontologists. While DNA is considered "an invaluable tool," dental X-ray comparisons continue to be the standard method of identification.

The anthropologists work "blind" when identifying remains and have no knowledge of the physical characteristics or even the number of individuals believed to be involved in a case. They develop a biological profile that includes the number of individuals represented, their age, race, sex, muscularity, height, indication of injuries before and after death, and any characteristic abnormalities prior to death. Once a profile is established, it is compared with known, recorded characteristics of a missing individual or individuals supplied by the Casualty Data Analysis Section. DNA analysis is often used as a final determinate.

CILHI isn't the only group involved in the search for the World War II missing. MIA Hunters, a private Minnesota-based group led by Bryan Moon, a former Northwest Airlines vice president, actively searches for missing American servicemen from World War II. Moon's group recently discovered the body of Lt. Theodore Thompson, a Minnesotan missing for fifty-eight years, in the cemetery of a small Sicilian town. MIA Hunters began the search at the request of Lieutenant Thompson's family and located the grave by speaking to elderly Sicilians who remembered the crash and the burial. One woman identified Lieutenant Thompson from photographs, and the caretaker of the village cemetery remembered burying him.

Moon's group also traveled to New Guinea to recover the remains of Lt. Harold Wurtz, Jr., a fighter pilot, and Harriet Gowen, twenty-eight, a Red Cross worker from Stillwater, Minnesota. The pair took off in a P-47 Thunderbolt fighter from the Nadzab airfield in Papua New Guinea on May 12, 1945, and never returned from a joyride. Despite extensive searches by the Air Corps, neither the plane nor the couple's remains were found. It was later determined that the fighter had just returned from a combat mission when Lieutenant Wurtz and Ms. Gowen flew off. The plane had not been refueled and ran out of gas.

In a current endeavor, MIA Hunters is searching for a missing navy pilot who bailed out during a dogfight with Japanese planes over the islands of Amami-Ō-shima and Kikai Jima north of Okinawa in the Ryukyu chain. Moon began the search by locating the Japanese pilot, Hayao Fujimoto, who shot down the American on April 3, 1945.

The U.S. Navy had dispatched a rescue team to retrieve the downed American but found an empty dinghy and concluded that he had drowned. Moon, however, developed a different theory based on his experiences growing up in Southampton, England. He watched dogfights between German and RAF fighters over the English Channel during the Battle of Britain in 1940 and noticed that whenever a parachute was seen coming down, rescue boats were sent out to pick up the pilot, regardless of whether he was British or German. Moon believes the Japanese responded likewise and picked up the downed American and took him to Kikai Jima where he probably died in captivity. Moon's team is searching for the flyer's remains on the island.

MIA Hunters locates missing servicemen but turns all identification work over to CILHI. Once Lieutenant Wurtz's identity was established, he was buried at Arlington National Cemetery, and Harriet Gowan was buried in her hometown of Stillwater, Minnesota, in a plot between her mother and father. They had left an empty grave for their daughter in hopes that someday she would come home.

2 0

Kipling and the Lost Children

"We remember and must charge our children to remember," Rudyard Kipling wrote in 1921 of the British dead of World War I. Kipling knew well the need to remember. He lived the same nightmare in World War I as Dr. Franks did in World War II. Kipling's only son, John, disappeared at the Battle of Loos in 1915. Lt. John Kipling was one of scores of thousands of British Empire soldiers, about a quarter of all those killed, who were lost, many without a trace. His story is not unique, but it became notable because of his father's fame and because it represented the plight of so many families on both sides. It also was a story that repeated itself again and again for families around the world a quarter of a century later during World War II.

John Kipling was rejected for service in the British army in 1914 because he was underage and had poor eyesight. He was only seventeen and could have been deferred from military duty. But John was eager to fight for king and country, in part because of his father's strong support of empire and Rudyard's stand against German aggression against Belgium and France.

Rudyard used his influence to obtain a commission for his son in the Irish Guards, an infantry unit in training for the western front. Less than a year later, in 1915, the Guards were deployed to France and immediately went into action at Loos. John courageously led his men in an assault on German positions, ducking machine gun and rifle fire as he advanced on German positions. It was his first, and last, combat action.

Rudyard and his wife Carrie received word soon afterward that John was missing in action. Like Dr. Franks, Rudyard was devastated by the news and refused to accept the government's report that his son was presumed dead. He investigated every piece of evidence relating to his son's fate. He learned that John was last seen wounded in the leg, and the Kiplings believed that their son could still be alive, either in a field hospital somewhere near the front or even in a German POW camp.

The Kiplings traveled to France to interview men who had served with John, they visited hospitals and spoke to soldiers wounded in the fighting near where John was last seen, and they compiled a minute-by-minute chart of his final movements on the battlefield and plotted these on a map. They became convinced that they would find John. Rudyard also used his connections to contact German officials to learn if John were being held prisoner. But these efforts were unfruitful.

As time passed, it became increasingly clear that John had been killed. There were reports that comrades had seen John screaming in pain from a serious head wound near German lines. A member of his unit reported that he had seen John dead with his head covered with blood. Most frustrating of all was that John's body had not been recovered. Like Red Franks twenty-eight years later, John Kipling had vanished on the battlefield.

John's fate remained elusive. Presumably he had been swallowed up between the trenches in the mud of no-man's-land. His disappearance changed Rudyard's life; he was emotionally drained and he aged considerably.

After the war, Rudyard became a member of the Imperial War Graves Commission and visited the battlefields of the western front and in the

Near East to oversee the cemeteries and monuments for the British war dead. In his later years, Kipling transferred his grief to his literature and to his poetry. One of his most quoted epitaphs was written from the perspective of the soldier:

If any question why we died,

Tell them, because our fathers lied.

In another Rudyard wrote:

I have slain none except my Mother. She

(Blessing her slayer) died of grief for me

One of Kipling's more moving poems was "The Children" with its pathetic cry,

These were our children who died for our lands: they were dear in our sight.

We have only the memory left of their home-treasured sayings and laughter.

Neither Alien nor Priest shall decide on it. That's our right.

But who shall return us the children?

Rudyard Kipling died in 1936 never having found his son. Shortly before his death he wrote the short story, "The Gardener," in which he describes how John had likely died. "The next shell uprooted and laid down over the body what had been the foundation of a barn wall so neatly that none but an expert would have guessed that anything unpleasant had happened."

In 1992, seventy-seven years after John Kipling's disappearance, the Commonwealth War Graves Commission announced that it had "succeeded beyond a reasonable doubt" in establishing that John Kipling had been buried in St. Mary's field hospital cemetery at Loos in a grave inscribed as an unknown "Lieutenant of the Great War, Irish Guards." To those who admired Kipling and followed this great tragedy in his life, the discovery of John's body "closed one of the war's most tragic family histories." A new headstone, inscribed with the name of Lt. John Kipling, was placed over the grave.

But the fate of John Kipling still remains in doubt. Some historians claim that there are discrepancies in the new findings and that the body in the grave could not be John Kipling's. They believe the remains showed evidence that they belonged to a first lieutenant while John was a second lieutenant. They also contend that the location of the body when it was retrieved in 1915 does not match the spot where John Kipling was last seen alive. The answer may never be known and the mystery and pain of John Kipling's death lingers on nearly a hundred years after he died in France.

It was Rudyard Kipling who coined the phrase "known but to God," to be used on the headstones of the unidentified soldiers of the empire who died in the Great War. It came from the heart as did his perpetual endowment to have "Last Post," the British equivalent to taps, sounded every evening at Menin Gate, the memorial to the war dead at Ypres, Belgium.

2 1

Raising the Dead

The raising of the American dead after World War II was an epic unique in human history. Never before had a nation mounted such a monumental, worldwide operation to exhume the bodies of its war dead. The U.S. government had returned the dead from the Spanish-American War and from World War I, but the vastness of the U.S. effort after World War II has never been matched. The memorial division of the Quartermaster Corps, which was responsible for the repatriation and final disposition of the dead, had to deal with war-related fatalities of some 406,000 men, and some women, most of whom had been killed or died in military theaters of war overseas.

Prior to exhumation and recovery, the dead had been buried in 454 temporary military cemeteries or in "other registered burial sites" in eighty-six nations on six continents, "and on numerous islands scattered through the seven seas." All the bodies had to be identified, if possible, and removed to larger relocation cemeteries to await a decision about a final resting place for each man. The task was daunting.

Tarawa, an atoll in the Gilbert Islands in the central Pacific, exemplified the problems that graves registration teams encountered when they began to exhume the dead. More than two thousand Americans had died to take the atoll in 1943, and there were forty-three separate burial sites where marines had been interred immediately after the fighting. The majority of the dead were buried on Betio, an island that was the scene of the fiercest fighting at Tarawa.

Graves registration personnel operating throughout the atoll found many marked graves that yielded no bodies, and the landmarks to distinguish one temporary cemetery containing about four hundred graves had been removed. To retrieve the bodies of all the marines who died on Tarawa, search teams had to conduct thorough searches based on intuition supplemented by information supplied by men who had helped bury the dead after the battle.

The effort was made more difficult because many of the dead had been interred hastily during and immediately after the battle with bullets and live grenades still on their bodies. The grenades were particularly hazardous because the handles had rusted away and fell off when the remains were disturbed.

Tarawa was but one battleground among hundreds where recovery operations took place. A reporter for the *New Zealand Observer* wrote a vivid account of another American disinterment operation from the Waikumete Cemetery in Auckland.

"Sweating American soldiers were dragging soggy corpses out of the ooze last week. Thus 113 dead Americans began their last ride to a permanent resting place, following the decision of the U.S. Congress.

"It was a gruesome scene.

"In a tree-lined plot were opened graves. Coffins lay around to receive the decomposed dead. Shovels were rammed into mounds of mud piled besides the holes, and desolate white crosses stuck askew in the ground.

"In dungarees and gum boots, the grave gang worked. They were an average looking crew. . . . There were city men and small-town boys. In green-cloth denims, rubber gloves, and heavy boots, they pried from the sticky earth reluctant bodies, which had lain there for two and three years.

"They were obeying orders.

"The U.S. Congress had spoken. With very natural sentiment, it had ordered the disinterring of American dead overseas. But Congress did not have to do the job. Young men did and not many of them liked it, for this is not the first crop of corpses they have plucked from foreign soil. Nor will it be the last. . . .

"Doubtless, mothers of fallen soldiers will in some way assuage their grief if their sons come back to them. . . . At least, they can place flowers on their graves and feel a closer communion with their loved ones. But it will serve to reopen old wounds."

The same graves registration unit at work in Auckland moved around the South Pacific disinterring the remains of other American dead from their temporary graves. The unit moved to Suva, New Zealand, and then traveled to Samoa to disinter the bodies of 242 Americans and prepare them for shipment to the large national cemetery in Hawaii.

One team operating in New Caledonia in the Pacific retrieved some 557 American dead. Another 243 dead were disinterred on Ulithi atoll in the Caroline Islands, a sprawling naval base during the war. Operations to remove the dead went on all over the vast Pacific all the way to Mainland China. When the job was complete, more than seventy thousand remains of American dead had been disinterred and moved to "centralized, accessible burial places or to mausoleums where they awaited final repatriation or permanent overseas interment."

The situation was somewhat different in Europe. The fighting was not as dispersed over such large distances, and the battlefronts were relatively well defined, and the terrain generally accessible. The bodies of the dead were gathered and transported to large temporary cemeteries where thousands of men were interred. All but one of the temporary burial grounds in Europe became permanent cemeteries after the war.

The United States formally began bringing home the bodies of its dead warriors years after the war ended. The official program was initiated in the European theater on July 27, 1947, at the Henri-Chappelle American Cemetery, eighteen miles from Liége, Belgium, with the exhumation of the bodies for shipment to the United States. Initially, some 6,248 American dead were disinterred, embalmed, casketed, and shipped to the port of Antwerp, where they were to be loaded on the army transport ship *Joseph V. Connolly* for the final voyage to New York. The *Connolly*'s previous mission had been to transport boxed aircraft to various war zones around the world.

The operation revealed problems and deficiencies that had not been anticipated. The army faced a shortage of licensed embalmers, there weren't enough metal caskets because of the postwar civilian demand for automobiles and refrigerators, and the disembarkation port of Antwerp had inadequate storage space for all the casketed remains. Not until the fall of 1947 did the military have enough caskets to bring home all its war dead from overseas. Despite these difficulties the operation proceeded smoothly, and eventually a total of 7,060 remains were disinterred from Henri-Chappelle and shipped home.

The *Connolly* was one of nine vessels that were converted at a cost of more than $1.3 million each to carry the thousands of heavy metal caskets. Five ships plied the Atlantic and four were assigned to the Pacific. Designated a "mortuary ship," the *Connolly* was refitted in Hoboken, New Jersey, where she was reballasted and equipped with special racks to transport the coffins.

Prior to the *Connolly*'s sailing from Antwerp to New York, Belgian and American officials held a solemn ceremony in the Antwerp's Grand Place to memorialize the American dead. The flower-covered, flag-draped casket of an unknown American soldier was placed in the square where Joseph Cardinal van Roey, primate of Belgium, said a blessing over the body as church bells tolled in the nearby Notre Dame Cathedral. Hundreds of Belgians attending the memorial service fell in behind the procession as a caisson bore the casket to a pier on the Scheldt River. The casket was then loaded aboard the *Connolly*, which was strung with flowers from bow to stern. P-47 Thunderbolt fighters flew aloft as the ship steamed slowly down Scheldt, its banks lined with Belgian citizens paying their last respects to the Americans who had died for Belgium's freedom, most in the battles for northwest Europe, including the Aachen campaign and the Battle of the Bulge. There was one woman aboard, an army nurse, who had also died in combat.

Time Magazine noted that when the *Connolly* and the other transport ships carrying the dead arrived in the United States, "every U.S. city and town, almost every crossroads hamlet, would have a fresh reminder of the price of peace."

2 2

Going Home

In April 1945, as the body of President Franklin D. Roosevelt was being carried from his Warm Springs, Georgia, residence back to Washington, DC, to lie in state, navy musician Graham W. Jackson sang the Negro spiritual "Going Home" as Roosevelt's body was transported to a waiting train. The photo of Jackson, a friend of Roosevelt's, playing his accordion with tears streaming down his face, immortalized that moment of national grief.

Goin' home, goin' home, I'm a goin' home;

Quiet-like, some still day, I'm jes' goin' home.

It's not far, jes' close by,

Through an open door;

Work all done, care laid by,

Goin' to fear no more.

For the families of 233,181 American dead, home was where they wanted their sons and husbands to lie in eternal rest after the war. "I plead with you that you bring back our son to us," one woman wrote in a letter to the War Department in 1946. "He is our only son and we feel that his remains should be here so that we can console ourselves with frequent visitations to his grave."

The wife of a navy officer asked that her husband's body be returned so that their daughter would have tangible evidence that she had had a father. Otherwise, she feared he would forever be "a mysterious stranger whom she had never known and to whom she seemed unrelated."

Many soldiers wished to be buried at home if they were killed in battle. Daniel Unger, an infantryman with the Second Division, killed near Saint-Lô, France, on July 13, 1944, told his wife, Hazel, before he left for war that if he were killed, he wanted to be buried in Tower City, Pennsylvania.

The desire of warriors to come home in death is powerful and as old as civilization. Officers in the Roman legions asked that their cremated remains be sent back to Rome if they died in battle. Irish mercenaries, killed in the seventeenth century at the Battle of Fontenoy in France, asked that they be returned to Ireland if they were killed. According to legend, their prayers were answered as their souls return home every spring in the form of the wild geese that descend in migrating flocks on Ireland.

And I heard them say "Home!" and I knew them

For souls of the felled

So wrote Thomas Hardy in his poem, "The Souls of the Slain," about the dead of the Boer war.

The U.S. War Department was aware of the desire of many families to bring home their dead sons from World War II. It surveyed ceremonial and interment practices for war dead, ancient and modern, and found that many cultures had similar traditions. In ancient Greece, "that a Spartan should either return from battle bearing his shield, or be carried home upon it, reveals some sort of system for recovery and identification of the dead. The Athenian democracy achieved similar results with greater refinement of ceremony and deeper expression of feeling."

Thucydides described the procedures by which Athenian warriors were repatriated home for burial during the Peloponnesian War. "It was a custom of their ancestors," Thucydides wrote. The dead were returned to the city and borne to their final resting place in a funeral procession that included an empty bier "for those whose bodies could not be recovered." The dead are laid out "in the public sepulcher in the most beautiful suburb of the city in which those who fall in war are always buried, with the exception of those slain at Marathon, who for their singular and extraordinary valour were interred on the spot where they fell. . . . Such is the manner of the burying, and throughout the whole of the war, whenever the occasion arose, the established custom was observed."

For mothers the return of sons is instinctive. They were not "men," who died gloriously in battle, but mere boys hardly removed from childhood, and their lives were brutally taken from them by old men who prosecuted the war but did not fight. Boys as young as twelve served in the German army near the end of World War II, and Paul Fussell notes in his book, *The Boys' Crusade*, "the [American] army contained numerous illicit seventeen-year-olds, their presence as soldiers more or less regularized by false papers not rigorously inquired into." Fussell added, "Not a few soldiers hopeful of food packages from home specified Animal Crackers."

Erich Remarque weighed in on the subject of "men" in war when Paul Bäumer reflects about his infantry unit comrades. "I glance at my boots. They are big and clumsy, the britches are tucked into them, and standing up one looks well-built and powerful in these great drainpipes. But when we go bathing and strip, suddenly we have slender legs again and slight shoulders. We are no longer soldiers, but little more than boys."

The return of the dead offered families a measure of closure that comes with the rituals of the burial process. Many anthropologists note that the funeral service in all cultures is a ritualized version of the resurrection story; a young man dies in war, is buried, and then lives again. The family finds solace in the notion that their son is at home and at rest and existing in a better world.

Brenda Scalf Birchfield, whose father, Andrew James Scalf, was killed in Germany during World War II, believes the grief she experienced over his loss was greater because her family never went through the funeral process at home during or after the war. The Scalf family decided to have Andrew's remains interred in one of the overseas American cemeteries. "If my dad had been killed in an auto wreck at home, we would have had the funeral and we would all have gone through the grieving process. He would be someplace where we all could visit." Andrew Scalf is buried in the American cemetery at Margraten in the Netherlands.

Not all families asked that their sons and husbands be returned home. Some wished to avoid reliving the trauma and sorrow of death through the funeral and burial. Some were concerned for the future care of their sons and husbands, that once the immediate family was gone there would be no one to visit and care for the grave. They were relieved to know that their sons would be perpetually cared for in an American-administered cemetery overseas. The remains of some 93,342 soldiers who died in World War II are interred in these cemeteries alongside fallen comrades.

The parents of four sons, all killed in the war, explained to the War Department why they wanted the brothers buried overseas. In a letter to the War Department they wrote, "And now that the firing is over and quiet prevails in the valley and around our home, we have time to meditate over what has happened in the different battlefields and why our losses should be fourfold. However, we take consolation in the fact that our boys were brave and good servicemen, they were also fine sons, and . . . we are doing as well as anyone could be expected to do when such a catastrophe comes into the lives of a father and mother. . . . It is not our desire that our four sons shall be brought back to us for reburial. It is our sincere desire to visit the sacred spot where our boys are now resting and as we hope in peace unmolested."

"I feel soldiers should stay where they fell," said Gen. George S. Patton's widow, Beatrice. General Patton, who died as the result of an auto accident in December 1945, was buried in the Luxembourg American Cemetery and

Memorial amongst the graves of many of the soldiers he had commanded during the war.

Some families were divided in their opinions about the value and need to return a fallen member. "The cemeteries overseas are beautiful and it would have been good for my brother Hugh to remain with his comrades," Kenneth Mooney said. But Mooney's mother wanted her son brought home and buried in their hometown in New Jersey.

Various groups opposed the return of the dead to America after the war on religious and humanitarian grounds. The War Department was initially reluctant to bring back the dead because of the magnitude of the undertaking, but military officials recognized that it was virtually ordained by precedent established after the Civil War and followed during the Spanish-American War and World War I. In the report, *Final Disposition of World War II Dead*, the War Department concluded, "Although cold, practical logic may have dictated the choice of leaving the dead overseas in the beautiful, well-kept cemeteries of Europe and elsewhere, the sentimental desire of next of kin to have the earthly remains of their loved ones near them generally prevailed in post–World War II years, just as it had after World War I."

The Social Service Commission of the Protestant Episcopal Church in the Diocese of New York objected to repatriation because "its overemphasis of the mortal body is in conflict with the thoughts of the Christian Church from the days of the Apostles. It represents, initially, a basic misconception of the significance of our rapidly changing bodies, which on earth have been but the vehicle or vestment of immortal spirits. The souls of our war dead, freed from the limitations of the flesh, are even now being confronted with the opportunity to grow in spiritual stature and glory, a fact which our excessive concern over the bodily remains fails to proclaim."

The Episcopal commission also argued that repatriation was a "costly pagan venture." Along with the Department of Social Services of the Episcopal Diocese of Boston, it believed the $200 million price tag for the return of the dead could be better used for the "millions of people suffering and dying from lack of food, clothing, and shelter. . . . [T]he bereaved will, on reflection, conclude that it is more truly Christian for us as a nation to feed the hungry, clothe the naked, and administer to the living, than to yield to the natural desire to try to have the bodies of our beloved dead brought home." Despite the objections, the desire of the majority of Americans who suffered loss was to bring the remains of loved ones home, and their wishes prevailed.

For many, however, including Dr. Franks, there could be no return of the dead, no funeral, and no finality because their sons were missing in action or their remains could not be identified. A family's fear for a missing son, both real and irrational, was that he was condemned to wander restlessly either in this life or in an afterlife.

Millions of families in the warring nations of the twentieth century were traumatized because so many of their sons were missing and they had no grave site over which to mourn. Their dead could not be brought home. The bodies of some 361,650 out of 1,359,000 French soldiers killed in World War I were never recovered, and hundreds of thousands of young men from other nations also were unidentified or lost in battle.

In consequence, the French government erected monuments to the dead such as the Tomb of the Unknown Soldier, and it built ossuaries, like the vast structure at Verdun that displays the bones of thousands of French and German dead, piled in visible, random heaps. But monuments and ossuaries cannot replace the human need for a grave. At the inauguration of the Verdun ossuary in 1927, the presiding cleric expressed the sorrow and grief of so many families: "You whom we have seen wandering so many times through this labyrinth of death, in search of a name, the trace of your loved one, calling to him in a sobbing voice, come to the ossuary. Here is the tomb that probably contains some of him."

In contemporary America, families who lost members in the World Trade Center attack on September 11, 2001, sought the bodies of relatives to deal with what Dr. Robert A. Neimeyer, professor of psychology at the University of Memphis, calls the "phenomenon of absence." He notes, "the presence of a body helps to confirm the reality of the loss."

Like Dr. Franks, the 9/11 families grabbed at anything that would reveal the whereabouts of a body, even fragments of a body. "Details that would normally be nightmarish became almost comforting because they might lead to the fulfillment of the burial ritual: that some remains had been found on a rooftop; that workers were sifting for bone fragments on a garbage dump; that the medical examiner's office was preserving 20,000 body parts in refrigerated trucks," wrote *New York Times* reporter Dan Barry.

The need to return the dead home from war is also interwoven with the almost universal belief, held throughout history, that there is no greater glory than death in battle. War dead become mythic heroes whose souls their families and their nations wish to be enshrined at home. The Japanese shrine of Yasukuni Jinja in Tokyo is home to the souls of several million Japanese soldiers who died in national conflicts since 1869. Thus, Japanese war dead are returned home in spirit, if not in body.

In *The Epic of Gilgamesh*, the heroic poem dating back to 2,700 BC, glorious war dead of the Babylonian kingdom are described with reverence. "In this, oldest surviving epic poem, men are shown as already according a particular honorific status to death in war, a form of death which will guarantee them an enduring name, a memorial much to be preferred to any other form of record and achievement in life," writes Jon Davies in *The Christian Warrior in the Twentieth Century*.

Davies adds, "Herodotus describes how Solon regarded the Athenian Tellus as the happiest man who ever lived partly because 'he had a glorious death. In a battle he fought for his countrymen, routed the enemy, and died like a soldier; and the Athenians paid him the high honor of a public funeral on the spot where he fell.'"

In the twelfth-century epic poem, *The Song of Roland*, warriors find salvation through death in combat. "Roland is dead. God has his soul in heaven." And in the fifteenth-century work, *Le Jouvencel* by Jean de Bueils, "God is described as favoring those who make war upon the wicked because 'war is a proper and useful career for young men, for which they are respected by God and man,'" Davies writes.

The equivalents of war dead for early Christians were their martyrs, including Christ, who gave their lives for the faith. "Greater love hath no man than this, that a man lay down his life for his friends," Jesus says in the Book of John. Text from the Gospel of John appears on many war memorials including a plaque at the site of the Battle of Gettysburg: "Rest On Embalmed and Sainted Dead/ Dear As The Blood Ye Gave/ No Impious Footstep Here Shall Tread/ The Herbage Of Your Grave." Davies notes, "These words, and Jesus's words in John 15, attest to the strength of the doctrine of sacrifice in Eurochristian culture."

There are similar themes found in Pericles' funeral oration during the Peloponnesian War around 425 BC, and in President Abraham Lincoln's Gettysburg Address in 1863, more than two thousand years later.

"The whole earth is the tomb of heroic men, and their story is not graven in stone over their clay, but abides everywhere without visible symbol, woven into the stuff of other men's lives," Pericles said in his panegyric for the Athenian dead of the Peloponnesian War. These words were later inscribed on the walls of Edinburgh Castle in eulogies to the Scottish dead of the Great War.

At Gettysburg Lincoln referred to the same world community that "can never forget what they did here." The sacrifices of the Union troops at Gettysburg were equally invisible but gave the nation a new birth of freedom.

As a practical matter throughout history, however, most war dead could not be returned home from far-flung wars and empires. The Romans could not repatriate large numbers of their dead to Rome from Gaul or the Near East. Two millennia later it was British tradition that its fallen soldiers were buried where they fell. The body of Admiral Lord Nelson, victor at the Battle of Trafalgar in 1805, was one exception; his body was pickled in brandy and returned to England for burial. The British Empire was too vast to collect the remains of dead soldiers and return them to Britain. The graves of redcoats dot the American landscape from Boston to Princeton to Virginia where British soldiers are buried from the Revolution. Burial in some far-off land, in fact, became a symbol of the power and breadth of the empire as burial sites sprang up in British colonies around the world. The tradition was immortalized in the war poem of Rupert Brooke, "The Soldier":

If I should die, think only this of me;

That there's some corner of a foreign field

That is forever England.

There were compelling reasons for the British and similar empire builders to leave their soldiers where they fell. Prior to the raising of large conscripted, civilian armies, the ranks of many nations' military forces were filled with mercenaries who were often men with unsavory backgrounds, and there was no outcry for the return of their bodies as heroes. "If you look at the time of Waterloo, soldiers were viewed as one step from criminals," says Peter Francis, with the Commonwealth War Graves Commission in Maidenhead, England, which maintains the graves of about 1.7 million British and Commonwealth soldiers in burial sites around the world. The smallest such site is on Ocracoke Island, North Carolina, which contains the graves of five British seamen who were killed off the coast of the United States in World War II.

The nineteenth century brought radical changes to warfare and the way people viewed their military dead. Nations began drafting massive civilian armies and arming them with far more lethal weapons than had existed before. These civilian soldiers were no longer regarded as society's outcasts; they were the boys next door called to duty often against their will, and when they died in battle, their families expected proper burial and respect from the state. The status of soldiers had changed and, with it, public attitudes about the return of the dead.

During the early days of World War I, British and French families traveled to the battlefields of Belgium and northern France to exhume the bodies of their dead and return them home for burial. In one celebrated case in the British army, the body of Lord Lieutenant Gladstone, the grandson of the former British Prime Minister W.E. Gladstone, was exhumed from the battlefield at the request of powerful and highly placed relatives. The case gained notoriety because ordinary British soldiers had to conduct the exhumation under German fire. The incident served to confirm the belief among many, including General Sir Fabian Ware, founder of the Imperial War Graves Commission, that there should be complete equity in the burial of fallen British soldiers regardless of rank and position.

The British government quickly forbade battlefield exhumations and ruled that no remains of British dead could be returned home from France or from any other British theater of war. All soldiers, regardless of class, were to be interred near the battlefields where they fell. All were to be treated equally in death even if they had not been so treated in life. "It was felt immediately that if you allowed repatriation of remains, you would break that principal of equality because all the wealthy families would have repatriated their sons while the poor stayed in France," says Peter Francis.

As the war progressed, the sheer number of men killed also precluded the repatriation of the dead to Britain. The British Empire lost just under a million men during World War I, and the logistics of returning each body to the homeland would have been next to impossible and would have seriously interrupted the prosecution of the war. To this day the landscape around the old battlefields of the Somme and in Flanders is dotted with British military cemeteries, and the number of headstones staggers the imagination.

After World War I, hundreds of thousands of French families lobbied their government for the return home of their dead sons and husbands. The government refused and decreed that the dead should remain buried on the battlefields where they fell, in part because it believed it more fitting for the dead to rest with comrades. But officials were also sympathetic to the many families who would have no bodies to bury, and the ban on repatriation was established to be fair to them.

But the French government could not stop the tide of popular sentiment to bring the dead poilus home. Many families circumvented the government ban by hiring grave diggers, and so many bodies were being exhumed that the cemeteries near the old battlefields were in a constant state of chaos.

The French government relented in 1920, and bereaved families were allowed the right to repatriate the dead at state expense. The reburial program ran into problems over identity of the dead and jurisdictional disputes between parents and wives, but by 1923, some 300,000 French soldiers of the 1,359,000 who died were returned to their village cemeteries.

Placed in historical and cultural perspective, the American practice of returning its war dead from overseas, begun after the Spanish-American War, was not unique; it was the magnitude of the efforts after World Wars I and II and the distances involved that made them stand out. One British writer, Stephen Graham, belittled the American operation to return its war dead from Europe to America after World War I, in ignorance of British and French attitudes and policy. In his book, *The Challenge of the Dead,* he wrote,

> At Calais now the boxes are stacked on the quays with the embalmed American dead. At great cost of time and labor the dead soldiers are being removed from the places where they fell and packed in crates for transport to America. In this way America's sacrifice is lessened. For while in America this is considered to be America's own concern, it is certain that it is deplored in Europe. The taking away of the American dead has given the impression of a slur on the honour of lying in France. America removes her dead because of a sweet sentiment towards her own. She takes them from a more honourable resting place to a less honourable one. It is said to be due in part to the commercial enterprise of the American undertakers, but it is more due to the sentiment of mothers and wives and provincial pastors in America. That the transference of the dead across the Atlantic is out of keeping with European sentiment she ignores, or fails to understand. America feels that she is morally superior to Europe. American soil is God's own country and the rest is comparatively unhallowed. To be one in death with Frenchmen, Italians, Negroes, Chinamen, Portuguese does not suit her frame of mind.

The logistical difficulties of repatriation governed American policy for disposing of the dead during World War II. To have contemplated a return policy during the fighting would have been an organizational and logistical nightmare requiring the services of thousands of men who otherwise could be used to fight the war and tying up valuable space on cargo ships taking supplies to and from America.

The repatriation program began as the war ended. Under the terms of Public Law 383 of the Seventy-ninth Congress on May 16, 1946, families could request the return of sons and husbands for burial in a national cemetery in the United States or in a private plot. The family also could request that they remain buried with comrades in overseas cemeteries administered in perpetuity by the American Battle Monuments Commission (ABMC).

Most nations involved in World War II were devastated and financially incapable of such an expensive repatriation operation. Germany, in particular, was unable to retrieve many of her dead, and millions of German soldiers were buried in the Soviet Union and in territory that was soon behind the Iron Curtain. The British maintained their policy of burying their dead where they fell. Even if they had wished, the British probably could have ill afforded to return their dead from far-flung cemeteries.

One Englishman recalled how Great Britain suppressed the story of the repatriation of American war dead from English soil in fear that the British people would demand a similar program. According to a 1982 article in the newspaper, the *Daily Mail*,

> The bodies were dug up, identified, and placed in bronze caskets. They were loaded in a siding at Cambridge Station onto a special train, which was so long and heavily laden that it had to meander on a 200-mile journey to Wales to avoid tight bends and steep gradients. At a special enclosure at Cardiff Docks throughout 1948 and the next spring, America's dead were taken aboard US transport ships for the journey to New York. . . . It was not reported in British newspapers at the time. Confidential Foreign Office and Home Office files, now open to public scrutiny, reveal how Prime Minister Clement Atlee and Foreign Secretary Ernest Bevin were fearful that news of the huge project might leak out. In a 1948 letter, a Foreign Office official, Mr. J. G. Spicer, says, "We must be anxious to avoid giving publicity to the American repatriation operations, as the Imperial War Graves Commission has decided not to adopt

the same policy, and if the American scheme became known, it might have serious repercussions." His colleague, Mr. C. G. Kemball feared indignant complaints to newspapers and members of Parliament from "irate next of kin of British war dead who will ask why American corpses are treated differently from ours."

Even sixty years after the end of World War II, the return of American dead from that conflict goes on as it will probably continue for decades to come as bodies are recovered and brought home for burial. In 1996 the remains of Flight Officer Frank D. Miller, a P-47 fighter pilot, were recovered from the Zuider Zee in Holland. His plane crashed into the water after a mission over Germany in 1943, and twenty-nine-year-old Miller was reported missing.

In 1995, the propeller of a dredging vessel hit Miller's plane resting on the sea floor ten feet down. Divers investigated and found his skeletal remains still in the pilot's seat. Miller's body was returned to his home in Millersburg, Ohio, where he was buried with full military honors by an army honor guard from Fort Knox, Kentucky.

As the honor guard approached the cemetery, Maj. David Deckard, the casualty officer who had organized the ceremony, expressed concern that there would be more press people than mourners in attendance. But as the procession crested a hill overlooking the cemetery, he was surprised. "There, parked along the road to the cemetery, were cars and pickups, Suburbans, and minivans as far as the eye could see."

Frank Miller had finally come home to friends and family, and his nation.

2 3

America's National Cemeteries

It was on a cold, windswept day in January 1951 when Lt. James Schaen finally came home to Sarah six years after World War II. An honor guard accompanied his body to its final place of rest in Arlington National Cemetery. Snow blanketed the ground and obscured the marble headstones that stretched in symmetric rows across the gently rising and dipping landscape. A small group of black-clad mourners contrasted sharply with the tableau of white as they stood before Jim's flag-draped casket on a knoll within sight of the capitol dome in Washington, DC. Sarah and Jim's parents were present as was Jima, Jim's five-year-old daughter whom he had never known, and David Naugher, Sarah's second husband whom she had married in 1948. Sarah had come to Arlington to bury Jim out of obligation and out of love. He was no longer her legally recognized husband, but she was still his wife, and she would not forget the love they had once shared. Jim had once been the promise of her youth, and now all that was left of him were memories and his fragile remains.

Jim was killed October 27, 1944, when his B-24 plunged to earth near Gerstungen, Germany, where he was buried in the village cemetery. After the war Sarah asked that his body be permanently interred in Gerstungen with several comrades from his crew. But it was War Department policy that all the dead be retrieved, identified, and sent to consolidated cemeteries in Europe and the Pacific prior to being sent home or buried permanently overseas. Gerstungen was also in the Soviet sector of Germany and was closed to American families. Sarah selected Arlington as the place where she wanted Jim to be buried.

Jim was given a full military funeral, but Sarah was too upset to remember much of the ceremony. It was simple and short. An army chaplain conducted the service, and as he concluded, a firing party of soldiers delivered the traditional three-volley salute over the grave. A bugler sounded taps, and just before Jim's body was lowered into the grave, members of the honor guard removed the flag from the coffin, folded it, and presented it to Sarah.

"It was a beautiful place, a hillside looking out over the Pentagon," Sarah remembered. "The chaplain said a few words, somebody played taps, and there were gunshots. That's all I remember."

Taps had been sounded many hundreds of thousands of times at Arlington and the other national and overseas cemeteries over the graves of fallen soldiers and veterans of America's wars. The piece was first used a short time after being composed in 1863 at the funeral of a young Union artilleryman, killed in action. The soldier's commanding officer called for a traditional military funeral to include three memorial shots fired over the grave. But because Union and Confederate lines were only a few hundred yards apart, the officer ordered the playing of taps lest the nearby Confederates think the rifle fire presaged a Union infantry assault and order a preemptive counterattack.

After Jim's funeral Sarah returned to her life in Pontotoc, but she never forgot her first husband. Lieutenant Schaen was among the last American soldiers of World War II to be returned for burial in the United States between 1946 and 1951. Thirty-seven thousand dead were interred in one of the many national cemeteries located in thirty-eight states and Puerto Rico, ranging from Arlington to the National Memorial Cemetery of the Pacific and the Honolulu Memorial, commonly known as the Punchbowl, located in the Puowaina Crater in Honolulu.

Arlington National Cemetery is the best known of all the cemeteries on U.S. soil. It was the estate of General Robert E. Lee until the federal government confiscated the Custis Lee mansion and its surrounding grounds during the Civil War. It became a cemetery in May 1864 when the military needed burial space for the growing number of Union army dead. Pvt. William Henry Christman, Sixty-seventh Pennsylvania Infantry, was the first soldier interred in Arlington National Cemetery on May 13, 1864. Through the years Arlington has become America's greatest shrine, not just to the nation's war dead, but to past presidents, generals, diplomats, and honored civilians. It is also the site of the Tomb of the Unknown Soldier.

The Punchbowl is another well-known national cemetery dedicated to America's war dead from World War II, Korea, and Viet Nam. It lies within the crater of an extinct volcano near downtown Honolulu where one has the feeling of remoteness even in the midst of the bustling city. Along the crater's rim the visitor looks out to the city and the calm Pacific beyond. The tombstones all lie flat, which gives the Punchbowl the feel of a quiet, public park. Among the graves of sailors and soldiers are many who were killed during the Pearl Harbor attack on December 7, 1941. Ernie Pyle, America's favorite war correspondent from World War II, is also interred in the Punchbowl.

In all there are 136 national cemeteries in the United States. The U.S. Department of Veterans Affairs administers 120, fourteen are run by the Department of the Interior, and two, including Arlington, are under the jurisdiction of the Army.

After World War II, the majority of Americans who suffered loss chose to bury their dead in private family plots. Across America, in small towns, in cities, and in the countryside, they were buried near their homes to the peel of church bells, the crack of rifle volleys, and the mournful sound of taps. In all, some 141,000 dead were buried in hometown cemeteries.

Alita Howard was among the grieving family members who received Western Union telegrams notifying them that the remains of a husband, son, or brother were coming home. Alita was informed on October 24, 1946:

DEPARTMENT OF THE ARMY WILL DELIVER REMAINS OF LATE LIEU-
TENANT COLONEL CLARENCE A. HOWARD IN NEAR FUTURE. RECORDS OF
THIS OFFICE INDICATE YOU WISH REMAINS ESCORTED TO HAZEN AND
JAEGER FUNERAL HOME NORTH 1306 MONROE STREET SPOKANE, WASH-
INGTON. PLEASE INSTRUCT FUNERAL DIRECTOR TO MAKE ARRANGE-
MENTS TO ACCEPT REMAINS AT RAILROAD STATION UPON ARRIVAL.
PRIOR TO SHIPMENT FUNERAL DIRECTOR WILL BE NOTIFIED OF RAIL
ROUTING AND SCHEDULED TIME REMAINS WILL ARRIVE AT RAILROAD
STATION. REQUEST IMMEDIATE CONFIRMATION OF ABOVE SHIPPING IN-
STRUCTIONS BY TELEGRAM COLLECT TO AUBURN GENERAL DEPOT AT-
TENTION AMERICAN GRAVES REGISTRATION DIVISION AUBURN,
WASHINGTON. IF YOU DESIRE MILITARY HONORS AT FUNERAL YOU
SHOULD ASK LOCAL PATRIOTIC OR VETERANS ORGANIZATION OF YOUR
CHOICE TO MAKE ARRANGEMENTS. NECESSARY YOU INCLUDE NAME OF
DECEASED IN REPLY TELEGRAM.

    VERNON LEWIS LIEUTENANT COLONEL QMC

The procedure for the delivery of the dead was standardized. Once remains were removed from one of the nine mortuary ships, they were transferred to one of 118 special railroad cars that had been converted from hospital cars after the war to funeral coaches. The dead were shipped to major rail transfer centers from which their bodies were rerouted to their hometowns. One such small town was Pontotoc, Mississippi.

David Naugher was a member of a volunteer VFW honor guard that participated in private funerals of the war dead being returned to Pontotoc County, Mississippi. David grew up on the family's cotton farm on the outskirts of town and served as an infantryman in numerous campaigns in Europe where he was wounded in action. His brother, Eldridge Naugher, a captain in the 101st Airborne Division, was killed in Normandy in June 1944, and the family chose to leave his remains overseas to spare David's mother the pain of reliving his death when his body was returned. Eldridge is buried in the Normandy American Cemetery.

The Pontotoc VFW honor guard met the casket at the local funeral home after it had been delivered from the town train depot.

"We had one family determined to open the casket," said Howard Stafford, a member of the Pontotoc guard. "They felt like it was their son or their brother and they wanted to open it. But we'd been through that before and we weren't going to let them. We knew that all that was left was bones and dog tags." It was the custom of many families in Pontotoc to have the funeral and wake at home, and the family was with the coffin night and day until the body was buried.

After the funeral service the honor guard rode with the casket to the cemetery, sometimes miles into the country. "The preachers got long winded and some of those churches were just small tabernacles that had a roof on them and no heat. It was rough during the services with the wind and sleet blowing, but that was part of it," Stafford recalled. Summer wasn't much better because of the oppressive Mississippi heat.

"Some of the ceremonies got pretty touching," Naugher said. "We knew many of the dead, or if we didn't know them, we knew their families." When the service ended, the guard swung into action by firing a rifle salute, and the family was presented with the flag.

In one burial service in Missouri, the bodies of three brothers were returned to their hometown of Hurley on November 4, 1948, for burial in the local cemetery. The soldiers were Sgt. Frank H. Wright, killed during the Battle of the Bulge, Pvt. Harold B. Wright, who died of his wounds in a German POW camp on February 3, 1945, and Pvt. Elton E. Wright, killed in Germany on April 25, 1945, two weeks before the Germans surrendered. Their bodies were forwarded simultaneously from Kansas City to Hurley, where they were met by the local funeral director. The brothers were taken back to the family farm where their father, Henry A. Wright, a stooped, gray-haired widower, asked that the caskets be carried into the bedroom where all three boys had been born. Throughout the day on November 4, friends and neighbors called on the father and laid floral offerings of roses, carnations, and chrysanthemums on the floor in front of the caskets. Mr. Wright was with his two surviving sons and three daughters as the tributes were paid.

A memorial service was held the next day in the high school auditorium, and afterward the funeral procession moved to the Hilltop Cemetery, six miles southwest of Hurley, where interment services were held in a biting wind and under a gray, overcast sky.

An army history noted, "At the close of the ceremony, the flags were removed from the caskets and the escorts stepped forward to present them. Two went to the father and one to the widow of Pvt. Elton E. Wright. The nation and the community of Hurley had done all that could be done."

The VFW provided a standard eulogy for all military funerals that was fashioned after Lincoln's Gettysburg Address. It was read at the burial of Daniel Unger in Tower City, Pennsylvania, and began, "In many places throughout this great land of ours the following tribute is being read over the bodies of returned comrades. . . . We are assembled here today to pay tribute to Daniel Unger, who gave his life in the defense of our country. We say that he has made the supreme sacrifice. . . . We stand here humbly because he has contributed more than we the living to preserve American ideals. It is an honor for us to pay homage to his memory. . . . This man's return in the silence of death speaks far more powerfully than anything we might say. Each of us ought to be deeply influenced by his presence and should long remember this solemn moment."

The families of some 93,245 men who lost their lives in World War II elected to have their remains buried in one of fifteen World War II American military cemeteries overseas, administered by the American Battle Monuments Commission. The most famous of these twenty-four permanent American burial grounds on foreign soil is the Normandy American Cemetery near the town of Colleville-sur-Mer. To many, these places around the world are beautiful monuments to the sacrifices of American soldiers during World War II. The Normandy American Cemetery is located on the site of the temporary American Saint Laurent Cemetery, established by the U.S. First Army on June 8, 1944, the first American burial ground on European soil in World War II. It covers 172 acres and contains the graves of 9,386 Americans, most of whom gave their lives during the landings and ensuing operations of World War II. Within the Memorial from the Gardens of the Missing are inscribed the names of 1,557 missing Americans. Their remains have never been located nor identified.

24

The Empty Grave

First Lieutenant Gilbert B. Hadley came home in the fall of 1946 to be laid to rest three years after *Hadley's Harem* crashed into the Mediterranean Sea off the coast of Turkey as it was returning to Benghazi from Ploeşti. Lieutenant Hadley was trapped in the wreckage and drowned.

"Gib," as he was nicknamed by family and friends, was buried by his family in the Hadley's family cemetery plot in Arkansas City, Kansas, next to his kid brother, Perry, who was killed in a bicycle accident in 1936. A simple headstone marked Gib's grave.

But Gib Hadley came home in spirit only. The funeral brought the Hadleys a measure of closure for the loss of their son in World War II, but it was a small measure. Gib's grave was empty and the burial was purely symbolic since his body was not recovered. The Air Corps listed him as missing in action and presumed dead after military investigators interviewed surviving crew members and determined that Gib almost certainly did not escape from his plane before it sank in about ninety feet of water. By 1946, the family decided that it was time to get on with their lives.

Unlike Dr. Franks, the Hadley family at least knew the approximate location of Gib's final resting place in a watery grave less than a mile from the Turkish coast. Seven members of the crew escaped from the sinking plane and saw it go down with Gib and copilot James Rex Lindsey still on board. The family could visualize the grave site, they could visit the area if they chose, and they could pray for Gib close to where he lay entombed.

Nevertheless, Gib's mother never completely believed that her son died, and she mourned for him until her own death in 1973. A part of her clung to the notion that Gib had somehow gotten out of the plane and that she would someday hear the familiar sound of the door opening, listen for the singular rhythm and beat of his footsteps, and hear his booming, cheerful voice when he burst into the house.

"She was sure Gib would come home," said Bill Hadley, Gib's younger brother.

Gib was an irrepressible young man who grew up to resemble Clark Gable and who swashbuckled through life like Errol Flynn. The oldest of four children, three brothers, and a sister, Gib seemed cut from the pages of an adventure novel. He loved rowdy parties and once threw an all-night poker game at his family's house when his parents were in Kansas City on vacation. He smoked a pipe even as a teenager, dressed impeccably, and wore hand-tied bow ties, pressed shirts with French cuffs, and homburg hats. Bill Hadley has a lasting memory of his mother making Gib's breakfast with one hand while ironing one of his shirts with the other.

In a 1936 photo, taken with his grandmother and his brothers, Gib is shown with his grandmother's cane hooked around his brother Perry's leg, ready to yank it out from under him. The photograph reflected the joker in Gib Hadley. Perry was killed a few months later when a car struck his bicycle.

Gib joined the Air Corps in November 1941 after a stint in junior college in Arkansas City that came to an end when his father could no longer afford the expense of schooling. Gib qualified for pilot training and was stationed near home and buzzed his neighborhood on training flights, first in trainers and later in lumbering bombers. As a full-fledged pilot, Gib took his B-24 crew on harrowing low-level, cross-country flights on which crew members wondered if they would ever live long enough to see combat.

Outrageous behavior came naturally to Gib. He is said to have returned to his hotel room one night in El Paso, Texas, and flopped on the bed, too drunk to rouse himself to turn off the light. Instead, he reached for one of his pearl-handled revolvers and shot it out. The revolvers were Gib's trademark, and he carried them on combat missions, sometimes firing them out the pilot's window at German fighter planes that zipped by. He was also known to wear cowboy boots in place of the heavy fleece-lined ones provided by the Air Corps.

Gib's crew loved him. "There wasn't anything we wouldn't have done for him," said Roy Newton, a nineteen-year-old gunner on *Hadley's Harem*. Gib considered himself an equal among the crew and chewed out any member who saluted him, and he sometimes permitted his men to fly the B-24, contrary to regulations, when they were on training missions.

Gib's devil-may-care attitude attracted the attention of Col. John Kane, leader of the Pyramiders, the bomb group to which *Hadley's Harem* had been assigned in North Africa. Colonel Kane selected Lieutenant Hadley and *Hadley's Harem* to fly into Ploeşti as Kane's wingman because Lieutenant Hadley was a pilot who knew no fear. Flying with Killer Kane was a good omen and brought good luck because the colonel always managed to bring his plane, *Hail Columbia*, back from hellish combat missions. The crew of *Hadley's Harem* hoped some of Kane's luck would rub off on them over Ploeşti.

After the *Harem*'s bomb run over the refineries, Lieutenant Hadley immediately joined a formation of five other B-24s that included Killer Kane's battered *Hail Columbia* as the scattered elements of the Tidal Wave force headed for home. Without the protection of sister ships, *Hadley's Harem* was a sitting duck for enemy fighters. The plane was badly damaged from anti-aircraft fire, leaking fuel, with engines streaming smoke and fire and the greenhouse section of her nose blown apart by a direct hit from a heavy-caliber antiaircraft shell. The body of bombardier Lt. Leon Storms lay lifeless and torn on the nose deck. The rest of the plane was blackened by fire and riddled with holes.

The quintet flew toward Libya, low over villages and farms. They buzzed a Sunday excursion train as passengers hung from the windows and waved gaily upward at the incredulous bomber crews. The small formation stayed intact, climbing steadily over Bulgaria, Yugoslavia, and Greece, then weaving and dodging through open mountain passes and down valleys to Thrace and finally to the sea.

As *Hadley's Harem* reached the Aegean, her number three engine went out. The plane was at five thousand feet, and Lieutenant Hadley ordered the men to brace for ditching as her speed slowed to 125 miles per hour. They would never make North Africa, and Lieutenant Hadley turned his ship toward Cyprus. Then the supercharger in engine number four began to burn a brilliant blue-white and *Hadley's Harem* was doomed. Carefully Lieutenant Hadley set a course for Turkey, which was closer than Cyprus, while the *Harem* inexorably sank toward the sea as dusk approached over the eastern Mediterranean. The crew prepared to ditch, and Lieutenant Hadley worked the wheel and controls to settle the plane as gently as possibly into the sea, less than a mile from neutral Turkey.

The *Harem* skimmed the sea, struggling to make it to a patch of sand dead ahead. Sgt. Russell Page, in his normal position just behind the pilots, anticipated a hard landing and opened the escape hatch just behind the cockpit on the upper side of the plane. Once *Hadley's Harem* came to a stop in the water, he and the two pilots would scramble out through the open hatch. Sergeant Page's normal duties on landing were to call out the airspeed as the pilots brought the plane in for an approach, but this time Gib told him to sit down and to brace himself against his seat. It would be a hard landing, no matter what.

The coastline was visible some nine hundred yards off as *Hadley's Harem* strained to reach the safety of a sandy beach. Then her luck ran out as her left wing dipped into the water, and the big bomber cartwheeled into the sea and the cockpit filled instantly with seawater.

"We didn't ditch; we crashed," said Sergeant Page. "We went in nose and left wing first." *Hadley's Harem* hit the sea with a grinding crash that slammed the crew against bulkheads and armor-plated seats and brought tons of hurtling metal to a sudden, wrenching halt. *Hadley's Harem* went from nearly 100 to 0 mph in a second or two.

"We were under water almost instantly," Sergeant Page remembered, "and Hadley, Lindsey and I were thrashing around the flight deck underwater." Sergeant Page turned to the escape hatch, but the force of the landing had wrenched it shut and unmovable. Loose cables and wires snared the men as they struggled to get out. "It was the end as far as I was concerned," Page said. He was in a frenzy, pushing and kicking at the escape hatch. He lurched into the top gun turret where he vainly tried to smash his way through the Plexiglas. "My God, I'm going to die here," he screamed. Then, in semiconsciousness, he followed a gleam of dull light to his right and burst out gasping on the surface. The B-24 had split on impact, and Page went out where the two sections had broken apart.

When Sergeant Page emerged on the surface in the dwindling daylight, he looked in vain for Lieutenant Hadley and Lindsey but saw no sign of them as the bomber hissed and gurgled as it sank. Within minutes the plane slid under the surface to leave seven men bobbing in the sea several hundred yards from shore. The bedraggled crew members took stock and went to the aid of those more seriously injured. The group dog-paddled toward land, and Sergeant Page offered assistant engineer, S. Sgt. Pershing Waples, a portion of his life vest as they made their way to the shore. Waples was so appreciative of Sergeant Page's lifesaving assistance that he later named his son Russell Page Waples.

The survivors were a battered lot, suffering from broken bones, deep cuts, and abrasions, and they were immediately accosted by Turkish peasants who forced them to kneel and stripped them of their possessions. The crew members tried to tell the uncomprehending Turks that they were Americans, but the menacing peasants didn't understand. Turkish soldiers finally arrived at the same time as a British naval party that had been dispatched to the area in a rescue boat when a picket plane picked up *Hadley's Harem* m'aidez signals. The Brits tried to negotiate the immediate release of the crew, but the Turk soldiers took the men into custody.

C.L. Sulzberger of the *New York Times* wrote a lengthy article about the saga of *Hadley's Harem* over Ploeşti and her crew's travails in Turkey. It appeared in the Sunday Magazine section in late 1943 and was titled, "Life and Death of an American Bomber." Sulzberger concluded, "Thus ends the story of *Hadley's Harem*. Its epilogue has not been written."

The epilogue would never have been written had it not been for the curiosity and persistence of Roy Newton, the *Harem's* former gunner, who returned to California after the war. The Turks classified Newton and the rest of the crew as "shipwrecked mariners" because the plane had crashed at sea and not on Turkish territory, and they were handed over to American authorities shortly after the plane went down. The men made their way through Lebanon and Israel and into Egypt, where they were reunited with Colonel Kane.

Newton put the war and *Hadley's Harem* behind him until he attended a fiftieth anniversary reunion of Tidal Wave raiders in 1993. His interest in the plane and the fate of Gib Hadley and Don Lindsey was rekindled when he saw a photograph of himself among the seven surviving crew members, taken on the beach just after the *Harem* crashed.

"I've got a couple of coins and nothing else to do," he said to himself and set out to find his old plane. He went back to Turkey in 1994 and began searching along the Mediterranean coast, looking for the spot where *Hadley's Harem* had gone down. A Turkish newspaper wrote about Newton's quest, and the story caught the attention of a Turkish fisherman who had found a wreck twenty years before while diving in nearby waters. He contacted Newton and sent him pieces of a downed warplane. The parts were identified as belonging to *Hadley's Harem*, and Newton returned to Turkey where the fisherman took him to the exact spot where the plane was resting in ninety feet of water.

Newton set out to raise *Hadley's Harem* and eventually succeeded in bringing the nose section to the surface. The old B-24 was in remarkably good condition because it had settled to the seafloor where two freshwater rivers empty into the Mediterranean. The remains of *Hadley's Harem* were cleaned and stabilized and are now displayed in a Turkish museum.

The nose yielded numerous personal effects including a wristwatch that Newton identified as Gib's and his pearl-handled revolvers and cowboy boots. Also found were human remains that were sent to the CILHI in Hawaii, where DNA samples taken from Gib's sister Pat, and his brother, Bill, and from James Lindsey's brother, Don, were later matched with those taken from the bones found in the plane. The remains were identified as belonging to lieutenants Gib Hadley and Don Lindsey.

No one in the Hadley family ever expected that Gib's body would someday be coming back to Arkansas City. But in 1995, Pat received a telephone call from Roy Newton informing her that he had found her brother's remains off the coast of Turkey. She did not know Newton and called her brother Bill for advice. "Don't give him any money!" Bill Hadley warned. Bill didn't know Newton either and assumed that he was an imposter seeking to extort money. But the news was genuine and the military began planning to return Gib's body to his family in Arkansas City, and the remains of James Lindsey to his family in Texarkana, Texas.

The Army assigned Maj. Pamela Weishaar, stationed in Broken Arrow, Oklahoma, as the casualty assistance officer to help the Hadley family through the funeral and the grieving process. She explained the DNA findings from the central identification lab and arranged for a funeral detail from Fort Riley, Kansas, to act as honor guard. One of Major Weishaar's responsibilities was to see that Gib's remains were buried with a full uniform inside the casket, and she arranged that the uniform be historically accurate, khaki trousers, called pinks, a brown blouse or top, and a World War II officer's cap. Major Weishaar also arranged for a B-2 bomber flyover during the ceremonies and even suggested that the family could invite President Bill Clinton to the funeral. The Hadleys declined to invite the president.

Gib Hadley finally came home on January 9, 1996, for his second funeral in Riverview Cemetery in Arkansas City, fifty-three years after he died in World War II. This time there were hundreds of friends, family members, media, dignitaries, and military personnel in attendance.

The local newspaper, the *Ponca City News,* noted the number of World War II veterans in attendance.

> Their silver hair gleamed in the sun and blended with the white snow covering nearby graves as they stood, stoic and respectful, with hats removed in spite of the bitter cold. Rock solid, they shed no tears, but on closer look, the discerning heart could find—reflected in aging, but alert eyes—memories and shadows of many fallen friends, family members, and fellow soldiers lost in the great war. . . .
>
> Small children, stamping their feet in the wet snow—perhaps some great-nieces and nephews who never got to know their "Uncle Gib," assembled with the family. When the 21-gun salute was presented and taps was performed, those same children stood perfectly motionless with mouths open in awe. Adults attending seemed to be similarly affected, their faces reflecting a mixture of pride, sadness, and finality.

That same January, hundreds of mourners attended James Rex Lindsey's funeral in Gilbert, Texas. "You couldn't hardly get in the cemetery for all the people," said Don Lindsey, James's brother. "It was the biggest funeral they ever had in Gilbert."

James was buried in full uniform in the family plot next to his mother, who never accepted his loss. "She never got over it," Don Lindsey said. "She had the idea that he might come back. She talked about him all her life." She died in 1990.

Don Lindsey remembers the last time he saw his brother. James was passing through Louisiana to pick up *Hadley's Harem* and join the crew. He got off the train long enough to chat with Don for a few minutes. The conductor called out, "All aboard," and James got back on. "Good luck," he said to Don.

Bill Hadley also vividly remembers the last time he saw Gib. Nineteen-year-old Bill was boarding a train for Army Air Corps cadet training. "Gib just wished me good luck and said, 'See you later.' You never think it's going to happen to your family, but Lord, people were being killed every day. I never thought about it happening to Gib."

When the remains of Gib Hadley and James Lindsey were recovered, it meant that nine of the ten-man crew had been accounted for. The remaining crew member, bombardier Leon Storms, is still listed as missing in action. When *Hadley's Harem* crashed, Storms's body floated away from the wreck, and it was believed to have washed ashore where Turkish peasants probably buried it. The grave has never been found. The only official memory of Lieutenant Storms is his name inscribed on a plaque to the missing at the American cemetery in Carthage, Tunisia.

2 5

Coping

Whenever Sarah Schaen Naugher hears the lonely and solemn notes of taps, it is as though a spell is cast and once again she is a young woman of twenty-one on the threshold of life. The notes drift like a requiem through the distant reaches of her mind; it is 1943 and her husband, Lt. Jim Schaen, is as real in her memory as though he were still beside her. She can feel the cold wetness of the snowflakes melting on her face in Casper, Wyoming, as she and Jim walk to the preacher's house on Christmas Eve to be married. She relives their happiness as gypsies living in shoe box apartments and moving from one air base to another in the mountains of Wyoming and on the prairies of the Midwest in their old Packard automobile. She sees Jim outfitted in his flying gear as he turns away from her on the air base in Topeka, Kansas, and fades like a ghost as he walks to his B-24 bomber and disappears into the mists of a long-ago war. It was the last time she ever saw him.

Sarah remembers January 27, 1945, when she was eight months pregnant with her daughter, Jima, and she read the War Department telegram. It said something about the German Red Cross notifying the American Red Cross that Jim had been killed when his plane was shot down, September 27, 1944, over Kassel, Germany. Sarah stared blankly ahead as she tried to absorb the tragedy that had just befallen her. She cried for weeks as she recalled images of her once happy life. It was gone forever, and Sarah was never the same again.

Sixty years later Jim is still with Sarah, in her heart, in her thoughts, and in her memory. Jim's death is still almost as unbelievable to her today as it was on that day in January 1945, and Sarah still wonders if he really was killed. She wonders too if it was Jim's body that was in the casket that she buried in Arlington National Cemetery in January 1951. Jim was confident that he would return from the war, and Sarah never once doubted his word. He was listed first as missing in action in October 1944, but she was sure he had survived. When the families of other crew members received word in November that they were being held as POWs and there was no word about Jim, she still believed he would come home. After the news came that he had died in his plane, "my heart was broken. It still is," Sarah says. She still dreams that he will be coming home.

Sarah is a strong, practical woman. "You do what you have to do. You do the best you can and you move on," she says. She relied on her faith, her church, and her friends in the community. She became a teacher and married David Naugher, a dairy farmer and a combat veteran of the war, raised another family, and lived another life, a good life. But every time she hears taps, the emotion starts all over again. "You never get over it," Sarah says, and she is thankful to have married a man who could understand the pain and attachment she still has for her former husband; she needed that kind of understanding.

For Hazel Minium time also did not erase the pain and sadness of the loss of her husband, Daniel. "It's been more than fifty years now since he went away, and sometimes when there's a knock at the door I think, well, maybe Daniel's come back to me," Hazel said. "But I know it's not going to happen, and I've cried enough over the years to fill the Atlantic Ocean."

Death from war is often more difficult to accept than ordinary death. Young men like Daniel Unger and Jim Schaen were killed in the fullness of youth with the promise of life still before them. They died alone and violently far from home and far from the comfort of family and friends. No one could reach out and hold them as they died. For the families, there were no remains over which to mourn, no immediate funeral ceremony to bring some small measure of closure, and the grieving process that ordinarily takes place after a death was postponed. And when the dead came back, their families were never certain that the man in the casket was their son, brother, or husband.

The pain from loss in World War II still lurks just below the surface for many families, and belies the suffering of the bereaved and the myths that grow around the sacrifice and the glory of that war. "This thing that these men gave up their lives gladly makes me want to throw up," says Alita Howard. "They didn't give up their lives; their lives were torn from them."

A mother and father who lost a son, a widow who lost her husband, a daughter who lost her father, and a sister who lost a brother, all still weep. "The pain doesn't go away. It's always there," Hazel said.

"I don't think my parents ever got over it," said Ellie Pope Dodwell "If they came back to life tonight, they would well up in tears and talk about Billy. You would think that he had died just months before."

A one-time war widow, now an elderly woman who attended a 2002 Lehigh University reunion memorial service in Bethlehem, Pennsylvania, for alumni killed in World War II, burst into tears upon hearing taps sounded at the end of the service. "It's been so many years and I've had a wonderful second marriage. I don't know why I was so overcome," she said. Taps has come to symbolize the pain of death in war. It is so emotively powerful and haunting that many weep at the memories it evokes.

Alita Howard slowly resumed her life without Cory after the war and found renewed spirit by communicating with him on "the other side." Her life's work became relating to others that it is possible to speak to the dead. "My experience of darkness ended long ago when some concerned people— people who had already 'died'—cared enough to offer help at a time when sorrow weighed heavily upon me. . . . Since that time, my life has had meaning; my feet have taken a certain pathway. . . . It is as if great lights were helping to point the way. Not everyone finds this certain pathway," Alita says. "It is not well traveled. But there are others on it—other happy people. I am not alone."

Vera Brittain found a similar pathway in remembering her fiancé, Roland Leighton, killed in World War I. "For if the dead are their own subconscious selves, they can surely hear us and know that we are thinking of them even though we cannot know that they know or are thinking of us. Always at 11 P.M. on the 23rd day of the month, I mean to pause in whatever I am doing & let my spirit go out to His. Always at that hour I will turn to Him, just as the Mohammedans always turn to Mecca at sunrise," Brittain wrote.

Alita also finds solace in knowing that the dead warriors of World War II "understand that their deaths were not in vain." She says, "I know that my man and those great flyers who were killed are very happy with what they have done. My God, think of what we'd be going through if we were still living with Hitler." She learned to cope in her own way, as did the others, but they never could forget. And now in old age, Alita awaits the time soon when she will be reunited with Cory.

"You do get through it, but you never get over it," Ellie said. The weeping stopped, but only when Ellie's mother died. Billy is buried at the Normandy American Cemetery in France.

Donald McCluskey's mother became "very silent" for a year after her son was reported missing after his LST was sunk, and her patriotism waned. But time brought some healing to the McCluskey family. "We just didn't talk about it much," Donald said.

Kenneth Mooney's mother blamed Roosevelt for the death of her son but was consoled by frequent trips to the cemetery to visit Hugh Mooney's grave. "She felt more at peace having him back here where she could go and tend to his grave," Kenneth said. Today she lies buried next to her son.

Brenda Birchfield, whose father Andrew James Scalf was killed in Germany in 1945 when she was four years old, also finds solace near his grave in the American Cemetery in Margraten, in the Netherlands, which she visits frequently and where she has a dialogue with his spirit. "For some strange reason I feel a great deal of comfort near him even though I realize probably not all his body is in there."

Brenda has finally read her father's letters from before and during the war that she for a long time could not bring herself to read. "I took a week off and sat there and cried as I read them," Brenda said. She discovered her father, the jokes he told, the food he liked, the movies he watched, his passions and desires, and even the clothes he wore. "Before, he was a shadowy figure and I pretended I didn't care about him."

In 1998, after finding her father's grave, Brenda wrote, "I finally found Andrew James Scalf . . . my dad, and there he was in the Netherlands Cemetery . . . in Margraten, Holland. Far away from his home in Tennessee. I cried for him for the FIRST time that day . . . for my dad and for myself . . . and for what we both had missed . . . loving and knowing each other . . . and for what our lives could have been."

"It's absurd to say time makes one forget; I miss Him as much now as I ever did," Vera Brittain wrote. "One recovers from the shock, just as one gradually would get used to managing with one's left hand if one has lost one's right, but one never gets over the loss, for one is never the same after it. I've got used to facing the long empty years ahead of me. But I have always before me the realization of how empty they are and will be, since He will never be there again. One can only live through them as fully and as nobly as one can, and pray from the depths of one's lonely heart."

2 6

News from Red

When Dr. Franks arrived in Europe in 1947, he would never have imagined that his new position with the church would take him so many places and be so rewarding and enriching. He threw himself into missionary work with his customary zeal and tirelessness as he traveled extensively throughout Europe offering aid and assistance to refugees, meeting with church officials, and recruiting seminary students to project the Baptist faith.

But his quest to find Red was like a dark secret that haunted his waking moments. Red would have been twenty-nine in 1948, still a young man in the full of life, and not a day went by that Dr. Franks did not think of Red's open, smiling face. He felt a certain comfort in knowing that his son was somewhere within a few hundred miles of where he lived in Switzerland and not the thousands of miles away he had been from Mississippi. Dr. Franks also traveled to some of the places that Red had bombed during the war.

Dr. Franks had planned to leave Europe in 1949 and return home to the United States to find another pastorate or to teach at a college or university, but the church had other plans for him. It wanted to establish a theological seminary in Switzerland to train Baptist ministers for southern Europe, and he was asked to help. Founding a seminary and filling it with students would be a challenge since there were few Southern Baptists in Europe and even fewer in Switzerland, which had a Baptist population of only thirteen hundred. Augusta recorded some of her husband's progress in her diary: "These were very busy, hard, trying days, but wonderfully interesting and inspiring. We were plowing new ground for the denomination." But such challenges had never deterred Dr. Franks before. He had only to recall how thorny a job it had been to persuade his own church board in Columbus to build the educational center for the First Baptist Church, which eventually helped recruit hundreds of new worshipers.

Initially his job in Switzerland required finding a suitable location for the seminary, and he settled on an eight-acre site in Zurich with a forty-two-room mansion and two smaller adjacent buildings. But once this task was accomplished, he was asked to stay on and become the seminary's business manager, its director of public relations, and director of relief and rehabilitation for the Southern Baptist Church in Europe. Any thoughts of going home were put to rest. Still, he was thriving. "I am having a great experience here, thinking, dreaming, working in the language and land of much human distress and suffering," he wrote and added, "Mrs. Franks and I moved yesterday to our new seminary property. I am sitting here this morning for the first time in my office, and I am very happy at last to be settled. This is a lovely place. The wonderful panorama of snowcapped mountains are in full view. Last night was a wonderful moonlit night."

Despite his newfound peace of mind, the intensity of his search for Red increased. The mystery of his son's disappearance grew in complexity in 1947 as all records, American and enemy, were searched, former POWs were interviewed, and government officials and civilians in former enemy-held territory were questioned about lost American servicemen. Graves registration teams were also at work uncovering many of the dead. Still, there was no word of Red.

In early 1947 the bodies of 185 unknown American flyers were exhumed from Romanian graves around Ploeşti and transferred to the American military cemetery at Neuville-en-Condroz about eight miles outside of the city of Liége, Belgium. Neuville was the site of the army's central identification laboratory where forensic specialists were attempting to identify some eight thousand unknown American dead from all over the European theater. Each set of remains from Romania was marked with an identification number and was accompanied by an identification checklist.

Dr. Franks was not informed of the transfer of bodies until February 11, 1948, when he received a letter from Col. E. V. Freeman in the army's memorial division. "Although no conclusive information has been received in this office regarding the burial of the remains of your son, the remains which were recovered from Ploesti, Rumania, have been removed to the United States Military Cemetery Neuville-en-Condroz, Belgium. Information received from the American Graves Registration Command indicates that the remains of your son may be among these remains, which were recovered. However, the records of your son must be checked against all identifying media of those recovered from the cemetery, before positive identification can be established." The letter cautioned, however, that most of the bodies were so badly decomposed that identification could be difficult. To Dr. Franks the information was more of the same; the Army just didn't know where Red was.

Still, the military held out hope that there could be a break in the case; there were some promising possibilities that Red might be found among this group of unknowns. One set of remains was that of an American flyer, designated X-5191, who had been retrieved from a cemetery near Ploeşti by the Romanian detachment, the 347th Quartermaster Battalion (M) on January 30, 1947. The body was reported to have been found wearing the remnants of a wool OD sweater, remnants of a suntan shirt with an Air Corps insignia, remnants of suntan trousers, and a gabardine flying suit. The suntan shirt on X-5191's remains also bore the gold bar of a second lieutenant on the collar.

The army's forensic team at the central investigating point in Neuville-en-Condroz noted, however, that it had been unable to obtain fingerprints from the remains of X-5191; the body was "too decomposed." The chief investigator also remarked, "fluoroscopic examination unnecessary. Remains recovered in skeletal form, badly fractured and partially burned. Est. weight of remains: 20 pounds." Despite the possibility that X-5191 might be Red Franks, the forensic team concluded, "As processing at CIP revealed no positive identifying clues, this case remains 'unknown' as previously classified by another graves registration unit."

Attached to the forensic report was a diagram of a skeleton depicting X-5191's missing bones. The entire right hand from the wrist forward was lost. A section of the pelvic bone was missing, as were both kneecaps, a section of the left thighbone, and all the finger bones of the left hand.

X-5191 made the journey from Romania to Neuville-en-Condroz, where his skeletal remains, cloaked in a mattress-cover shroud, were buried in a wooden casket in a special plot for unknown dead. The burial took place at 3 P.M. on March 17, 1947, and was conducted by three chaplains representing the Protestant, Catholic, and Hebrew faiths, a procedure followed for all unknowns. A simple wooden cross, marked with the identity number, adorned the grave.

Dr. Franks continued to press government and military officials to investigate further. In early 1948, due largely to Dr. Franks's inquiries and pressure from Congressmen Rankin and Whittington, the military reopened the case of Red Franks. An army memo took heed of the power of Congress: "A Congressional request for information relative to the burial location of Lt. Franks was the basis for a review of all reports for unresolved casualties of the area of Ploeşti, in an effort to find which one could be associated with Lt. Franks."

The army's new review turned up an intriguing clue that had somehow been overlooked for more than a year. X-5191 had red hair. In a memorial division memo the following was reported:

"Army records of Lt. Franks; tooth chart, red hair, rank (2/Lt) and height were thoroughly compared with all Burial Reports received in this office of crew members who were casualties during 1 August 1943, over

Ploeşti, Romania. Unknown X-5191 is the *only* Burial Report (of 1 August 1943, Ploeşti bombing) that has the following:

a. an almost identical tooth chart
b. red hair
c. 2nd Lt. bar
d. agrees in height (estimated)

    All other Burial Reports for 1 August 1943, Ploeşti oil raid do not contain the above facts and, therefore, are eliminated."

Each set of remains returned from Romania came back with a checklist for physical characteristics, as well as those for clothing and equipment found with the body. The height listed for X-5191 was estimated to be five feet ten inches, roughly Red Franks's height. Under the category "Hair—color, length, quantity, curly, wavy, straight, whorls, or definite parting" was typed the word "red." The mention of red hair should have immediately alerted investigators that this was a unique and easily identifiable characteristic. Additionally, the fact that the dead airman was approximately Red Frank's height and wore the gold bar of a second lieutenant should have further narrowed the search for the identity of X-5191. Comparison of tooth charts would have served to confirm the identity.

How could the army's forensic investigators have overlooked the red hair, which was such an obvious clue to the identity of Red Franks? And why didn't its forensic specialists compare Red's tooth chart, which it had in its possession since 1943, with the tooth charts of all the unknowns from Romania? These are questions that will never be answered.

On April 21, 1948, Maj. Richard B. Coombs of the memorial division notified Dr. Franks that the army had concluded that X-5191 was Red. "The official report of burial discloses that the remains of a deceased military person were recovered from the Civilian and Military Cemetery of Bolovan, Ploesti, Rumania, by American graves registration personnel, and properly identified as the remains of your son as a result of a subsequent investigation. I am therefore gratified to inform you that his remains are now resting in Plot V, Row 8, Grave 177, in the United States military cemetery at Neuville-en-Condroz, Belgium. You may rest assured that the interment was accomplished in the solemn and dignified manner traditional for our honored dead, with military honors and appropriate religious services."

Major Coombs concluded the letter by writing, "I realize that it has taken a seemingly long time to forward this verified information to you, but I believe you will understand that this apparent delay was brought about by our endeavor to be absolutely accurate in our information. I am trusting, however, that this letter will assure you of the identification of your son's remains and will serve as a measure of relief from some of the anxiety and distress you have suffered."

But Dr. Franks had learned not to accept the military's word at face value. Now he had discovered additional information that he believed cast doubt on the army's finding. He wrote to Major Coombs at Neuville-en-Condroz:

> In the course of my present duties in Europe I hope before long to visit Rumania. While there I should like to interview the Rumanian natives who gave the information which led to evidence upon which the Department of the Army bases its conclusion that my son's remains have been definitely identified. I would therefore greatly appreciate your giving me the names and addresses of these natives.
>
> Your letter states that the plane had a "crew of eleven," and that one of the three survivors "visited the crash site, under guard, and reported that he saw five bodies." That leaves six men of the crew instead of four, as I had thought, who must have bailed out or in some manner left the plane before it crashed. Please give me again a complete list of the names of the crew's personnel, indicating the names and addresses of their nearest of kin, particularly designating the two others besides my son now listed as survivors among the six who left the plane.
>
> I would also appreciate complete copies of the testimony given in my son's case by the three surviving members. I can understand how their reports would vary as to details, though not necessarily conflict; but I cannot see why any one of these would be led to contradict himself.

The case dragged on. In late August 1948, Dr. Franks again wrote military officials at Neuville seeking evidence that would convince him that Red's body had been found.

> Thank you for the full explanations of the evidence which has been used in supporting the conclusions of the Department of the Army concerning my son's identification. To my way of thinking the most valuable and reliable evidence you offer is that concerning his teeth. Without that, the rest of the evidence would be of little value, as I see it. Barring alterations from dental work—extractions, fillings, etc., one's tooth chart should be almost as definite and convincing as one's fingerprints.
>
> I believe I would be able to recognize my son's teeth, particularly the occlusion of the upper teeth with the lower. If you will be kind enough to send me a copy of the chart which you have I would greatly appreciate it. If not, I expect to be in Paris in the early part of September, and while there I can visit the USMC offices where I will be able to see that chart. I understand a complete record of all the evidence is in that office, and that I would have the privilege of studying it.
>
> Until I know more definitely about all the evidence used in his case, particularly the tooth chart, I shall not be able to answer, giving my final conclusion. We can inform you later, I assume, if we are convinced that the identification of his remains is correct, as to what disposition we desire as his final resting place.

The memorial division obliged and sent Dr. Franks a copy of Red Franks's tooth chart on September 2, 1948.

A few days later, with the search for his son in its sixth year, Dr. Franks's quest to find his son ended. It was a quiet, prayerful moment, also sorrowful, but uplifting. A great weight had been removed from his shoulders and, with it, the anxiety, frustration, and resentment associated with the search. He now could find peace for both their souls even as he still grieved so deeply. He knew the pain of loss would be inextinguishable for the rest of his life. On September 13, Dr. Franks took a once unimaginable step when he wrote to the quartermaster general's office in Washington to verify the information that the memorial division had used to identify his son's remains. "Thank you for sending me a copy of the teeth chart which your department used as evidence in determining the identification of my son's remains. I also have had opportunity to investigate the records held in Paris concerning that evidence. I am convinced from these records that the department's conclusion is correct, that my son's remains have been definitely and positively identified. I am satisfied on this point."

The long night had ended. Dr. Franks's letter to the quartermaster general continued:

> It has been a long, drawn-out process. On my part and that of my family, it has been years of bitter anguish and of sorrowful suspense, at times of great disappointment and of resentful impatience. On your part I am now certain that there has been abundant grounds for you to exercise patience as the department has relentlessly pursued its work, running down every possible clue that might lead to a solution of the problem. I thank you for everything you have done to clear up the mystery that has surrounded my son's case from the very beginning.

While the military had ultimately been correct in stating that Red Franks had died at Ploeşti, it never had pulled together the evidence until 1948 to be able to verify its findings. The army's decision to classify Red as killed in action in 1943 was based on supposition from information passed on by the Romanians through the International Red Cross. The Romanians had based their conclusions about the fate of Red Franks on supposition as well. They had no proof that they had retrieved Red Franks's body or his dog tags, and evidence suggests that they never knew whether they had even buried Red's body.

Three weeks after the Tidal Wave attack, Jack Warner was surprised to find Romanian authorities by his hospital bedside seeking information about Red. Lieutenant Warner gave a statement to the International Red Cross on February 8, 1944: "Three weeks later [after *Euroclydon* had been shot down]

Romanian officials came to the hospital in search of Lieutenant Franks. The only way they could possibly have come in possession of his name was by finding his discarded parachute on which he had his name stenciled upon the cover."

Only after the war when graves registration personnel began recovery operations around Ploeşti did information begin to filter in about what happened to Red, but the information at first was largely hearsay. *Euroclydon* crew member S. Sgt. James R. Vest told army investigators when he was returned to Allied custody that he "was told by members of the Ninety-third Bomber Group that Lieutenant Franks jumped, but his parachute failed to open."

The graves registration team interviewed a Romanian engineer named Stiuca, who visited the *Euroclydon* crash site moments after it struck the ground. The team's report stated,

> He later saw five carbonized corpses laid out on the ground, and because he could speak English, he was asked to question two airmen [captured] who parachuted safely, in an attempt to find out the identity of the five bodies. The airman, however, did not disclose this information. Engineer Stiuca vaguely remembered the name of one of the prisoners as Lieutenant "Werner," and that there was another member of this aircraft who parachuted, and whose body was found near an antiaircraft battery. Stiuca found out that the dead airman's name was Second Lieutenant "Jesse Dee Franks, Jr.," A.S.N. O-734444. He did not state his source of this information and did not know where this airman was buried.

The graves registration report continued, "The report of the investigation group, however, states that in their opinion, the deceased was buried in the Bolovan Cemetery, Ploesti, but as an unidentified person because of inefficiency on the part of the local [Romanian] authorities."

But this information does not appear until late 1948 in the voluminous file the memorial division kept on Red Franks. It was disclosed in a letter to Dr. Franks on August 16, 1948.

As late as the 1980s information relating to his death was discovered by Bryan Moon, the MIA searcher who traveled to Ploeşti to gather information for a painting he was completing that depicted the Tidal Wave attack. He placed an ad in a local newspaper asking for information and artifacts from the Ploeşti raid. Moon was surprised the next day when a large number of people showed up at his hotel.

One of those who came forward was a man who had been a boy at the time of the attack and had watched as several B-24s went down around his family's farm not far from the refineries. When the last of the attacking bombers had headed home, the boy cautiously ventured out to inspect the wreckage of a plane that had crashed into a nearby schoolhouse. By the time he reached the burning B-24, Romanian police and military personnel had cordoned off the site, but he came across the body of an American airman lying a short distance from the wreck of his plane. The Romanian did not describe the condition of the body, but he said he stripped the man of all his possessions including his wallet and his belt. Years later he handed the wallet and belt over to Moon, who paid him a small sum for the items. Moon opened the wallet and found two well-preserved photographs and a business card. The photos were snapshots of a young American lieutenant and a pretty, dark-haired young woman in a winter coat sitting on the steps of a one-story house. These were the photographs of Dottie Turner and Red, sitting side by side and smiling into the camera, probably in Tucson, Arizona, where Red was stationed in the winter of 1943 just before being shipped overseas.

The business card was inscribed with the name, "Jesse D. Franks Jr., Lieutenant, Air Corps, Army of the United States." On the backside of the card Red had scribbled, "Send to Dr. Jesse D. Franks, Sr., Columbus, Mississippi." Moon carried the artifacts back to Nancy Lee, who kept them in memory of her brother.

In 1984 another Romanian who also had been a boy at the time of the Tidal Wave attack revealed that he too had come across the body of an *Euroclydon* crew member. Ioan Grigorescu was fourteen in 1943 when he witnessed "those skimming bombers flying into the heavily defended refineries, so low they were pulling the roofs off of houses. I saw bombers on fire, with young Americans trapped inside. I saw a river on fire from a crashed bomber. I saw a dead American in a walnut grove looking up into the sky, not far from his burning bomber." The bomber was *Euroclyden* and the crew member very likely was Red Franks.

Grigorescu also picked up a book to add to the English language volumes in his library. It was the copy of Shakespeare's *As You Like It* that Lieutenant Dickson carried on the flight to Ploeşti. But Dickson never bailed out of *Euroclydon* and died in the plane's wreckage. The book was probably thrown clear of the plane by the force of the crash. Of the four men who got out, Red Franks was the only one who did not survive.

Identifying X-5191 as the remains of Red Franks did not end Dr. Franks's travails with the Army. Before he knew that the unknowns from Romania had been transferred to Belgium in 1947, Dr. Franks asked the memorial division that if his son's remains were among those found at Ploeşti, Red should be buried in Romania near where he had been killed. When he learned that Red's remains had been transferred to Neuville, he asked that his son be buried in the American military cemetery at Cambridge, England. He stated his reasons in a letter to the memorial division.

1) There is to be no permanent overseas military cemetery in Romania, where my son met his death. I should have preferred that location, as my first choice.

2) The major part of my son's brief stay in Europe before he was killed was with the Air Force stationed in England. He was never in any of the fighting over Belgium, where his remains are temporarily buried.

3) Some of his dear friends among the airmen are interred in the Cambridge cemetery, including his next-door neighbor and boyhood playmate, Howard Noland of Columbus, Mississippi.

He ended the letter, "Thanking you for your every consideration."

But the memorial division informed Dr. Franks that the Cambridge American Military Cemetery was reserved only for those who had already been buried in England. "I can readily understand your desires, and I regret that I must inform you that it will not be possible to grant you this request," a memorial division official wrote.

Dr. Franks replied that he wanted Red to be buried with comrades overseas, and if he was to be buried at Ardennes, "I shall want a formal burial service at the cemetery, when Mrs. Franks and I shall hope to be present."

Once again the Army thwarted his request. The memorial division replied,

> Because interment operations are currently in progress in the United States military cemetery, Neuville-en-Condroz, Belgium, the cemetery is closed to visitors. The Department of the Army cannot authorize any request for permission to visit this cemetery until this work has been completed.
>
> After final interment of your son's remains have been accomplished, you will receive a permanent grave location letter from our office. Upon receipt of this letter you might write us to learn whether the work is near enough completion to permit visitors in this cemetery.

Dr. Franks made one last request of the Army, and this time there was immediate acquiescence. On January 27, 1949, he wrote the memorial division.

> In the War Department's earliest correspondence with me concerning my son's case, his rank was given as "First Lieutenant," not "Second Lieutenant." His Purple Heart Medal also carries his rank as "First Lieutenant," as do the formal statements of sympathy from President Roosevelt and Chief of Staff Marshall. Later correspondences began to refer to him as "Second Lieutenant."
>
> Inquiring of the Department of War as to this discrepancy this fact was revealed: That my son had actually been awarded his promotion to the rank of First Lieutenant shortly before his death, but before it passed through the required formalities which would have officially elevated him to that rank, he was killed. . . . I mention this matter here because I think

his rank should be definitely determined before the permanent inscription on his grave marker is made.

A short time later Dr. Franks received approval of his request in a letter from the memorial division. Major James F. Smith responded, "I am gratified to inform you that under date of 25 January 1949 the Secretary of the Army issued formal orders directing the promotion posthumously of Jesse D. Franks, Jr., 0-734444 to the grade of First Lieutenant, Army of the United States, effective 31 July 1943. All records have been amended and the permanent grave marker will be inscribed accordingly." Dr. Franks had been Red's advocate one last time.

The story of Red Franks had ended but it would be retold in Dr. Franks's memory for as long as he lived. "It was the greatest tragedy of his life," Nancy Lee said. One year's intended service with the church in Europe had stretched into five, and then to seven as Dr. Franks pursued his duties with the new seminary and with refugee concerns. "Had I been told when we left America that we would be gone seven years I think I would not have believed it," Augusta wrote. They had only been back to the States a few times, once in 1950 when Dr. Franks presided at Nancy Lee's marriage to Thomas Goodall in the First Baptist Church in Columbus.

In 1954, Dr. Franks was nearly seventy, well past the board's retirement age of sixty-five. He and Augusta took stock of their seven years in Europe and found their experiences beyond their wildest dreams. As they made plans to return to the United States, one European Baptist wrote Dr. Franks a note of thanks and praise when he learned of his immanent departure:

"Dear Dr. Franks, we are not competent to judge another man, only God can do that, but we were hungry and you fed us. Many of us were naked and you clothed us. Surely we were sick and you visited us. Really we were in prison and you came to us.

"This about sums up the joy of the relief program, which gave Dr. Franks such a sense of usefulness and caused our Baptist Foreign Mission

Board to speak words of love and commendation about our seven years in Europe," Augusta wrote.

Dr. Franks himself reflected on his years in Europe. He called it "one of the happiest periods of our Christian ministry, one of the richest, most satisfying in religious experience and service."

Doctor and Augusta Franks made several trips to the Ardennes American Cemetery in the 1950s and 1960s to visit Red's grave before leaving for the United States in June 1954, as did Nancy Lee and her husband, Thomas, an attorney in Gallatin, Tennessee. "We were satisfied with the place where he was. A lot of people want to bring their loved ones home, but it was such a beautiful place where Red rests that we felt comfortable with leaving him there," Nancy Lee said. Dr. Franks had chosen not to return Red's body home to Friendship Cemetery in Columbus or to a grave next to his mother, Sallie, and sister, Elizabeth, in Ripley, Mississippi.

There was an air of peace and serenity in the cemetery that satisfied Dr. Franks; Red was with comrades, the unnamed heroes of the war who had paid the price for freedom and salvation with their lives. In this sense they were Christlike, and these thoughts soothed Dr. Franks.

But more earthly thoughts intruded as well. He often wondered how different his own life and Red's life might have been had Red chosen to stay in seminary and gone on to receive his divinity degree. Red probably would have survived the war, but it was like him to join the fray. Dr. Franks also relived the last seconds of Red's life. If he had just moved a moment or two sooner, his parachute might have had time to open. How is it that some men survived and others didn't? He knew the answer; it was God's will and Dr. Franks had learned accept it.

As Dr. Franks stood over his son's grave before returning to the United States, he saw the complete simplicity of life after death. It was boiled down to a plain white cross that revealed nothing of the young man buried beneath it, none of his complexities, none of his hopes and dreams. Red and the hundreds of his comrades lying in this field in Belgium were mute. It remains for the living to speak for those killed in war. Dr. Franks comforted himself that the body was merely a vehicle for the spirit that now resided somewhere in the firmament.

Dr. Franks placed a bouquet of flowers next to the cross that bore the inscription:

JESSE D. FRANKS JR.

1LT

328 BOMB SQ. 93rd BOMB GP/HEAVY

MISSISSIPPI

AUGUST 1, 1943

He stepped back and communed with Red. He could hear him speak and hear him laugh as they recounted stories of their lives together in Columbus, sad and funny. He heard Red's voice reading from his last letter: "I love you, and am so proud to be your son. . . . [T]ake good care of yourself, little Sis, and don't let this get you down, because I would never want it that way. Never change—be the same swell Dad always. Remember, you are doing the best job in the world now, and you always have done the best one."

Dr. Franks took his final leave from Red's grave. He looked back briefly at the white cross, knowing it would be the last time he would ever be near his son again in this life. Some might say that now there was closure for this proud, humbled man of God. But it was not to be. "Closure is not proclaimed," writes Thomas Lynch. "It is achieved—and rarely."

A year after Red's body was identified, Dr. Franks wrote why closure is so difficult to attain: "How difficult it is to understand and to believe that a loving, heavenly father has permitted this to happen." Then he added:

Not now, but in the coming years—

It may be in the better land—

You'll know the meaning of your tears

And then understand.

Dr. Franks found some solace for his loss in the memories and recollections of others who knew his son. Everyone had liked Red, and those who knew him well adored him. Lt. Jack Warner praised Red when he learned that his comrade had probably been killed in the Tidal Wave attack. Lieutenant Warner was still a POW in Romania and recovering from his wounds when he wrote Dr. Franks in late 1943: "I can say at this time a few things that should give you, as Red's father, pleasure. Everyone who ever came in contact with Red was dearly influenced and improved by a perfect example of the Christian life he led. He was deeply devoted to our Lord, to you, and to Dot. His life was a mirror of that devotion. I am proud that he considered me as a friend just as I know that you are proud to be his father."

Red's boyhood friend from Camp Ridgecrest, Dick Burts, remembered Red's simple, direct way. "Let's you and me be friends," Burts remembered Red saying at their first meeting in their early teens. For Burts, this summed up Red's character: "Everybody loved Red Franks. What you saw was what you got. He didn't put on any pretenses. He wasn't particularly religious or pious, but he was religious in his caring and in his consideration for others. Everybody around him knew he was their buddy and they could look to him if they needed him. He was who he was, solid, loyal, and straightforward and just a great guy. He was true blue."

In June 1954 Dr. Franks returned to America. He and Augusta settled in Wake Forest, North Carolina, where he had been asked to assist in the establishment of the new Southeastern Seminary. Two years later Dr. Franks accepted a teaching position on the faculty of Bethel College in Hopkinsville, Kentucky. He planned to teach religion as long as he was physically able, and there was no age limit to his tenure at Bethel. The Frankses were drawn to Hopkinsville because it was near Nancy Lee's home in Gallatin, Tennessee, and the Goodalls had two daughters. Dr. Franks and Augusta purchased a wooded lot where they built a small cottage. Winters were spent teaching at Bethel College and summers were spent studying in New York and traveling to world mission conferences. It was an ideal retirement for both.

In 1959 Dr. Franks experienced the symptoms of a heart attack, but thought little of it and continued his life almost unfazed. In March 1960, he had another bout of angina and was hospitalized for more than five weeks. He returned home in April and suffered a massive heart attack five days later. He was rushed to the hospital and died the next day. "Quietly and peacefully he went to meet his Lord," Augusta said.

Augusta wrote of her husband a few years later: "He was a man of real worth and depth and vision. He was a man who loved deeply. He loved people, his family and his country. He never wavered from the conviction that God had called him to preach. He left a legacy to all who knew him of unblemished character and honesty."

All who knew him remembered him with love and respect. "Reverend Franks was the kindest, gentlest, most loving person I've ever known," said Betty Holland, Nancy Lee's lifelong friend. "He loved his two children enough for two parents, and when Red was killed, it broke his heart for sure, for sure."

Long after Dr. Franks's death, Charles Reed, one of three airmen who bailed out of *Euroclydon* and survived, remarked on a parent's anguish for a son in war. He and crewmate Sgt. Bernard Lucas became good friends before "Luke" was killed when *Euroclydon* was struck by antiaircraft fire over Ploeşti. It took thirty years before Reed could write a letter about Ploeşti to Luke's family. Luke's parents lost two sons in World War II and never knew where his body was interred, if it was interred at all. The Air Force briefly reopened the search for Luke in the 1970s, but in vain. Today his name is among those listed as missing on a plaque in the Florence American Cemetery in Florence, Italy.

In a letter to the Lucas family Reed said that only years afterward could he understand a parent's heartbreak over the loss of a son in war. He and his brother were both listed as missing in action during the war and while both were safe and survived, the strain seriously affected his mother's health for the remainder of her life. And only when Reed's own son served in Viet Nam did he fully comprehend the true anguish of war.

Reed said he had never told anyone, including his own family, of the horror he experienced over Ploeşti. "The Lord smiled on the Reed family," he concluded in his letter to Luke's family. "My son came home."

2 7

Memorial Day

In the spring of 1866, a year after the Civil War ended, four women from Columbus, Mississippi, set out for the city's Friendship Cemetery to decorate the graves of some 2,194 Confederate soldiers who had been killed in the Battle of Shiloh in Tennessee in April 1862. The women also adorned the graves of forty Union army troops buried nearby who had died in the battles for control of Mississippi. The Friendship grave sites of both Union and rebel dead had been neglected after the collapse of the Confederate states in 1865.

Friendship Cemetery was established in 1849 a mile or so south of Columbus on a bluff overlooking the Tombigbee River. Many of Columbus's leading citizens are buried there, as are others who had shaped the history of Mississippi and the nation. Among the dead are four congressmen, two Mississippi governors, presidents of Mississippi State College for Women, soldiers from all America's wars, and generals, including Lt. Gen. Stephen Dill Lee.

After the Battle of Shiloh, wounded Confederate soldiers were shipped south by railroad to makeshift hospitals in cities and towns in northern Mississippi. Those who reached Columbus were cared for in houses and buildings throughout the city including, some believe, in the original First Baptist Church and the Frank Noland home. Many of the wounded died and their bodies were removed to Friendship Cemetery.

Without anyone to care for the graves, four women, Mrs. Augusta Murdock Sykes Cox, Mrs. Frances Jane Butler Garrett Fontaine, Mrs. Kate McCarthy Hill Cooper Heath, and Miss Martha Elizabeth "Matt" Morton, organized an annual memorial day for the war dead in Friendship Cemetery. The group's first gathering was held on April 25, 1866, when the women assembled, with great pomp, outside the cemetery. The local newspaper, the *Mississippi Index,* made the event front-page news: "First marched in twos, the young ladies and girls, dressed in immaculate white, each bearing her bouquet or chaplet of flowers. Next came the matrons, dressed in mourning, like the others with flowers in their hands, their black dresses typical of the southern heart in gloom for its beloved dead—the fair flowers emblematic of women's admiration and affection for all that was gallant and chivalrous in patriots. Lastly, came the procession of carriages bearing the elderly ladies." The *Index* added with pride: "No distinction had been made between our own dead and about forty federal soldiers, who were sleeping their last sleep next to them."

The April 25, 1866, ceremony in Friendship had a lasting, unintended effect on every corner of America. By many accounts this was the nation's first Decoration Day, which has become Memorial Day. Other communities, including Columbus, Georgia, lay claim to initiating Memorial Day celebrations. Several women of the Ladies Memorial Association in that Georgian community honored their Confederate war dead on April 26, 1866. But the ladies of Columbus, Mississippi, were one day ahead of their sisters in Georgia.

The observances in Columbus, Mississippi, also were reported in newspapers around the country, particularly in the north, where former foes were praised for honoring the war dead of both sides. The women themselves were bereaved, having lost sons, husbands, and brothers in the Civil War.

The Columbus, Mississippi, ceremonies are also said to have inspired a New York lawyer, Francis Miles Finch, to write the poem, "The Blue and the Gray," that was published in the *Atlantic Monthly* in September 1867. The poem appeared with the following note: "The women of Columbus, Miss., animated by noble sentiments, have shown themselves impartial in their offerings to the memory of the dead. They strewed flowers on the graves of the Confederate and the National soldiers."

The ladies of Columbus, Mississippi, still honor the war dead each year. The graves of the Union soldiers are long gone, having been removed in 1867 when the bodies of all Union soldiers were exhumed and collected from the battlefields of the Civil War and interred in one of the numerous national cemeteries established after the war. The gravestones of the long-dead Confederate soldiers remain and stand in ranks shaded by towering magnolia trees that were planted when the soldiers were first interred in 1862.

Near the graves of the Confederate soldiers is a newer headstone, placed there nearly a century after the Civil War. It is the grave of Dr. Jesse Dee Franks, who was laid to rest in Friendship Cemetery in 1960. His second wife, Augusta, lies nearby.

Dr. Franks is still remembered in Columbus more than a half century after he left his ministry at the First Baptist Church in 1947. His old friend, Bernie Imes, the former editor of the *Commercial Dispatch,* occasionally wrote about Dr. Franks in the years after his death. His columns formed an ongoing epitaph to Dr. Franks.

"The longtime pastor will be remembered as one of the strongest characters to fill a pulpit in Columbus," Imes wrote in 1979. "With Dr. Franks there was absolutely no compromise. Typical of Dr. Franks, he fought fiercely for every inch in a losing battle. Even though the cause was a certain loss, he never wavered for a moment.

"I suppose you expect it of strong wills, the rocky path they must travel.

Dr. Franks had his share. Probably the hardest blow of all came when his son Red Franks was lost in a World War II bombing mission over Romanian oil fields." Imes reported that Dr. Franks "was almost beyond belief that his son was dead."

But in the greatest battle he ever waged, Dr. Franks did not lose. Without his uncompromising character, he would never have unraveled the mystery of his son's disappearance. He found Red and knew that he had been given a Christian burial and was not condemned to eternal anonymity. A number of Tidal Wave flyers lost over Ploeşti, including three from *Euroclydon*, are listed as missing to this day. Their remains may rest in the Ardennes American Cemetery in Belgium, but they have never been identified. They had no advocate, family or friend, who searched for them to the ends of the earth.

Dr. Franks is buried not far from the monument in Friendship Cemetery to a former and equally beloved pastor of the First Baptist Church of Columbus, the Rev. Thomas Teasdale. The monument bears the image of the Angel of Grief, the guardian spirit that stood by Dr. Franks's side during his long search for Red.

2 8

A Promise Kept

On March 8, 1985, Dottie Turner Furr celebrated her sixty-fourth birthday at her home in Pontotoc with her cousins, the Anderson sisters, Genevieve Yancey, Eleanor Rayburn, and Julia Holmes. Spring was coming to Mississippi and had lightly brushed the fields and woods with green and gently awakened the magnolia trees. Soon the kudzu would spring back to life and blanket the countryside with its gargantuan shapes. The coming of the new season stirred memories of the women's childhood in Pontotoc, in times before the war, when they were girls and young women, before Dottie became so ill. In recent years she had been crippled by a series of strokes and was in a serious battle with cancer. There was little time left and the Anderson sisters knew this probably would be Dottie's final visit to Pontotoc and the last time they would see her alive. She and her husband Dick were returning to Orlando the next day to their permanent home in Florida. They came to Pontotoc only periodically to see old friends and to check on their house.

As Dottie and the sisters chatted, the telephone rang. Dottie waited briefly for Dick to take the call and then maneuvered her wheelchair into an adjacent room to answer the phone when it was apparent he was outdoors and did not hear the ring. Her cousins heard her soft voice as she said, "Hello," and then only silence as the caller carried on most of the conversation. A half hour passed before Dottie returned to her cousins' company, dazed and pale. The sisters worried that she was deathly ill.

"You won't believe who that call was from," Dottie whispered as she composed herself. "It was from a boy who was in the crew with Red."

Genevieve, Eleanor, and Julia needed no explanation about Red. They had known him well and loved him as the charming young man from Columbus who captured Dottie's heart nearly a half century before and who had won her hand over many other suitors, including her husband Dick Furr. Dottie seldom spoke of Red during her forty-year marriage, but her cousins knew that she had never forgotten him.

The caller was Jack Warner; he was keeping a long-held promise made to Red years before in the Libyan Desert just before the Tidal Wave raid. Everyone in *Euroclydon's* crew knew how he adored Dottie and about their plans to be married after the war. Red knew his chances of surviving the attack were slim, and he made all the crew promise that if anything happened to him, those who survived were to contact Dottie to express his enduring love and to ask if she needed anything. Warner told this all to Dottie as he reminisced about his friendship with Red so many years before. He recalled their fun times on leave and the frightening moments they experienced on bombing missions. He spoke about Red's last moments in *Euroclydon*, just before the plane went down. They had been soul mates in the nose through its many missions before the fateful raid on Ploeşti.

Warner's call revived painful memories that Dottie had buried after Red's death. She had moved on to a new life, but she could never forget the wonderful part Red had played in her youth. There were always reminders of him, a strain of music, a glimpse of his handwriting, a long-forgotten photograph, or their last days together before he went off to war. She would never forget those moments, and at times throughout her life she recalled their parting. She remembered his touch, their last embrace, his voice, and the moment he walked away for the last time. Sometimes as the years passed, she looked back and it seemed that her time with Red had been a dream from which she had awakened to find that he had never existed. Those last days with Red were some of the most cherished of her life; she would never forget.

Beyond the cheerful moments, she and Red both felt the stark reality of war. It drew them closer together than they'd ever been as they realized that their brief times together might be their last.

Dottie had been visiting her aunt Genevieve Maxedon in Corinth, in northern Mississippi not far from Memphis, Tennessee, when she received a telegram from Dr. Franks informing her that Red's plane had been shot down over Ploeşti and he was reported missing in action. Her cousin Eleanor Anderson was among the relatives present to console Dottie. Word of Red's loss quickly spread through Corinth, where many of the townsfolk knew Dottie, and they converged on the Maxedon's home to share her pain. She was immobilized by grief and collapsed in her bed for several days.

For many months afterward, Dottie prayed that Red was alive. But with each passing day and no word about his fate, she realized that he probably would not be coming home. In September 1943, when Red was officially reported killed, she refused to believe it. He had to be alive; she was sure of it and believed he would be found, maybe in a prison camp or, as she sometimes fantasized, fighting with partisans in Romania or Yugoslavia. She tried not to think of his suffering.

Several weeks after Red's disappearance, Dottie received his last letter, and for a moment everything was right again and he was suddenly with her. She held it in her hands, anticipating. It was Red's handwriting. He had written the letter the night before the Ploeşti raid and told Dottie of his love for her that nothing could change, not even death. Dottie wept at Red's calm bravery as he faced death a few hours away.

Dottie anticipated every telephone call and eagerly awaited the letter that might bring word from Red. "She kept hoping he was coming back," Genevieve remembered. "She talked a lot about him then, and she always held out hope for a long time."

By the spring of 1945 it was apparent to her that Red was not coming home. Dottie's dreams of their future were destroyed and her faith in God's grace tested. She was overwhelmed by the hideous truths of war.

The Ploeşti POWs had been released the autumn before, and Red was not among them. Dottie wept until she could mourn no more. She grieved for Dr. Franks as well, a brave and devout man whose faith and belief in God never faltered even as he suffered.

Dottie stayed in touch with Dr. Franks, and although he would never stop searching for his son, he knew as the war neared an end she could not sacrifice her life on the slim hope that Red was alive. She was twenty-four and Dr. Franks counseled her to move on, and with his urgings, Dottie took the bold and symbolic step to begin a new life by returning Red's engagement ring. She knew what the ring meant to Dr. Franks; it was a memory of both his first wife Sallie and of Red. Dottie also understood that by returning the ring she was acknowledging that Red was gone forever. The ring was passed down to Nancy Lee's daughter.

Dick Furr had come back into Dottie's life before the war ended. She had turned down Dick's offer of marriage several years earlier, and Dick had finished college and joined the Air Corps. He became a pilot and flew P-38 fighter planes in the Mediterranean theater and ironically flew bomber escort missions on B-24 raids over Ploeşti in the months after the Tidal Wave attack. The Air Corps had changed its tactics after the costly August 1 low-level attack and returned to high-altitude missions against the target. Up high, the big, lumbering bombers were vulnerable to fighter attack, and the P-38s stationed in Italy protected the B-24s and B-17s. Dick had tangled with the enemy and scored at least one kill of a German fighter. He wrote back home: "Those Jerries were swarming around our bombers, and as one bounced off I caught him with a burst. He exploded in midair."

Dick was dashing in his A-2 flying jacket and his officer's cap rakishly tilted to the side of his head, as he posed next to the nose art on his P-38 that depicted a Felix the Cat figure underscored with the inscription "Furr's A Flyin." Dick came home in 1945 and began dating Dottie again when she came to Pontotoc to visit her mother. He proposed and they were married in the summer of 1945.

Dick and Dottie settled in Pontotoc where their three children were born, two sons, Dickie, in 1947, and Robert, in 1949, and daughter Dawn, in 1951. Dick had taken his degree in horticulture at Mississippi State College in 1941 and joined his mother, Estelle, in her floral business when he returned from the war. The Furrs became the most popular couple in town, always ready for a party, and they took up residence in Estelle's house until the family got too big. Then Dottie demanded a house of their own, which Dick built on an adjacent property facing the Oxford Road.

But Dick missed flying and the days of jockeying a P-38 around the skies. After the Korean War began, he rejoined the Air Force in 1951, and Dottie became an "army wife," accustomed to moving about the country and the world. The Furrs lived in Maine, where Dick was stationed as a B-52 pilot, and in Germany and Hawaii, and Dick did two tours in military intelligence at the Pentagon in northern Virginia. Dottie loved the Air Force, the travel, and her friends. Occasionally, she and other wives would explore Europe, leaving their children in the care of German nannies. Dottie traveled through France, Germany, England, and Italy and was drawn by the culture, the history, and the arts and music. She even suggested to her daughter, Dawn, that she marry an air force officer so that she too could travel the world.

To Dottie, family was paramount, and she devoted herself to raising her children and supporting Dick's career as the impeccable hostess wherever they were stationed. She entertained and dressed stylishly. Dottie gave music lessons until her children were grown and then became a kindergarten teacher to indulge her love for kids.

The Furr household was always filled with music. If Dottie was not playing the piano, Dawn would come home from school to strains of music coming from the living room as her mother sat patiently at the piano with a young pupil. Once a year her students gathered at the home for a recital. "She was a wonderful teacher," Dawn remembered. "She played beautifully; she had music in her soul." Dawn always marveled at her mother's ability to sit down at the piano and play any tune just by ear.

Dick retired from the Air Force as a lieutenant colonel in 1969 and moved his family back to Pontotoc to manage his family's floral shop. Dottie longed to stay in the Washington, DC, area among friends, where life was vibrant and exciting, but she was the dutiful wife and knew the family business was important to Dick. Pontotoc, with its few thousand residents, was a major readjustment after Europe and Washington, but she went back nevertheless. Miss Lila had long since died, but they had many relatives and old friends in Pontotoc.

Her life was good and full, and Dottie was not one to wallow in the past. But she never forgot Red. Her Anderson cousins believed that his memory often lurked just below the surface of her life. "She always had a spot in her heart for him, and there were reminders like the Ninety-first Psalm that were very, very sensitive and that she could barely touch on. The Furrs also made regular trips to the Columbus Air Force Base for medical care and to shop at the post exchange. We just didn't talk about Red a lot," Genevieve said.

"I don't think she ever completely recovered from it, although she had a happy marriage and three wonderful children. But she never did forget Red Franks," Julia Holmes said.

"Everybody knew that Red was the one she really loved," said her cousin Sarah Gillespie.

To her daughter Dawn, Red was a somewhat mythical character inhabiting a shadow land. Only occasionally did Dottie mention him and usually "in a melancholy way when she was at a time in her life looking back and thinking what might have been," Dawn said. "She would speak of him timidly, particularly to me, her daughter, about a man that she had loved who wasn't my dad," Dawn added. Dottie also didn't mention Red around her family out of respect for Dick.

There were remnants of Red and Dottie's lost love, but not on display: a book of poetry inscribed, "To Dottie from Red," and a few photographs.

One was the snapshot of Dottie in her dorm room at Belhaven College in 1940 sitting next to a large portrait of Red.

Dottie kept the silver pattern she and Red had chosen, Prelude, in her marriage to Dick. She and Red didn't have the money to add to her silver set in any significant way while he was in the Air Corps. They would have to rely on others' gifts. She recorded each entry that showed that whenever he could, Red gave her small pieces of silver to help complete the set. In March 1941, and again in December 1941, he gave her a teaspoon. In December 1942, he gave Dottie a salad fork and a soup spoon, and in April 1942, he bought a dinner bell and a lemon fork. In April 1943, just before he left for war, Dottie recorded Red's last silver gift, one cream soupspoon. It was also to be her last entry.

When Dottie married Dick Furr, her mother-in-law, Estelle, suggested that she give up the Prelude pattern and choose the same one as Estelle's. But Dottie declined. She would stick with Prelude. It reminded her of her love of music, but Dawn believes she may also have kept it as a reminder of Red.

"I finally came to realize how significant Red's life—and death—were in the life of my mother. I know that she loved Red dearly," Dawn said. After Dottie's death, Dawn opened her mother's Bible and discovered that it contained memorials and mementos of three people in her life whom she had lost and dearly loved.

Stashed between the pages was her father's Rotary card from 1929. She adored Jim Turner, who died when Dottie was fourteen. There also was a copy of the memorial service from her son's funeral in 1978. Dickey had died in an auto accident near their home in Pontotoc.

"Dickie's death was a horrible tragedy," Dawn said. He was the oldest of the Furr children and was building a house several miles outside Pontotoc. Dickie had married a girl in his mother's image, a young woman even more petite that Dottie. Everything in the house was diminutive and set low so that Dickie's bride could manage. To Dawn, it was a doll's house.

Dickie was returning from working on the house late one night when his car veered into the path of an eighteen-wheeler. He died instantly. Dickie's death was almost too much for Dottie to bear, but she bore her grief internally just as she had when she lost Red.

Also in Dottie's Bible was the bulletin from a church service at the St. Charles Street Presbyterian Church in New Orleans, dated December 26, 1943, after Red had been shot down. A poem, "A New Start," was printed on the front cover, and the "Roll of Honor" of the young men and parishioners from New Orleans who were serving in the war was on the back. "I will start anew this morning," the poem begins. "I will try to find contentment in the paths that I must tread." Five months after Red's loss Dottie was beginning to realize she was now alone.

"Red is not mentioned specifically in the bulletin," Dawn said. "But this was a very difficult time for her and she was relying on her faith to get her through. It would have been so like her to hold on to his memory in this very quiet and personal way. She had a broken heart and she needed to mend and she needed to find happiness again. She knew she had to move on with her life, but she needed to remember his."

Dottie always faced death and adversity privately and stoically. She had a stroke at the age of forty-seven in 1968. She was left paralyzed on her left side, but refused to be bowed, and once back home she turned to music for salvation and therapy. Dawn watched her mother struggle to make her hands work. She would lift her paralyzed hand onto the keyboard and will it to play as it once had. "When she used to play, her hands were all over the keyboard," Dawn said. Now she could barely make them move. Dottie was determined and calm. "Well, I guess this hand just isn't going to work anymore," she would declare as though it were a recalcitrant child who needed rehabilitation through patience and understanding. Eventually she made her limp left hand move, forcing feeling back into the fingers to play and to reach for an octave. Slowly she regained the full use of her hand and body. And she played beautifully once again. But success was fleeting. She suffered a series of strokes over the next decade, and by the time she was in her mid-fifties, Dottie was too crippled to play the piano, but she was uncomplaining.

"I heard my mother say more than once when I was growing up that if you were unhappy about something, you didn't make everyone else around you unhappy," Dawn said. Dottie lived according to the precepts of a poem, "Perspective," that appeared in the book of poetry, *Light of the Years,* by Grace Noll Crowell, given to her by Red just before he left for war. It was a religious poem about going through life with the hand of God.

"It's almost like my mother's voice telling me that you have to keep perspective in all things," Dawn said. "That's the kind of person my mother was, and I have the feeling that was the kind of person Red was."

Dawn always wondered if her mother's stoicism was a factor in her illnesses. Just as she had held her sorrow in check around friends when Red had been killed, she kept all her emotions under tight reign throughout her life. Dottie suffered from high blood pressure, which doctors did not discover until after her first stroke. She also was a heavy smoker most of her adult life. The blood pressure contributed to her strokes and the smoking to her final illness. In 1983 Dottie was diagnosed with lung cancer and by 1985 she was an invalid and critically ill; the cancer had invaded her brain.

Dottie Turner Furr died a few days after Jack Warner delivered Red's last message. To Dawn it almost seemed as though she had been waiting to hear from him after all the years. The number of coincidences that merged at that one moment when the telephone rang surprised Dawn. It was only by chance that Dottie answered the phone. Dick normally did, but he did not hear it ring. If he had answered, he probably would have told Jack Warner that Dottie was too ill to take the call. Dottie's cousins had just happened to drop by; otherwise no one might know of Jack Warner's call. Dottie also was seldom in Pontotoc. Dawn wonders, was it chance that Dottie heard from Jack, or was it ordained?

Dottie was buried in Pontotoc, Mississippi, in the Furr family cemetery plot. Dick Furr died in 2002, but chose to be buried in Georgia next to his second wife. Dottie rests alone as does Red.

Dawn believes that Dottie may have made her final peace with Red over his grave at the Ardennes American Cemetery in Belgium. While she and Dick were stationed in Germany, the Ardennes cemetery would not have been far away. Dawn has a photograph of Dick placing flowers on the grave of a cousin, William Furr, an army sergeant who was killed in Germany in 1945.

He is buried at the Margraten American Cemetery in the Netherlands. "I think she may also have visited Red's grave," Dawn said.

Dawn spoke an epitaph for Dottie, one that Red Franks would have written had he lived. "She was the loveliest person I ever had the pleasure of knowing, and her sixty-four years were simply not enough. I take comfort in the thought that maybe she was ready and she knew Red was waiting for her."

2 9

Greater Love Hath No Man

August 1 was a day of celebration for Jack Warner and his family for many years after World War II. The day commemorated Operation Tidal Wave, the defining event of his life and the day in 1943 when he missed his rendezvous with death.

Warner retired to a suburb of Dayton, Ohio, in 1966 after serving twenty-five years in the Air Force. He returned home from captivity in Romania after the war and decided to reenlist in the Air Force where he continued as a navigator on strategic bombers. He flew in EB-29s and in new jet EB-47s before being assigned to the XB-70, in the supersonic bomber program. Warner attained the rank of lieutenant colonel before retiring to Fairborn, Ohio, with his wife Wanda. His daughter Karen lived nearby.

The Warners made an annual pilgrimage to the United States Air Force Museum in Dayton, Ohio, every August 1. The museum holds one of the largest and best collections of military aircraft in the world, including the

B-24D, *Strawberry Bitch,* that flew with the 376th Bomb Group, the Liberandos. The museum also maintains an exhibit of artifacts, photographs, and letters devoted to the Tidal Wave raid in which Lieutenant Warner's OD GI shirt that he wore on the mission is prominently displayed. Clearly visible is the stitching around the shoulder and down the back where Romanian nurse Elana Andreise sewed up the thirty-five tears and holes from shrapnel. He kept it as a reminder of his brush with death and later donated it to the museum.

Lieutenant Warner barely survived the battle at Ploeşti. He bailed out seconds before *Euroclydon* crashed, and his parachute opened an instant before he slammed into the ground. He was knocked unconscious by the force of his landing. When he came to, he was taken captive by Romanian soldiers and paraded through nearby villages in the back of an ambulance for the benefit of curious onlookers who came to see this badly shot-up and burned American.

Doctors believed Lieutenant Warner to be too seriously wounded to survive and left him to die among the bodies of American airmen lying on bloodied parachutes in the "dead corner" of a hospital ward. But he lived through the night, and only the next day did doctors attend to his injuries. He clung to life with the help of a fellow American airman who provided him with water and summoned nurses when his fever spiked. He recuperated slowly but was unable to use his left hand and arm because of his wounds. Nurse Andreise wrote his letters home to family, friends, and Dr. Franks in the weeks that Lieutenant Warner remained in the hospital.

For the Franks family August 1 was always a day of mourning, especially immediately after the war when Dr. Franks struggled to unravel the mystery of what had happened to Red. In 1945, shortly after Lieutenant Warner returned home from prison camp, Dr. Franks visited him at his Lexington, Kentucky, home, seeking answers about Red's disappearance. Dr. Franks was accompanied by Bob Caldwell, a family friend and an FBI agent from Columbus who, Dr. Franks believed, might be able to elicit more detailed information about Red's fate. But the trip proved fruitless; Jack Warner recollected only that Red bailed out of the plane as it plunged to earth and that he believed his chute had opened. After that Warner said he had no knowledge of what had happened to Red other than what he had been told by the Romanians and Germans.

One version of *Euroclydon*'s last seconds suggested that Red bailed out first before Warner jumped. If that were true, Dr. Franks wondered why Red's chute hadn't opened in time? If Lieutenant Warner had gone out after Red, he would have been the one killed. The story of *Euroclydon*'s final moments came to light only after the war in debriefings of surviving crew members, in books, in magazine articles, and in interviews, an extensive one with Jack Warner published in 1998 and 1999 in the *Friends Journal* of the Air Force Museum Association.

Jack Warner told his daughter Karen that "someone" pushed him from the plane and saved his life. Warner said he did not know who it was, but realized that it was an act of self-sacrifice that cost the man his life. Red and Jack were fast friends and had made a pact to help one another if the plane was shot down.

In 1995 Jack Warner called Nancy Lee at her home in Gallatin, Tennessee. She had never spoken to him in all the years since the war, although she knew that her father and Warner had become friends. Warner wanted to apologize for the misunderstanding that led Dr. Franks to believe that Red had bailed out and survived. Nancy Lee has always remembered the day in 1943 when her father summoned her home from college and presented her with Jack Warner's letter saying that Red was alive.

Warner told Nancy Lee that his conclusion that Red was alive had been supposition. Warner then said, "Red pushed me out of the plane and we were too close to the ground for his chute to open." Warner never explained why he was revealing this information a half century after the war, but Nancy Lee believed he was motivated by guilt. Red had died and Warner had lived.

"We talked for two hours," Nancy Lee said. "I sat down on the floor because he talked for so long. He was getting it off his chest. He sounded remorseful." Nancy Lee asked her husband, Thomas Goodall, to pick up an extension phone to listen in. By the time the conversation ended, Nancy Lee was consoling Jack Warner. "I'm not holding it against you. Don't cause yourself grief over something that happened fifty years ago. I had to comfort him," she said.

Warner's daughter Karen said that her father always spoke of Red with regret because they had been such good friends. And he lived the rest of his life knowing that he had survived because of a twist of fate and the helping hand of a true friend.

Warner would never forget. *Euroclydon's* last moments were terror filled, wracked by stupefying confusion, explosions, flame, and death. The B-24 streaked over the target, her engines screaming at full bore, her machine guns reverberating in a hellish clatter through the plane.

Sgt. Reed remembered the moment *Euroclydon* entered the battle zone. He and "Luke" had steeled themselves as best they could to the terror and mayhem they knew was coming. Suddenly antiaircraft guns were firing on the plane but the crew could not spot them. *Euroclydon* was in the lead element and would be the first or second plane over the target. Surprise was the crew's only weapon that day, and it had been lost.

Almost at the same moment that Red released the bombs, an explosion staggered the plane, detonating near the bomb bay, ripping apart her auxiliary gas tanks, and setting off a firestorm that swept through the aircraft.

The hit in the midsection killed Sergeant Lucas, serving as a waist gunner that day, and severed communications between the crew in the rear of the plane and the pilots, navigator, and bombardier. Immediately the plane was on fire and only fifty to seventy-five feet off the ground, Sergeant Reed remembered. With flames racing through the fuselage the crew had no alternative but to bail out or perish. Sergeant Reed and the left waist gunner, Sergeant Vest were the first to get out, Reed through the bottom hatch and Vest through the left waist window. More shells hit the plane. A 37 mm antiaircraft shell burst in the nose, jamming Lieutenant Warner's gun.

Euroclydon was doomed. To save the crew, the pilots pulled back on the wheel and sounded the alarm bell for every crew member to jump. The plane rose from fifty to about 180 feet, streaming fire.

In the greenhouse Red and Lieutenant Warner looked through the crawl space beneath the pilot's platform to see flames racing toward them from the bomb bay. They needed no prodding to jump as the alarm bell clanged away. Both men instantly moved towards the nosewheel hatch just as another 37 mm shell exploded, wounding both men. Lieutenant Warner yelled out in pain as shell fragments shattered his shoulder and arm. Red was still able to function even though he too had been wounded by the blast that severed hydraulic and gasoline lines. Fire erupted in the crawl space as flammable fluids ignited and were fanned by burst oxygen tanks. The nose compartment became engulfed in flame.

Red and Lieutenant Warner were desperate. The more heavily built Red grabbed his friend and shoved and pulled him toward the hatch. The spring-loaded doors swung out with a kick, but the narrow opening often snagged men in full flight suits and bulky parachutes on their backs. The plane was also rising at a steep angle, making the few feet from the navigator's platform to the hatch a desperate uphill struggle. The navigator's platform became the floor as Red lifted Lieutenant Warner and pushed him to the small hatch opening. Lieutenant Warner's arm was useless as Red began to squeeze his friend through the opening. Just before Lieutenant Warner went out, Red instructed him to pull the rip cord as soon as he was outside the plane. *Euroclydon* reached the zenith of her rise and began to heel over and fall to earth. Lieutenant Warner popped out just as the plane began her descent. The plane spun and twisted as she fell and Red jumped through the hatch. Suddenly he was free and instantly yanked his rip cord. It was too late.

Several crew members in an accompanying plane saw Red's chute fail to open in time to slow his descent, but in the heat of battle they were unable to identify him as *Euroclydon*'s bombardier. They flew by the stricken aircraft and saw the B-24 break in two just before it crashed into a building on the outskirts of Ploeşti.

Lieutenant Warner told Air Corps intelligence after his release from prison camp that Red had been wounded from antiaircraft shells exploding in *Euroclyden*'s nose. No one will ever know the seriousness of Red's wounds, but they could have been severe. Army forensic specialists analyzing Red's remains years later at Neuville-en-Condroz noted that he was missing his left hand and the fingers of his right hand.

Sergeant Reed summed up the fate of Red Franks and the many Americans killed that day over Ploeşti. "Our youth could not overcome the dangerous mission we were on."

When Dr. Franks wrote the eulogy for Red that he delivered before the congregation of the First Baptist Church in late 1943, he spoke of Red's "triumphant Christian faith . . . that should inspire and challenge to highest courage and to noblest and most self-sacrificing patriotism, both on the home front and on our many battlefronts."

But Dr. Franks never knew the extent of his son's Christian devotion. Red's action in giving his own life so that a comrade could live was the noblest gesture that one man can give to another.

The remains of Lt. Jesse D. Franks, Jr., were finally committed to a permanent grave in 1949. Dr. Franks recalled that every summer night as a teenager attending Camp Ridgecrest in the 1930s, Red sounded taps on his bugle as the campers crawled into their bunks. The simple, haunting beauty and significance of this deeply moving call was probably lost on him as it echoed across the rolling mountains of North Carolina. He never would have suspected that the same piece would be sounded over his own grave in Belgium only a few years later.

It had been a long journey from the prairies of northeast Mississippi, from a lonely place called Ploeşti, to a haven among comrades. The unspoken words of taps drifted across the Ardennes American cemetery:

Day is done,

Gone the sun,

From the hills, from the lake, from the skies,

All is well,

Safely rest,

God is nigh.

Epilogue

Col. John Riley Kane, leader of the Ninety-eighth Bomb Group, the Pyramiders, who won the Medal of Honor for heroism during the Ploeşti raid, and, like Red Franks, the son of a Baptist minister from the Old South, left a memorable eulogy to Red and the American airmen killed on the August 1, 1943, mission. Colonel Kane survived Ploeşti and the war and died more than a half century later in 1996 at the age of eighty-nine. The stars in the firmament had not moved in his lifetime, as he observed the night before the attack, but the world had changed dramatically since then, and the men who died on that mission are now part of the ages. Coming from a man nicknamed Killer Kane, the sensitivity of his tribute is particularly poignant.

TO THE FALLEN OF PLOEŞTI

"To you who fly on forever, I send that part of me which cannot be separated and is bound to you for all time. I send to you, those of our hopes and dreams that never quite came true, the joyous laughter and showery tears of our boyhood, the marvelous mysteries of our adolescence, the glorious strength and tragic illusions of our young manhood, all these that were and perhaps would have been, I leave in your care, out there in the Blue."

Bibliography

TELEPHONE INTERVIEWS WITH THE AUTHOR

Chebie Bateman 2002
Brenda Burchfield 2002
Dick Burts 2003, 2004
Dr. H. Reed Carroll 2003
Jennie Clements 2002
Terry Clements 2002
Steve Dean 2002
Ellie Pope Dodwell, 2002
Michael Edwards 2002
J. W. Fagan 2003
Peter Francis 2003
Fran Fuqua 2002, 2003
Herbert Gabhart 2002
Dawn Furr Gerakaris 2003
Sarah Gillespie 2003

Nancy Lee Goodall 2002, 2003, 2004
Larry Greer 2003
John Griggs 2003
Betty Holland 2002
Julia Holmes 2002, 2003, 2004
Alita Howard, 1994
Bernie Imes 2002
V. Joris 2003
Dr. John Kerner 2003
Florence Mars 2003
Marrietta McCarter 2002
Hazel Minium, 1994
Hartwell McPhail 2003
Bryan Moon 2002, 2003
David Naugher 2003

Sarah Naugher 2003

Frank Nemeth, 2003

Frank Noland 2003

Riley Noland 2002

Barbara Owens 2003

Russell Page 2003

Karen Warner Pearce 2003

Tom Peske 2003

Jake Propst 2002

Eleanor Rayburn 2002, 2003

Darrell C. Richardson 2004

Scott Serby 2002

John Siladie 2002

Shield Sims 2002

Lt. Col. Deborah Skillman 2003

Eleanor Slaughter 2002

General Jacob Smart 2004

Nannie Kate Smith 2002

Elizabeth Spencer 2002

Howard Stafford, 2003

Carroll Stewart 2004

Walter Stuart 2002, 2003

Wanda Sumner 2003, 2004

Kerry Sullivan 2003

Elizabeth Teass, 2003

Isadore Valenti 2003

Wanda Warner 2002

Maj. Pamela Weishaar 2003

Genevieve Yancey 2002

Maud Yeow 2002

Personal Interviews with Author

Col. Paul A. Bethke, Hickham Air Force Base, Hawaii, 2003

Ginger Couden, Hickham Air Force Base, Hawaii, 2003

Jack Davis, Easton, PA, 2002, 2003

Bob Fuqua, Columbus, MS, 2003

Fran Fuqua, Columbus, MS, 2003

Sgt. Sebastian Harris, Hickham AFB, Hawaii 2003

Julia Holmes, Pontotoc, MS, 2003

Nancy Lee Goodall, Gallatin, TN, 2003

Russell James, Columbus, MS, 2003

Ken Mooney, Easton, PA , 1993

Sarah Naugher, Pontotoc, MS, 2003

David Naugher, Pontotoc, MS, 2003

Frank Noland, Columbus, MS, 2003

Eleanor Rayburn, Pontotoc, MS, 2003

Johnnie Webb, Hickham Air Force Base , Hawaii, 2003

Genevieve Yancey, Pontotoc, MS, 2003

BIBLIOGRAPHY

Letters to Dr. Franks

Red Franks, March 1940
Red Franks, July 31, 1943
Frank Milley, August 22, 1943
Brig. Gen. V. H. Strahm, September 14, 1943
Maj. W. F. Hehman, October 26, 1943
Maj. W. F. Hehman, November 4, 1943
Rep. John E. Rankin, November 5, 1943
2nd Lt. William Hurwitz, November 17, 1943
Maj. Gen. J. A. Ulio, November 29, 1943
Maj. Gen. J. A. Ulio, December 9, 1943
Maj. Gen. J. A. Ulio, January 18, 1944
Rep. Will M. Whittington, January 26, 1944
Rep. Will M. Whittington, February 17, 1944
Rep. Will M. Whittington, March 8, 1944
1st Lt. G. H. Galvin, Jr., March 14, 1944
1st Lt. F. H. George, March 20, 1944
2nd Lt. R. E. Rodgers, March 25, 1944
Rep. Will M. Whittington, April 12, 1944
Rep. Will M. Whittington, April 14, 1944
2nd Lt. R. E. Rodgers, April 15, 1944
Rep. Will M. Whittington, April 22, 1944
Lt. Jack Warner, April 23, 1944
Col. A. W. Snyder, May 22, 1944
Rep. Will M. Whittington, May 24, 1944
Maj. A. W. Snyder, May 22, 1944
Maj. Gen. J. A. Ulio, July 4, 1944
Rep. Will M. Whittington, July 7, 1944
1st Lt. G. H. Galvin, Jr., July 7, 1944
2nd Lt. Frances L. Hartt, July 27, 1944
Maj. Gen. J. A. Ulio, August 8, 1944
2nd Lt. Frances L. Hartt, August 16, 1944
Rep. Will M. Whittington, September 1, 1944
Rep. Will M. Whittington, September 13, 1944
Capt. F. A. Eckhardt, October 23, 1944
Capt. F. A. Eckhardt, November 3, 1944

Brig. Gen. Edward Witsell, November 27, 1944

Lt. Col. Mayo Darling, March 30, 1945

Capt. F. A. Eckhardt, April 7, 1945

Col. E. C. Gault, May 29, 1945

Lt. Col. Mayo Darling, June 11, 1945

Brig. Gen. Edward F. Witsell, July 4, 1945

Brig. Gen. Edward F. Witsell, Nov. 14, 1945

Maj. James L. Prenn, December 20, 1945

Brig. Gen. Edward F. Witsell, January 19, 1946

Rep. Will M. Whittington, May 18, 1946

Rep. Will M. Whittington, May 31, 1946

Frank Leavell, July 5, 1946

Maj. James L. Prenn, August 20, 1946

Brig. Gen. Leon W. Johnson, October 29, 1946

Maj. Gen. Edward F. Witsell, January 1, 1947

Brig. Gen. Leon W. Johnson, January 13, 1947

Maj. James L. Prenn, January 16, 1947

Brig. Gen. Edward F. Witsell, January 17, 1947

Col. E. V. Freeman, February 11, 1948

Col. W. H. Hinman, Jr., February 14, 1947

Col. W. H. Hinman, Jr., February 17, 1947

Lt. Col. R. M. Bauknight, October 22, 1947

Col. E. V. Freeman, February 11, 1948

Maj. Gen. Richard B. Coombs, April 21, 1948

Maj. Gen. Thomas B. Larkin, April 22, 1948

Col. E. C. Gaupt, May 29, 1948

Maj. Gen. Richard B. Coombs, June 7, 1948

Maj. James F. Smith, August 16, 1948

Maj. James F. Smith, September 2, 1948

Maj. James F. Smith, September 23, 1948

Maj. James F. Smith, January 27, 1949

Maj. Gene H. Feldman, June 29, 1949

BIBLIOGRAPHY

LETTERS FROM DR. JESSE FRANKS

First Baptist Church Deacons, June 10, 1923
Bernie Imes, December 24, 1943
1st Lt. G. H. Galvin, March 17, 1944
1st Lt. G. H. Galvin, March 28, 1944
Rep. Will M. Whittington, April 7, 1944
2nd Lt. Frances Hartt, August 4, 1944
Rep. Will M. Whittington, September 6, 1944
Capt. F. A. Eckhardt, November 1, 1944
Capt. F. A. Eckhardt, November 8, 1944
Brig. Gen. Edward F. Witsell, December 4, 1944
Brig. Gen. Leon W. Johnson, December 5, 1944
Brig. Gen. Edward F. Witsell, December 9, 1944
Quartermaster General, December 27, 1944
Lt. Col. Mayo A. Darling, April 16, 1945
Lt. Col. Mayo A. Darling, May 17, 1945
Graves Registration Service, November 20, 1945
Mr. and Mrs. Howard Noland, March 1, 1946
Maj. Gen. Edward F. Witsell, June 12, 1946
Brig. Gen. Leon W. Johnson, September 30, 1946
Brig. Gen. Leon W. Johnson, November 5, 1946
Brig. Gen. Leon W. Johnson, November 6, 1946
Brig. Gen. Leon W. Johnson, January 10, 1947
Col. J. McDonald, January 15, 1947
Adjutant General, Army Air Forces, October 16, 1947
First Baptist Church, Christmas, 1947
Quartermaster General, March 4, 1948
Quartermaster General, May 28, 1948
Maj. Richard Coombs, August 4, 1948
Maj. James I. Smith, August 26, 1948
Quartermaster General, September 13, 1948
Dr. S. R. Woodson, February 5, 1951
Col. Robert G. Fuqua, no date
Ruth, no date
First Baptist Church—on occasion of dedication of Freedom Memorial Endowment, no date

293

OTHER LETTERS

S. L. Robinson to Red Franks, August 8, 1937
Red Franks to R. C. Gresham, May 26, 1943
Red Franks to R. C. Gresham, July 17, 1943
R. C. Gresham to Red Franks, July 12, 1943
Gen. H. H. Arnold to officers and men of the 9th US Bomber Command, August 20, 1943
Maj. Gen. J. A. Ulio to Mr. And Mrs. Joseph Lucas, October 26, 1943
Charlotte Johnson to Rep. John Rankin, November 3, 1943
1st Lt. G. H. Galvin, Jr., to Joseph Lucas, November 10, 1943
M. C. Clarkson to Army Effects Bureau, November 18, 1943
Maj. W. F. Hehman to Joseph Lucas, November 25, 1943
M. C. Clarkson to Kansas City Quartermaster Depot, November 29, 1943
2nd Lt. M. S. Pool to Joseph Lucas, December 4, 1943
Lt. Jack Warner to Dot Turner, January 1, 1944
1st Lt. Frank H. George to Mr. Robinson, January 16, 1944
National Society of the Red Cross of Romania to Dorothy Turner, January 21, 1944
Maj. Gen. J. A. Ulio to Rep. Will M. Whittington, February 15, 1944
1st Lt. G. H. Galvin, Jr., to Joseph Lucas, March 14, 1944
Joseph Lucas to 1st Lt. G. H. Galvin, Jr., March 21, 1943
2nd Lt. R. E. Rodgers to Joseph Lucas, March 30, 1944
Brig. Gen. Robert Dunlop to Rep Will M. Whittington, April 18, 1944
Brig. Gen. Robert Dunlop to Rep. Will M. Whittington, May 22, 1944
Maj. Gen. J. A. Ulio to Rep. Will M. Whittington, July 5, 1944
Capt. S. N. Greenstein to Joseph Lucas, August 11, 1944
Chaplain Thomas Dunleavy to Mr. and Mrs. Joseph Nemeth, January 15, 1945
Chaplain E. F. Shumaker to Joseph Nemeth, January 15, 1945
Lt. Commander N. Helvestine to Elizabeth Nemeth, January 27, 1945
Rep. Will M. Whittington to Maj. Gen. Edward F. Witsell, June 19, 1946
Col. J. McDonald to Rep. Will M. Whittington, June 27, 1946
Rep. Will M. Whittington to Maj. T. B. Larkin, June 29, 1946
Maj. Gen. Edward F. Witsell to Rep. Will M. Whittington, July 6, 1946
Maj. Gen. Edward F. Witsell to Rep. Will M. Whittington, July 9, 1946
Col. J. McDonald to Rep. Will M. Whittington, July 10, 1946
Col. J. McDonald to Rep. Will M. Whittington, July 27, 1946

BIBLIOGRAPHY

Maj. Martin G. Riley to Commanding Officer, Graves Registration, February 7, 1947

Isle Beale to Prisoner of War Service, July 25, 1947

Col. M. Banknight to Isle Beale, October 22, 1947

Col. A. D. Fisken to Adjutant General, October 27, 1947

Lt. Col. Edward D. Comm to Rep. Will M. Whittington, April 28, 1948

Joseph Lucas to the Adjutant General, July 18, 1948

Capt. J. F. Vogl to Joseph Lucas, October 11, 1948

R. F. Beckman to Vincent B. Lucas, October 16, 1959

Charles A. Reed to Mrs. Hapgood, October 12, 1973

R. A. Hakala to American Battle Monuments Commission, October 25, 1973

R. A. Hakala to Sen. Gale W. McGee, March 8, 1974

Lt. Col. William E. Ryan to R. A. Hakala, November 1, 1973

Col. William Denison to Sen. Gale W. McGee, March 8, 1974

Alita Feeback to Hazel Unger Minium, January 21, 1996

James S. Hardy to Fran Fuqua, August 17, 2002

Mrs. Malcolm Heard to Fran Fuqua, August 23, 2002

Betty Holland to Fran Fuqua, August, 2002

LETTERS, FAXES, AND E-MAILS TO AUTHOR

Chebie Bateman, June 26, 2002

Don Morrison, July 18, 2002

Ellen Jones, July 26, 2002

Brenda Scalf Burchfield, July 26, 2002

Robert W. Sterfels, July 29, 2002

Robert W. Sterfels, August 7, 2002

Peter Francis, August 20, 2002

Alita Feeback, August 11, 1995

Richard Boylan, August 12, 2002

Peter Francis, August 20, 2002

Fran Fuqua, July 15, 2002

Fran Fuqua, August 27, 2002

Herbert Gabhart, August 9, 2002

Donald Singer, August 20, 2002

Donald Singer, September 13, 2002

BIBLIOGRAPHY

Brenda Scalf Burchfield, October 25, 2002
Brenda Scalf Burchfield, October 27, 2002
Fran Fuqua, January 4, 2003
Dawn Furr Gerakaris, December 18, 2002
Elizabeth Spencer, January 6, 2003
Dawn Furr Gerakaris, January 8, 2003
Dawn Furr Gerakaris, January 15, 2003
Tatuc Macea, January 28, 2003
Bill Fill, February 15, 2003
Dawn Furr Gerakaris, March 30, 2003
Dawn Furr Gerakaris, March 31, 2003
Dawn Furr Gerakaris, April 1, 2003
Lana Ragsdale, April 10, 2003
Dawn Furr Gerakaris, April 10, 2003
Don Lindsey, April 24, 2003
Alice Smith, June 4, 2003
Chris Brooks, June 5, 2003
Dawn Furr Gerakaris, June 9, 2003
Dawn Furr Gerakaris, June 11, 2003
Fran Fuqua, July 17, 2003
Dawn Furr Gerakaris, June 23, 2003
Bryan Moon, July 24, 2003
Teri Newsome, August 5, 2003
Dawn Furr Gerakaris, November 16, 2003
Sylvia Kenrick Brown, December 3, 2003
Sylvia Kenrick Brown, December 8, 2003
Robert Suggs, December 18, 2003
Ron Springs, December 18, 2003
Dawn Furr Gerakaris, December 27, 2003
Ron Springs, January 17, 2004

Telegrams

Dr. Jesse Franks from Red Franks, May 8, 1943
Dr. Jesse Franks from Red Franks, July 23, 1943
Mrs. Margaret Lucas from Gen. J. A. Ulio, August 11, 1943

BIBLIOGRAPHY

Dr. Jesse Franks from Gen. J. A. Ulio, August 16, 1943
Dr. Jesse Franks from Gen. J. A. Ulio, September 23, 1943
Mrs. Margaret Lucas from Gen. J. A. Ulio, October 23, 1943
Hazel Unger from the Adjutant General, August 3, 1944
Alita Howard from Lt. Col. Vernon Lewis, October 24, 1946

RADIOGRAMS TO QUARTERMASTER GENERAL REGARDING SEARCH
FOR REMAINS OF 1ST LT. JESSE D. FRANKS

February 6, 1947
February 7, 1947
February 13, 1947
February 14, 1947
September 25, 1947
October 1, 1947
October 21, 1947

BOOKS

AAF The Official Guide to the Army Air Forces. Pocket Books, New York, 1944.

Ambrose, Stephen. *D-Day.* Touchstone Books, New York, 1995.

Ardery, Philip. *Bomber Pilot.* The University Press of Kentucky, Lexington, KY, 1978.

Beeker, Annette, and Gudoin-Rouzeau Stephanie. *Understanding the Great War.* Hill & Wang, New York, 2003.

Birdsall, Steve. *Log of the Liberators.* Doubleday, New York, 1973.

Brittain, Vera. *Testament of Youth, An Autobiographical Study of the Years 1900–1925.* Penguin USA, New York, 1994.

Catledge, Turner. *My Life and Times.* HarperCollins, New York, 1971.

Collins, V. H. *Poems of War and Battle.* Oxford, Clarendon Press, New York, 1914.

Crowell, Grace Noll. *Light of Years.* Harper & Brothers, New York, 1936.

Davies, Jon. *The Christian Warrior in the 20th Century.* Edwin Mellen Press, Lewiston, NY, 1995.

———. *Death, Burial and the Rebirth in the Religions of Antiquity.* Routledge, New York, 1999.

Davis, Larry. *B24 Liberators in Action.* Squadron/Signal Publication, Carrollton, Texas, 1987.

Dugan, James, and Stewart, Carroll. *Ploeşti.* Random House, New York, 1962.

Federal Writers Project of the Works Progress Administration. *Mississippi.* Viking Press, New York, 1943.

Feeback, Alita. *Breaking the Death Barrier.* Eternity Unlimited Publications, Escondido, CA, 1974.

Freeman, Roger A. *The Mighty Eighth.* Doubleday, Garden City, NY, 1973.

Fussell, Paul. *The Boys' Crusade.* Modern Library, New York, 2003.

———. *Doing Battle.* Little, Brown & Co., Boston, 1996.

———. *The Great War in Modern Memory.* Oxford University Press, New York, London, 2000.

Gibson, Edwin, et al., *Courage Remembered.* McClelland and Stewart, Toronto, 1989.

Goodwin, Doris Kearns. *No Ordinary Times.* Simon & Schuster, New York, 1994.

Graham, Stephen. *The Challenge of the Dead.* Cassell & Co. Ltd., London, 1921.

Gushwa, Robert. *The Best and Worst of Times.* Office of the Chief of Chaplains, Department of the Army, Washington, DC, 1977.

Hill, Michael. *Black Sunday, Ploeşti.* Schiffer Publishers, Ltd., Atglen, PA, 2001.

Holt, Tonie, and Valmai. *My Boy Jack.* Leo Cooper, Barnsley, South Yorkshire, 1998.

Kaplan, Philip, and Smith, Rex Alan. *One Last Look.* Abbeville Press, New York, 1983.

Kershaw, Alex. *The Bedford Boys.* De Capo Press, Cambridge, MA, 2003.

Lipscomb, Dr. W. L. *A History of Columbus Mississippi.* Press of Dispatch Printing Co., Birmingham, AL, 1909.

MacCloskey, Munro. *Hallowed Ground.* Richards Rosen Press, Inc., New York, 1968.

Magnan, Philip. *Letters from the Pacific Front.* Universe.Com, 2002.

Majdalany, Fred. *The Battle of Casino.* Ballantine Books, New York, 1957.

Newby, Leroy. *Into the Guns of Ploeşti.* Motorbooks International, Osceola, WI, 1991.

———. *Target Ploeşti.* Presidio Press, Nojato, CA, 1983.

The New English Bible. Oxford and Cambridge University Presses, Cambridge, UK, 1970.

Pogue, Forest. *George C. Marshall, Organizer for Victory.* Viking, New York, 1973.

Remarque, Erich Marie. *All Quiet on the Western Front.* Ballantine Books, New York, 1996.

Ross, William, and Romanus, Charles F. *The Quartermaster Corps, Operations in the War Against Germany.* USA WWII Series, Washington, DC, 1965.

Steere, Edward. *The Graves Registration Service of World War II.* Historical Section, Office of the Quartermaster, Washington DC, April, 1951.

Sanner, Richard. *Combat Medic Memoirs.* Rennas Productions, 1995.

Schneider, Richard H. *Taps.* William Morrow, HarperCollins, New York, 2002.

Sibley, Marlo Carter. *Mississippi Off the Beaten Path.* Globe Pequot Press, Old Saybrook, CT, 1996.

Spencer, Elizabeth. *Landcapes of the Heart, A Memoire.* Louisiana State University Press, Baton Rouge, LA, 2003.

———. *The Southern Woman.* Modern Library, New York, 2001.

Steere, Edward, and Boardman, Thayer M. *Final Disposition of Word War II Dead, 1945–51.* QMC Historical Studies, Washington, DC, 1957.

Stroup, Russell Cartwright. *Letters from the Pacific.* University of Missouri Press, Columbia, MO, 2002.

Sulzberger, C. L. *American Heritage Picture History of World War II.* American Heritage Publishing Corp., New York, 1966.

Thucydidies. *The History of the Peloponnesian Wars.* Viking Press, New York, 1954.

Tischler, Nancy. *Tennessee Williams.* The Citadel Press, Sacramento, CA, 1961.

Williams, Edwina Darkin. *Remember Me to Tom.* G. P. Putnam's Sons, New York, 1966.

Wolff, Leon. *Low Level Mission.* Doubleday & Co., Inc., Garden City, NY, 1957.

MAGAZINES

"The American Purpose." editorial, *Life,* July 5, 1943.

Anders, Dr. Steven. "With All Due Honors." *Quartermaster Professional Bulletin.* United States Army Mortuary Affairs Center Website http://www.quartermaster.army.mil/MAC/Autumn/Winter 1994.

Cannon, Florence. "Our Honored Dead." *The Quartermaster Review.* United States Army Mortuary Affairs Center Website http://www.quartermaster.army.mil/MAC/May/June, 1952.

Colley, David. "Going Home." *VFW.* pp. 32–35. November, 1995.

Dowling, Tom. "The Graves We Dug." *Army.* pp. 36–39. January 1989.

"Gold Star Honor Roll." *Mississippi College Alumni Bulletin.* pp. 1–2. April 1945.

"Graves Registration." *QM Review.* pp. 25–26, 95–96. May/June 1946.

McBane, Maj. Robert. "These Honored Dead." *Army Information Digest.* pp. 23–30. August, 1946.

Hillinger, Charles. "Mothers Who Wear the Stars of Gold." *VFW.* pp. 32–36. September 1993.

Life, cover, July 26, 1943.

"New Guinea MIA Search." *Soldiers,* pp. 42–43. April 1988.

Noyer, William L. "The Final Voyage." *The Retired Officer.* pp. 40–44. March 1989.

QMC Historical Studies: The Graves Registration Service in World War II. *QMC Historical Studies.* pp. 1–14. April 1951.

"The Return of John X." *Time.* October 13, 1947.

Quinn, Bernard. "The Private Who Lost and Won." *American Legion Magazine.* pp. 14–16, 48, 49. February 1963.

Schetter, Dave. "Introducing Josephine Nealona." *Vanguard.* p. 2. May/June 1992.

Schon, Herbert. "The Return of Our War Dead." *QM Review.* pp. 16–18, 85–86. July/August 1946.

"SOP on Burial and Graves Registration." *Military Review.* March 1944.

"Tragic History," *Quartermaster Review.* pp. 27–29. January/February 1946.

Unitt, Pete. "Ploesti at Low Level," *Friends Journal.* pp. 17–24. Winter 1998/1999.

———. "Ploesti at Low Level." *Friends Journal.* pp. 29–37. Spring 1999.

"The War Dead." *Life.* pp. 76–77. November 3, 1947.

NEWSPAPERS

Beall, Jon Baluh. "Making Sure Memories Don't Fade." *The Express Times.* June 30, 2002.

Barry, Don. "Death as a Constant Companion." *New York Times.* September 11, 2002.

Berger, Meyer. "400,000 in Silent Tribute as War Dead Come Home." *New York Times.* October 27, 1947.

Brett, Regina. "Caretaker of the Dead." *Akron Beacon Journal.* May 26, 1991.

"City to Pay Homage to War Dead Today." *New York Times.* October 26, 1947.

The News. Gallatin, TN, May 28, 1989.

"Commentary." *The Columbus Commercial Dispatch.* December 15, 1991.

Cooper, Clint. "Defense Officials Searching for POWs, MIAs." *Times and Free Press.* May 10, 2000.

Davey, Monica. "As Families Mourn, They Raise Questions Regarding Information." *New York Times.* April 20, 2003.

"Decoration Day Observance Set." *The Columbus Commercial Dispatch.* April 24, 1955.

Finger, Steve. "Putting Legend to Rest." *Wichita Eagle.* January 5, 1997.

———. "Remains of Flamboyant World War II Hero are Returned." *Knight Ridder Tribune News Service.* January 8, 1997.

Fooks, James. "Mission Accomplished, 53 years after Bomber Crashed, Texarkana Flier is Headed Home." *Dallas Morning News.* September 29, 1996.

———. "Remains of World War II Pilot to be Buried in Family Plot." *Dallas Morning News.* January 7, 1997.

Gettleman, Jeffrey. "Deaths in Iraq Take a Steady Toll." *New York Times.* November 2, 2003.

Goldman, Ari L. "Confronting Grief, Not Burying It." *New York Times.* September 7, 2003.

Hitt, Jack. "American Way of Death Becomes American Way of Life." *New York Times.* August 18, 2002.

Imes, Birney, III. "Jesse Franks' Letter." *The Columbus Commercial Dispatch.* July 21, 2002.

———. "Don't Let Us Forget Who Real Heroes Are." *The Columbus Commercial Dispatch.* June 2, 1991.

———. "Belt's Emergence Rekindles Belief in Wizards." *The Columbus Commercial Dispatch.* December 15, 1991.

Imes, Birney, Jr. "Potpourri . . ." *The Columbus Commercial Dispatch.* July 8, 1979.

"John J. Nemeth of Coast Guard Dies of Wounds." *Bethlehem Globe Times.* January 19, 1944.

Johnson, David. "War Hero." *The News Examiner* (Gallatin, TN). May 28, 1984.

Keegan, John. "Father Who Felt Guilt and Searched in Vain." *The Telegraph.* February 3, 1998.

"Memories Come Flooding Back on 58th Anniversary of D-Day." *The Express Times.* Easton, PA. June 7, 2002.

"Mississippians at War." *The Clarion Ledger.* September 29, 1943.

Monitor, Leigh Anne. "Crazy for Kudzu." *Birmingham Post Herald.* Fall 2003.

Mydans, Seth. "US Combs Indochina for Clues to Missing." *New York Times.* July 20, 2002.

Nuaroth, Tony. "Veterans Keep Memory of Sacrifice Alive." *The Express Times.* December 8, 2002.

Old, Hudson. "Downed Pilot Receives Hero's Return." *East Texas Journal.* February 1997.

Perl, Peter. "The Paper Trail. *Washington Post Magazine.* May 30, 2004.

Reavis, Ed. "GI Bulge Victim Well Remembered in Luxembourg." *Stars and Stripes.*

"Red Cross Elects Dr. J. D. Franks." *Columbus Commercial Dispatch.* October 22, 1945.

"Red Franks Reported Mission in Action." *The Clarion Ledger.* August 18, 1943.

"Remains of World War II Pilot to Be Buried in Family Plot." *Dallas Morning News.* January 7, 1997.

"Romanian Immigrant Dies at 85." *Akron News.* June 5, 1996.

Rosenthal, Andrew. "Accounting for the Invisible Casualties of War Shouldn't Be Matter of Politics." *New York Times.* November 14, 2003.

Sulzberger, C. L. "Life and Death of an American Bomber." *New York Times Magazine.* July 16, 1944.

Summers, Laura. "Remains of Pilot to be Returned." *Tulsa World.* December 26, 1996.

Truscott IV, Lucian. "A Call to Honor." *New York Times.* November 11, 2003.

Turner, Alan. "Years Later, The Burials They Deserve." *Houston Chronicle.* January 10, 1997.

Walker, Ian. "How the Americans Took 170,000 War Dead Home." *Daily Mail.* (London). 1982.

Winerip, Michael. "Five Decades Later, A Fighter Pilot's Final Flight Ends." *New York Times.* May 28, 1996.

Wirth, Gene. "Mississippians and War." *The Clarion Ledger.* Fall 1943.

Zehr, Kathy. "Final Farewell Paid WWII Pilot, Hero at Arkansas City Service." *Ponca City News.* June 12, 1996.

————. "Local War Hero Comes Home to Rest." *Ponca City News.* June 11, 1996.

The Columbus Commercial Dispatch, May 1943 to September 1945.

VIDEOS

Wing and a Prayer: The Saga of Utah Man. Spike Productions. 1999.

World War II with Walter Cronkite. CBS Video Library. 1983.

PAMPHLETS

Butte, Charles D. *Graves Registration during World War II in Europe: 603 Quartermaster Graves Registration Company.* Typescript, 1992.

U.S. Department of Army. *Escorting American War Dead.* August 1948.

U.S. War Department. *Military Escorts: Return of World War II Dead.* 1947.

BIBLIOGRAPHY

DOCUMENTS

Dental Chart, Joseph F. Minogue, March, 1942

Dental Chart, Enoch Porter, April 4, 1942

Dental Chart, Bernard R. Lucas, May 28, 1942

Dental Chart, Howard L. Dickson, June 8, 1942

Dedicatory Service for Christian, American, Service Flags, First Baptist Church, September 27, 1942

Dental Chart, Joseph E. Boswell, November 2, 1942

Report of Dental Survey, October 14, 1942

Dental Chart, Earl L. Frost, June 10, 1943

Flying Personnel Dental Identification Form, June 10, 1943

Dental Chart, Jesse D. Franks, June 10, 1943

Report of Dental Survey, May 28, 1943

Field Order NO58, Ploesti Attack, July 28, 1943

Aircraft Missing Report, August 12, 1943

Army Effects Bureau, October 6, 1943

Inventory of Effects, October 10, 1943

Inventory of Effects, October 13, 1943

Report of Death, War Department, Adjutant General's Office, October 13, 1943

Report of Death, War Department, October 29, 1943

Application for Effects of Deceased Soldier, November 1, 1943

Affidavit of Claimant, November 18, 1943

Army Effects Bureau, November 27, 1943

Report of Transactions of Personal Effects, November 27, 1943

Inquiry Concerning Missing American Personnel File, February 8, 1944

Order of Shipment, March 24, 1944

Inventory, March 27, 1944

Report of Death, War Department, Adjutant General's Office, March 6, 1944

Order for Shipment, March 21, 1944

Army Effects Bureau, April 3, 1944

Personal Effects Receipt, April 10, 1944

Report of Transactions Disposing of Personal Effects, May 1, 1944

Burial Information, June 17, 1944

Order for Shipment, July 4, 1944

Army Effects Bureau Inventory, July 14, 1944

BIBLIOGRAPHY

Missing Air Crew Report, July 11, 1944
CQMG Form 302, Burial Information, June 17, 1944
Order for Shipment, August 1, 1944
Personal Effects Receipt, August 3, 1944
Twenty-fifth Anniversary Recognition and Appreciation Service, July 7, 1946
Findings in Grave, January 7, 1947
Disposition Form, January 17, 1947
Identification Checklist, January 30, 1947
Skeletal Chart, January 30, 1947
Report of Investigation Area Search, February 11, 1947
Tooth Chart, February 11, 1947
Report of Interment, March 17, 1947
Dedicatory Service, Soldier Memorial Tablet and Freedom Memorial Endowment, First Baptist Church, April 27, 1947
Benediction Ceremony, United States Military Cemetery, Henri-Chapelle, Belgium, July 27, 1947
Case History of Unknown, March 23, 1948
Request for Disposition of Remains, April 22, 1948
RRE Form Number 43, September 20, 1948
Promotion Orders, January 25, 1949
Disinterment Directive, March 15, 1949
Deferred Search Certificate, March 31, 1950
Memorialization of Non-recoverable Remains of World War II, October 15, 1953
Overview of CICHI Laboratories, August 11, 2003
Overview of CICHI Operations, August 11, 2003

No Dates

List of Belhaven College Graduates, 1941–1943
Missing Air Crew Report Raymond Warner
Missing Air Crew Report Charles A. Reed
Missing Air Crew Report James Richard Vest
Casualty Report for Joe Boswell
Casualty Report for Howard Dickson
Casualty Report for Frank Farrell

BIBLIOGRAPHY

Casualty Report for Jesse Franks
Casualty Report for Earl Frost
Casualty Report for Bernard Lucus
Casualty Report for John Monogue
Casualty Report for Enoch Porter
History and Development of the National Cemetery System, Department of
    Veterans Affairs
National Cemetery System, Department of Veterans Affairs
Public Law 383, 79th Congress
Remains not Recovered or Identified

Memos

328th Bombardment Squadron, Personal Effects Office, September 2, 1943
328th Bombardment Squadron, Transmittal of Effects, September 7, 1943
1st Lt. Bryan Obertheir, Transmittal of Effects, September 21, 1943
328th Bombardment Squadron, Monetary Effects, September 23, 1943
Maj. W. F. Hehman, Army Effects, November 27, 1943
Maj. W. F. Hehman, Army Effects, December 13, 1943
Maj. W. F. Hehman, Personal Effects, May 1, 1944
Maj. W. F. Hehman, Disposal of Personal Effects, August 16, 1944
Capt. F. H. George, Disposal of Effects, September 13, 1944
Report of Investigation, February 6, 1946
Maj. Anthony Bayer, Report of Interment, June 27, 1946
Capt. Alvin I. Kochman, Burial, July 16, 1946
Identification of Unknown Deceased, July 18, 1946
Identification of Unknown Deceased, July 23, 1946
Maj. Walter B. Morrow, Isolated Burials, September 24, 1946
Maj. Martin G. Riley, Burial Information, October 10, 1946
Maj. Martin G. Riley, January 20, 1947
Interoffice Reference Sheet, February 2 –7, 1947
Maj. O. J. Murray, February 6, 1947
Report of Interment, February 7, 1947
Maj. Walter B. Morrow, February 8, 1947
Interoffice Reference Sheet, February 21–26, 1947
Proceedings of Board of Review, April 9, 1947

BIBLIOGRAPHY

First Field Command, Graves Registration, April 29, 1947
Interoffice Reference Sheet, February 11, 1948
Interoffice Reference Sheet, April 10–29, 1948
Identification of Unknown Deceased, April 15, 1948
Burial Information, May 20, 1948
Interoffice Reference Sheet, September 3–8, 1948
Interoffice Reference Sheet, January 26–27, 1949
Proposed Visit to Neuville-en-Condroz, Belgium, January 27, 1949
Request for Information, December 7, 1950

PERSONAL HISTORIES

Franks, Augusta E. *A Biography of Dr. Jesse Dee Franks.*
Franks, J. D. *Our Seven Years in Post-war Europe.* 1959.
Hale, Rev. Wallace. *Battle Rattle.* 2003.
Hale, Rev. Wallace. *The Dead Still Speak.* 1946.
Wood, Verda. *Meanderings in Memory.* 1989.

PAPERS

Hudson, Sadie. *First Decoration Day—Columbus, Mississippi.* undated (circa 1947).
Kilmer, Kento. *The Origin and History of Memorial Day.* The Library of Congress.
    May 21, 1958.
Naugher, Sarah Schaen. *Mississippian by Choice, Mississippians in the Mighty Eighth.*

FIRST BAPTIST EVANGEL/CHURCH NEWSLETTER

January 15, 1928
March 1, 1942
November 8, 1942
January 24, 1943
May 30, 1943
January 9, 1944
February 6, 1944

February 13, 1944
February 20, 1944
May 21, 1944
November 19, 1944
March 16, 1947
May 1947